Teaching Benefit-Cost Analysis

ELGAR GUIDES TO TEACHING

The Elgar Guides to Teaching series provides a variety of resources for instructors looking for new ways to engage students. Each volume provides a unique set of materials and insights that will help both new and seasoned teachers expand their toolbox in order to teach more effectively. Titles include selections of methods, exercises, games and teaching philosophies suitable for the particular subject featured. Each volume is authored or edited by a seasoned professor. Edited volumes comprise contributions from both established instructors and newer faculty who offer fresh takes on their fields of study.

Titles in the series include:

Teaching Benefit-Cost Analysis

Tools of the Trade

Edited by

Scott Farrow

Professor of Economics, University of Maryland, Baltimore County, USA

ELGAR GUIDES TO TEACHING

Cheltenham, UK • Northampton, MA, USA

Published by
Edward Elgar Publishing Limited
The Lypiatts
15 Lansdown Road
Cheltenham
Glos GL50 2JA
UK

Edward Elgar Publishing, Inc.
William Pratt House
9 Dewey Court
Northampton
Massachusetts 01060
USA

A catalogue record for this book
is available from the British Library

Library of Congress Control Number: 2018931659

This book is available electronically in the **Elgar**online
Economics subject collection
DOI 10.4337/9781786435323

ISBN 978 1 78643 531 6 (cased)
ISBN 978 1 78643 532 3 (eBook)

Typeset by Servis Filmsetting Ltd, Stockport, Cheshire
Printed and bound by CPI Group (UK) Ltd, Croydon, CR0 4YY

Contents

Contributors

Clive Belfield is a professor in the Department of Economics at Queens College, City University of New York. He is also principal economist at the Center for Benefit-Cost Studies of Education and a research affiliate at the Community College Research Center, Teachers College, Columbia University. He received his PhD in economics from the University of Exeter, England. His research interests are economic evaluation of education programs.

William K. Bellinger is Professor Emeritus at Dickinson College in Pennsylvania. He has a BA from Michigan State University, an MS from Cornell University's School of Industrial and Labor Relations, and a PhD from Northwestern University. His primary fields are urban and labor economics, with interests in cost-benefit analysis, small town and small city economic development, and research for South-Central Pennsylvania non-profit and government agencies.

A. Brooks Bowden is an Assistant Professor of methods and policy in the Educational Leadership, Policy, and Human Development department at North Carolina State University. She is the director of training and associate director at the Center for Benefit-Cost Studies of Education at Teachers College, Columbia University. She received her PhD in education policy with a specialization in economics from Columbia University. She specializes in program evaluation and economic analysis, focusing on applications and methodology of the ingredients method of cost analysis.

Gelsomina Catalano is a Research Fellow at the Department of Economics, Management and Quantitative Methods, Università degli Studi di Milano, in the framework of the study on the socio-economic impacts of CERN post-LHC scenarios. She is also adjunct Professor of Regional Economics and Policy at the University of Milan and Partner and senior Economist at CSIL. She has been participating in different evaluation studies of projects, programs and policies on behalf of the European Investment Bank, the European Parliament and the European Commission.

Chris Dockins teaches economics courses at Johns Hopkins University and the University of Maryland and is a Senior Economist with the National

Center for Environmental Economics at the US Environmental Protection Agency. His research focuses primarily on benefit-cost analysis, particularly for quantifying and valuing human health risks. From 2006 to 2010 he was the Director of NCEE's Science Policy and Analysis Division. He earned his PhD in economics from Duke University.

Susan E. Dudley is director of the George Washington University Regulatory Studies Center and distinguished professor of practice in GW's Trachtenberg School of Public Policy and Public Administration. She served as the presidentially appointed Administrator of the Office of Information and Regulatory Affairs, which reviews federal regulations before they are issued, and as president of the Society for Benefit-Cost Analysis. She is a member of the Administrative Conference of the United States and the National Academy of Public Administration.

Scott Farrow is a Professor of Economics at UMBC in the University System of Maryland. He was the founding editor of the *Journal of Benefit-Cost Analysis*. He has also served on the faculty at Carnegie Mellon University, as the Chief Economist of the GAO, twice in the Executive Office of the President, and in the Department of the Interior. He is also affiliated with the Woods Hole Oceanographic Institution (WHOI) and the University of Southern California-CREATE.

Massimo Florio is Professor of Public Economics at the Department of Economics, Management and Quantitative Methods, Università degli Studi di Milano. He has been awarded by the European Commission a Jean Monnet Chair of Economics of European Integration, subsequently the Jean Monnet Chair "Ad Personam" EU Industrial Policy, and recently the scientific coordination of a Jean Monnet network of six universities. His main research interests are in applied welfare economics, cost-benefit analysis, industrial and regional policies, infrastructure and growth, government expenditures regulation, privatization and public enterprise. Florio has led evaluation research and advisory work for the European Commission, the European Parliament, the European Investment Bank, the OECD, the World Bank and other institutions such as CERN.

David Greenberg is a Professor Emeritus of Economics at the University of Maryland, Baltimore County. He is a labor economist and cost-benefit analyst who received his PhD at MIT. Much of his research focuses on the evaluation of government programs. He has published widely on social experimentation, cost and cost-benefit analysis, employment, training programs, evaluation and other topics. With his co-authors, he has recently completed work on the fifth edition of a widely used textbook on cost-benefit analysis, which will be published in 2018 by the Cambridge University Press.

Charles Griffiths teaches economics courses at Johns Hopkins University and the University of Maryland and is a Senior Economist with the National Center for Environmental Economics at the US Environmental Protection Agency. His areas of research include valuing water quality improvements, the social cost of carbon, the evaluation of voluntary programs, and the benefits assessment of health improvements. He served as a Senior Economist at the Council of Economic Advisers. He earned his PhD in economics from the University of Maryland.

Arnold C. Harberger's teaching career spans more than 65 years. Applied welfare economics has been one of his principal fields, for which he was named a Pioneer in Development by the World Bank (1985). He is also a member of the US National Academy of Sciences and a fellow of the Econometric Society and the American Academy of Arts and Sciences. He was the first president of the Society for Benefit-Cost Analysis, and is also a past president of the Western Economic Association and of the American Economic Association. His books include *Project Evaluation, Taxation and Welfare*, and (with Glenn P. Jenkins and C.Y. Kuo) *Cost-Benefit Analysis for Investment Decisions*. He is currently the Gustavus F. and Ann M. Swift Distinguished Service Professor Emeritus of the University of Chicago, and Distinguished Professor Emeritus of UCLA.

Per-Olov Johansson, Stockholm School of Economics. Professor Johansson has previously held Professorships at the University of Oslo and the Royal College of Forestry, Umeå, Sweden (SLU). His publications include five books published by Cambridge University Press and two by Edward Elgar, and more than 100 articles and book chapters.

Bengt Kriström is Professor of Resource Economics and Head of the Department of Forest Economics at the Swedish University of Agricultural Sciences, Umeå. He has been a consultant to the Swedish Government and to the OECD on many occasions, and has been a member of the Prime Minister's Commission on Sustainability and Chair of the Expert Group on Environmental Studies at the Ministry of Finance.

Kerry Krutilla is a Professor of Public Policy at the School of Public and Environmental Affairs, Indiana University in Bloomington. His research focuses on the economic evaluation of federal regulations; optimal investment in cybersecurity; and distributional accounting formats for benefit-cost analysis. He has conducted contract research for the World Bank, the US Agency for International Development, and the US Departments of Energy and Agriculture, and offered training courses and curriculum consulting in Spain, Russia, Vietnam and Azerbaijan.

Henry M. Levin is the director of the Center for Benefit-Cost Studies of Education, the William H. Kilpatrick Professor of Economics and Education at Teachers College, Columbia University, and the David Jacks Professor of Higher Education and Economics, Emeritus, at Stanford University. He has been engaged in cost-effectiveness and benefit-cost studies in education and other fields since 1970. He is the author of 22 books and about 300 scholarly articles on these topics as well as others in the economics of education and educational policy.

John Mendeloff is a Professor at the Graduate School of Public and International Affairs at the University of Pittsburgh. He previously taught at UC-San Diego and SUNY-Albany. His PhD is from UC-Berkeley. His research has focused on government regulation of health and safety risks, including issues of enforcement as well as standard-setting. He is the author of *The Dilemma of Toxic Substance Regulation: How Overregulation Causes Underregulation at OSHA.*

Chiara Pancotti is Partner and Economist at CSIL – Centre for Industrial Studies (Milan, Italy). Her main fields of expertise are regional development, project evaluation and cost-benefit analysis, especially in the RDI, cultural and environmental fields. She has also been carrying out trainings on cost-benefit analysis targeting civil servants and practitioners in Italy and abroad – including Lithuania, Slovenia, FYROM – as well as graduate students. Currently, she is involved in a study on behalf of the European Commission concerning the *ex post* evaluation of major projects supported by the ERDF and CF between 2000 and 2013.

Emile Quinet is an academic scholar, member of Paris School of Economics and author of about 20 books and 300 articles, communications and research reports, and an expert in transport and public economics, working for national and international agencies. He recently completed a report to the French Government on "Cost benefit assessment of public investment in France" (Paris, Commissariat Général à la Stratégie et à la Prospective), whose conclusions have been implemented in the official guidelines.

Lisa A. Robinson is a Senior Research Scientist at the Harvard Center for Health Decision Science and the Harvard Center for Risk Analysis. Her work focuses on the conduct of benefit-cost analysis, particularly for policies with outcomes that cannot be fully valued using market measures. She was previously a Senior Fellow at the Harvard Kennedy School and is an Affiliate Fellow of its Regulatory Policy Program. She is a past President of the Society for Benefit-Cost Analysis and a Fellow of the Society for Risk Analysis.

David Salkever is Professor, School of Public Policy, University of Maryland, Baltimore County (UMBC) and Professor Emeritus, Bloomberg School of Public Health, Johns Hopkins University. He has published widely in health economics, including studies of hospital economics, regulation, pharmaceutical markets and economics of disabilities. Recent CBA-related work includes studies on marginal valuation of targeting and screening information in early childhood intervention programs, and on the application of Meltzer's societal CEA framework for programs to rehabilitate persons with severe mental illness. His current research foci include costs of environmental impacts and interventions for young children.

Stuart Shapiro is a Professor of Public Policy at the Bloustein School of Planning and Public Policy at Rutgers University. He teaches and writes about cost-benefit analysis and is the author of *Analysis and Public Policy: Successes, Failures and Directions for Reform* (2016), an examination of the use of various types of analysis in policymaking. Prior to coming to Rutgers, Professor Shapiro worked for five years at the Office of Information and Regulatory Affairs.

Nicolas Treich is Research Associate at INRA at Toulouse School of Economics in France. His research concerns risk and decision theory, environmental economics and benefit-cost analysis. He has published over 40 papers in peer-reviewed journals on various topics including the Precautionary Principle, the value of statistical life and climate policy. He has written various broad audience papers and reports on policy issues. He is Editor-in-Chief of the *Geneva Risk and Insurance Review*.

David Weimer is the Edwin E. Witte Professor of Political Economy at the University of Wisconsin–Madison, where he teaches cost-benefit analysis. His research focuses broadly on policy craft and institutional design. Although most of his recent research has addressed issues in health policy, he has done policy-relevant research in the areas of energy security, natural resource policy, education, criminal justice and research methods.

Richard O. Zerbe is the Daniel J. Evans Distinguished Professor Emeritus at the University of Washington, an Adjunct Professor at Washington University and currently a Fulbright Professor at the University of Bari Law School in Italy.

Preface: Teaching benefit-cost analysis

We teachers of benefit-cost analysis (BCA) face a continuing challenge to interest and ideally inspire our students. It is also challenging to keep up with the expanding body of theory and applications. Just preparing for multiple classes and dealing with evaluations seems to fill the available time. This volume, *Teaching Benefit-Cost Analysis: Tools of the Trade* (TBCA), provides 19 chapters from 24 experienced international authors who make available their teaching, research and practical skills at your disposal. Each contributor was asked to provide a teaching module, here presented as a chapter, to present their favorite topic or to provide key insights into conveying difficult topics. Each chapter is an independent essay; a teacher's digest from which you can select whatever is consistent with your style and interests. Abstracts for each chapter help you hone in on specific topics. And you can always assign chapters as supplemental reading!

But first, who are we teaching and how do we teach it? I asked contributors to provide their syllabi, and with the help of Nate Pritchard, found more on the Internet. Syllabi only provide an insight into the structure of the course, but what I found was:

- Most courses appear to be upper level undergraduate or applied graduate studies such as policy or health care. This book is targeted at that audience, with somewhat less attention to health care and to more advanced students.

- Most BCA teachers appear to provide conceptual and quantitative teachings, often with some case studies. *TBCA* provides such teachers with a wide array of specific topics in addition to those already mentioned. Teachers looking for material on more conceptual matters or course design might look at Harberger (on Harberger Triangles writ large) in Chapter 2, Robinson on valuing mortality risk reductions (the value per statistical life) (Chapter 8), Catalano and Florio on designing a short course for professionals (Chapter 7) and Shapiro on integrating cases into the classroom in Chapter 18 (with examples). Griffiths and Dockins bring their mixture of government and academic expertise to the issue defining the baseline in Chapter 3 along with Mendeloff on the arithmetic of efficiency and the challenges of marginal analysis (Chapter 9). Teachers looking for material on specific skills might consider a class exercise in simulation (Farrow, Chapter 19), or the challenge of finding a market failure from well-meaning students who just want to make something happen (Dudley, Chapter 6).

• Specific and controversial topics are included here as well. Addiction is addressed by Weimer (Chapter 13), distributional issues by Krutilla (Chapter 17), education by Belfield, Bowden and Levin (Chapter 16), land use and transport by Quinet (Chapter 14) and research infrastructure by Florio and Pancotti (Chapter 15).

• There is often a distinction between general BCA and health BCA. This is most obvious in the choice of textbooks. About 80 percent of the syllabi used texts (easily found on the web) such as Boardman, Greenberg, Vining and Weimer (Weimer on addiction writes in Chapter 13, Greenberg on labor writes in Chapter 10); Zerbe and Bellas (Zerbe writes on standing in Chapter 4), and Bellinger writes on decision rules in Chapter 1. However, almost 20 percent of the courses use health-based textbooks such as Drummond, Sculpher, Torrance, O'Brien and Stoddart or Brent. Teachers of those health classes may benefit most from the general skills chapters presented here, or the discussion of health, BCA and alternative utility measures presented by Salkever in Chapter 12.

• There are a few more advanced chapters such as those dealing with partial and general equilibrium (Harberger, Chapter 2; Johansson and Kriström, Chapter 5) and risk and uncertainty (Treich, Chapter 11) that may be most useful for the more advanced courses and students (or we faculty!).

Besides the essential inputs from the contributing authors, the book would not have become a reality without the encouragement of Alan Sturmer at Edward Elgar and the meticulous and timely assistance of Dr Mary Kokoski, an economist of note in her own right. Many of the authors are active with the Society for Benefit-Cost Analysis (SBCA) and publish frequently in its *Journal of Benefit-Cost Analysis*. Although there is no formal tie between the book and that organization, I think there is a commonality of purpose in improving and applying BCA. Ultimately, teaching is an exchange with students and I appreciate, more in the long run than the short run, the push from students to explain or develop topics more clearly. Additionally, I thank Kelly Hodges, Crystal Proctor, Jacqueline Pennisi and Nate Pritchard of UMBC for their important assistance at various points and the very professional support from multiple hands at

Edward Elgar throughout the process. Dr Elaine A. King, my spouse, provided encouragement and showed remarkable patience. Finally, there are the teachers who influenced me substantively or pedagogically over the years and to whom I owe a great deal of thanks; among them are Gregory M. Duncan, Maureen Cropper, Lane Rawlins, Francis Ferguson, Walter Butcher, Donald Bushaw and R.K. Goto. Robert (Bob) Hahn brought me back to BCA after many years' absence.

There is a certain humor as I recall telling one of my BCA teachers that I was uneasy with a BCA in the absence of distributional issues being treated in an integrated way. I still don't believe rigidly in the results of a BCA but it is indeed, as a colleague says, "Where the economic rubber meets the road." BCA was one of two themes I brought to my post as Chief Economist of the Government Accountability Office (GAO), although I called it economic performance in that setting, while the second theme was risk—also common in BCA.

It is in teaching the numerous assumptions and the connections between data, theory and results that I renew my appreciation for the intellectual construct of BCA and the power of its purpose. Ultimately, it is *your* students' hands that will hold the future of many investments, programs, policies and BCA itself; please teach them well.

Scott Farrow

Professor/UMBC,
Affiliate Faculty/University of Southern California-CREATE
Guest Investigator/the Woods Hole Oceanographic Institution

PART I

The big picture

1.   Decision rules

William K. Bellinger

ABSTRACT

Benefit-cost analysis is the cornerstone of the economic analysis of public policy, and is closely aligned with basic rational choice and market concepts from microeconomics. Information and other constraints often block the direct application of marginal decision rules for policy decisions, but the conceptual role of marginalism can still be useful in interpreting benefit-cost analysis. While all policy analysis texts that emphasize the economic dimensions of policy cover the basics of marginal analysis, the sources of market inefficiency, and basic decision rules for policy analysis, the connections between marginal and non-marginal policy decision rules are seldom emphasized. This chapter limits its discussion of marginal analysis to the concepts of optimal quantity and optimal allocation rather than the market-based concepts of surplus, equilibrium and elasticity which are discussed in later chapters. This chapter begins by reviewing marginal and non-marginal concepts and measures for policy decisions, and then discusses a set of basic decision rules that can be informed by these concepts. Student exercises are included and answered in the appendix to the chapter.

MARGINAL AND NON-MARGINAL FUNDAMENTALS

There are two marginal concepts that inform common policy decision rules. The first defines the optimal quantity of any activity as the point where marginal benefits equal marginal costs, given that net benefits are decreasing in the neighborhood of the equality. If these conditions apply, one should continue to invest in a project as long as the marginal benefits of the project are greater than its marginal costs, and should choose one's scale for the project where the marginal benefits and marginal costs are equal.

The other fundamental marginal decision related to policy analysis involves allocating resources across a set of policies, with or without a budget constraint. Ideally, one should allocate resources so that the marginal benefit of the last dollar spent on one project equals the marginal benefit per dollar for all others. In equation form, for any three projects X, Y and Z, the ideal allocation of funds between the projects would occur where:

$$\frac{MBx}{MCx} = \frac{MBy}{MCy} = \frac{MBz}{MCz},$$ (1.1)

where *MB* refers to marginal benefits and *MC* to marginal costs. This rule is analogous to various tangency conditions that define optimal choice for the individual, including the equal marginal utility per dollar rule that defines utility maximization in introductory microeconomics texts.[1] If one has no budget constraint, each of these projects should be funded until its marginal benefits equal its marginal costs, as in Figure 1.2. If each project's marginal benefits equal its marginal costs, each ratio in equation (1.1) will equal 1. We later refer to this option as an optimal budget. When an effective budget constraint exists, the ratios will be larger than 1 and some projects may not be funded at all, a case which will be covered in more detail further on.

For truly marginal analysis one would have to be able to costlessly compare a large number of policy options. If one could arrange these options in order of declining net benefits one would have a problem similar to Figure 1.1. Accurate marginal analysis requires complete and costless information and highly divisible units of measurement. A more realistic scenario involves comparing the net benefits of a much more limited set of policies with alternative budgets and/or designs. Comparing these policy options in order of budget size or quantity would involve a type of quasi-marginal analysis, but none of the mathematics of marginal economics would directly apply. However, there are lessons from marginalism in most comparisons of alternative policies.

The most fundamental non-marginal principles for analyzing the efficiency of policy alternatives are the Pareto improvement principle (a corollary to Pareto optimality), and the Kaldor-Hicks criterion or fundamental rule of policy analysis.

Definitions:
Pareto improvement: An action leads to a Pareto improvement if it makes at least one person better off without making at least one person worse off. A Pareto improvement can also be achieved if anybody who

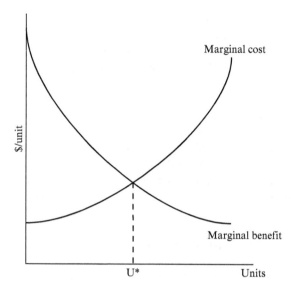

Figure 1.1 Optimal scale for one project

would otherwise lose due to a policy is fully compensated for his or her losses. Therefore a Pareto improvement requires that total benefits outweigh total costs, and that any losers be fully compensated.

The Kaldor-Hicks principle states that a policy should be adopted if the winners could *in principle* compensate the losers. This rule requires only that the total benefits outweigh the total costs.

NON-MARGINAL MEASUREMENTS

The Kaldor-Hicks principle can be applied to several different types of decisions, all of which are informed to some degree by the basic concepts of marginalism. These decisions can be made using one or more of the following measurements of benefits and costs. The three most common of these measurements are net benefits, the benefit/cost ratio and the rate of return. These three concepts are defined below:

Definitions:
Net Benefits = Total Benefits – Total Costs
Benefit/Cost Ratio = Total Benefits/Total Costs
Rate of Return = 100 percent • (Total Benefits-Total Costs)/Total Costs

In some situations, these measurements are consistent, but in others they can produce different rankings for alternative projects. In cases where these measurements are not consistent, a clear preference exists in economics for the net benefits measure. These measures will first be applied to an example.

Student Exercise 1: One design for a new windmill-based electricity complex costs $9 million to construct, will produce $15 million worth of power, and will require $2 million in operating and maintenance costs. A second design will cost $6 million to construct, produce $10 million worth of power, and will require $2 million in operating and maintenance costs. Find the net benefits, benefit/cost ratio, and percentage rate of return on each of these two projects. Answers are provided at the end of the chapter.

> **Project 1:**
> net benefits = ____ benefit/cost ratio = ____ rate of return = ____
> **Project 2:**
> net benefits = ____ benefit/cost ratio = ____ rate of return = ____

If you can only recommend one choice, which option is best according to each measure?

Every policy analysis text recommends the net benefit measure over the benefit/cost ratio. The primary reason for this preference is that net benefits are more consistent with the Kaldor-Hicks criterion. Net benefits attempt to directly measure the total net gain for society whether or not losers are compensated. There are also technical problems with the benefit/cost ratio and rate of return measures. For example, the benefit/cost ratio and rate of return measures are sensitive to how one categorizes operating expenses. One can include operating expenses as part of total cost, making the total revenue for the first windmill project in the previous example $15 million and the total costs $11 million. One may also define benefits as net operating revenue, or total revenue minus operating costs. Under this interpretation the benefits of the windmills would equal $13 million and the total costs $9 million. Both interpretations of operating costs produce net benefits of $4 million, but they produce different benefit/cost ratios and rates of return.

TYPES OF POLICY DECISIONS

Benefit-cost analysis is interpreted somewhat differently for different types of decisions. Among the types of policy decisions an analyst may be required to investigate are the following:

1. Should a single program be accepted or rejected?
2. Which one, at most, of a set of alternatives should be approved?
3. What is the optimal size of a budget covering multiple projects?
4. Which one or more projects should be approved within a fixed budget?
5. What is the ideal scale or scope of a particular project or program?
6. If multiple groups will receive benefits, how should the benefits be allocated?

Each decision will be considered below.

Accepting or Rejecting a Single Project

The decision rule when analyzing a single project is very simple. Approve the project if the net benefits are greater than zero, so that society experiences a net gain in well-being. If total benefits are greater than total costs, then the benefit/cost ratio will be greater than one and the rate of return will be greater than zero. All these outcomes will lead the analyst to recommend approval of the program.

Choosing One of Several Possible Projects

The second type of decision requires the analyst to choose at most one project among multiple alternatives. This type of situation occurs when determining the best use of a plot of land or a particular choice among competing designs for a building or highway project. The recommended rule for this decision is to **choose the project with the highest net benefits, assuming that at least one alternative has positive net benefits.**

Student Exercise 2: See Table 1.1. Assume that a particular plot of land could be developed as residential housing, an industrial park or a factory outlet mall. Only one alternative (at most) can be approved. Assuming that all relevant costs including opportunity costs are included, the ideal choice

Table 1.1   Real estate alternatives

	Housing	Industrial Park	Outlet Mall	Vacant Lot
Benefits	$1,000,000	$1,250,000	$1,600,000	$1,000
Costs	$1,100,000	$900,000	$1,200,000	$1,000
Net Benefits				
B/C Ratio				
Rate of Return				

in this simple case is to find the policy that will provide the highest net benefits to society. Students can be asked to rank these choices in terms of their net benefits, and choose the one that places first. Then they should calculate the benefit/cost ratio and rate of return for each alternative. Note that the benefit/cost ratios for the industrial park and the outlet mall are not consistent with the net benefit ranking. Given this information, which project should be approved?

Choosing an Optimal Budget

An optimal budget is an intriguing concept, but may be less impressive in political terms once it is defined.

> **Definition: An optimal budget** is one that maximizes possible net gains to society as a whole. Therefore an optimal budget will fund all projects with positive net benefits for society. If marginal analysis is possible, an optimal budget would be sufficient so that each project or department is funded to the point where its marginal benefits equal its marginal costs.

Student Exercise 3: What is the optimal budget for the set of projects in Table 1.1?

Choosing Which One or More Projects to Fund Given a Fixed Total Budget

If a person runs a charitable institution that funds health research or a transportation agency that allocates a fixed budget for highway repairs, she will face this kind of decision on a regular basis. The efficiency goal of this decision rule is to maximize the net benefits of a fixed budget.

Marginal analysis would suggest allocating funds so that the marginal benefit/marginal cost ratios are equal for all funded projects. Linear programming or other mathematical programming techniques may be used if sufficient production information exists or if multiple constraints are in force.[2] Assuming that information is too limited for marginal analysis and that only the budget is constrained, a viable method for making this choice involves the following steps:

1. Calculate the benefit/cost (B/C) ratio for each choice. Immediately reject any project which does not have a B/C ratio greater than one.
2. Rank the projects according to their B/C ratio.
3. Choose the highest B/C ratio, then the next highest, and so forth until you cannot go further without breaking your budget. This step is simi-

lar to moving from left to right on the basic marginal benefit-marginal cost graph in Figure 1.1.

4. If you must skip one or more projects due to budget considerations, choose the remaining programs with the highest B/C ratios that fit into the budget.

Because of the limited choices in such cases, the budget constraint is likely to not be fully spent, creating a case of complementary slackness in the budget constraint. The predetermined scale of each project also may imply a degree of inefficiency.

Student Exercise 4: See Table 1.1.

1. Assume that you have plenty of available land but only $3 million to spend. Following the four steps above, choose the projects from the table that should be approved within this budget. Then verify that these projects provide the greatest total net benefits.
2. Now assume that your budget has not been determined. Calculate the optimal budget for land development given this set of projects.

Choosing the Ideal Scale of a Project

A common question associated with many different types of policies is how large the policy or project should be. For social policies such as housing assistance or a job training program, the program's scale determines number of dollars spent and the number of people served. For an infrastructure project, the physical size as well as the cost of the project may be an issue. For example, the number of lanes in a new road is very much an issue of scale. Using marginal analysis, scale is simply a matter of finding the quantity of goods or services for which marginal benefits equals marginal cost. When information is not adequate for marginalism, exploring the net benefits of a finite number of production levels, and choosing the level with the highest net benefits, may partially serve the same purpose. This approach is a type of sensitivity analysis. If one orders the production scales by size, the comparison of each successive size is somewhat marginal in nature.

A scale example with limited information
In 1942 the US federal government established a 50 parts per billion (ppb) standard for the allowable amount of arsenic in drinking water. A 1999 report by the National Academy of Sciences concluded that the 50 ppb standard did not adequately protect public health, and provided a set of

Table 1.2   Alternate arsenic standard benefits and costs

Arsenic Standard	3 PPB	5 PPB	10 PPB	20 PPB
Compliance Costs (millions of 1999 $)	$698–792	$415–472	$180–206	$67–77
Estimated Health Benefits (millions of 1999$)	$214–491	$191–356	$140–198	$66–75
Cancer Cases Avoided	57–138	51–100	37–56	19–20

Source: US Environmental Protection Agency (2001).

estimated costs and benefits for a range of possible standards to replace the original.

Student Exercise 5: See Table 1.2. In 2001 the Environmental Protection Agency (EPA) chose one of the following maximum allowable levels of arsenic. Which one would you choose, if any, and why? EPA policy at that time was to assign a value of $6 million per life saved. If half of these cancer cases would result in death, what would the value of lives saved be worth in dollar terms? Use the high estimate of cancer cases avoided as an example.

Choosing an Optimal Scale and Allocation Among Different Programs: Marginal Analysis

Another common administrative decision involves determining both the total size of a program and how much funding should go to various agencies or constituencies who might benefit from the program. The basic efficiency issues involved in this relatively difficult decision consist of finding the optimal scale for the entire project and then allocating resources among the programs so as to maximize the net benefits of the entire budget. Examples of this allocation issue abound. When a police department decides how many patrol officers to hire and how many to allocate to each neighborhood, or a transportation authority adopts a total annual budget and a set of highway construction projects to fund within the budget, the efficient allocation of funds should be considered. Of course, political factors are also likely to be involved in such decisions.

Determining both the budget scale and allocation among various programs or constituencies involves elements of both the optimal budget concept and the optimal allocation of funds within that budget. Using marginal analysis, one can see some elements of this process more explicitly. The analysis of the total scale of the project and allocation involves

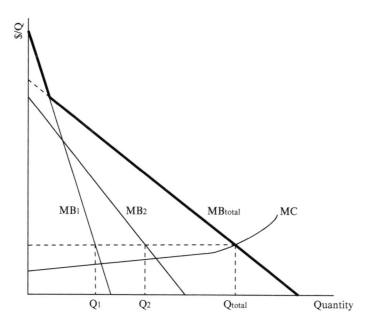

Figure 1.2   Allocating resources between two related programs

several steps (see Figure 1.2). First one needs to calculate the marginal benefits of the given programs. In Figure 1.2 there are two programs with marginal benefit curves MB_1 and MB_2. Then one adds the marginal benefit curves horizontally to find the marginal benefits of the total budget. One then finds the quantity where the sum of the individual marginal benefits meets the marginal cost (Q_{total}), as well as the dollar value of the marginal benefit or marginal cost at this quantity. Cumulatively, these steps involve the aggregation of individual programs into a total budget, and then the determination of the optimal level of total production. This completes the scale portion of the analysis.

The second phase of the analysis is to allocate the total budget among the various programs. To do this one sets the marginal benefits of each program equal to the dollar value of the marginal cost of the last unit produced. The quantities at which the individual marginal benefits equal the optimal marginal cost value dollar value (Q_1 and Q_2 in Figure 1.2) are the optimal levels of production that should be allocated to each group. One might also notice that if $MB_1 = MC_{total}$ and $MB_2 = MC_{total}$, this result also meets the marginal rule for an optimal budget, $\frac{MB_1}{MC_{total}} = \frac{MB_2}{MC_{total}} = 1$. For an example of this problem see Bellinger (2016), p. 181–2.

This section has introduced decision rules for several different situations, including approving or rejecting a single project, the optimal budget concept, choosing projects within a limited budget, and two related decisions involving the scale or size of a project. While the motivation provided by marginal analysis has been discussed, the key to most of these rules is to have sufficient information for estimating the benefits and costs of a reasonable set of alternatives. Most of the rest of the process involves a few concepts and a fair amount of common sense.

CONCLUSION

This chapter suggests that there may be value in relating the marginal and non-marginal decision rules for public policy in one's classes on the subject. The marginal and non-marginal decision rules used to analyze policy alternatives depend to some degree on the problem being addressed and the information available. Choices range from the approval or rejection of a single policy or project to the determination of an optimal budget and optimal allocation of resources across individual programs, constituencies or locations. In each case there is some role for economic rationality concepts in interpreting the decision rules, if instructors choose to draw this connection.

Neither the Kaldor-Hicks principle nor the marginal scale or optimal allocation rules discussed in this chapter actively consider equity, political practicality or other policy goals. Also, benefit-cost calculations are only as good as the information and numerical values that go into them. Since benefits and costs are often difficult to calculate, a substantial degree of humility is helpful when discussing your findings with experts, clients or the general public.

NOTES

1. Equation 1.1 is a variant of multiple optimal allocations rules that appear in undergraduate microeconomics texts. Most basically, the consumer equilibrium model states that a utility maximum exists when $MUx/Px = MUy/Py$, where MU refers to marginal utility and X and Y are two consumer goods. Similarly, a single person general equilibrium with production (often referred to as autarky) reaches an optimum when the marginal rate of substitution for consumption equals the marginal rate of product transformation. In equation form, the slope equality can be stated as $-MUx/MUy = -MCx/MCy$ which easily transforms to $MUx/MCx = MUy/MCy$, which is identical to equation 1.1 other than the non-monetary measure of marginal benefits.
2. Dayananda et al. (2002) provide a useful overview of linear programming as a tool for analyzing resource allocation with multiple constraints in Chapter 11.

REFERENCES AND RECOMMENDATIONS FOR FURTHER READING

Bellinger, W. (2016), *The Economic Analysis of Public Policy, 2nd Edition.* London: Routledge.

Dayananda, D., R. Irons, S. Harrison, J. Herbohn and P. Rowland (2002), *Capital Budgeting: Financial Appraisal of Investment Projects.* Cambridge: Cambridge University Press.

US Environmental Protection Agency (2001), 'National primary drinking water regulations: Arsenic clarifications to compliance and new source contaminants monitoring: Final rule', *Federal Register*, 50 DFR Parts 9, 141, and 142, Vol. 66 (January 22, 2001), 6975–7066.

US Environmental Protection Agency (2016), 'Drinking water arsenic rule history', (Last updated on November 2, 2016), https://19january2017snapshot.epa.gov/dwreginfo/drinking-water-arsenic-rule-history_.html (accessed January 8, 2018).

APPENDIX: ANSWERS TO STUDENT EXERCISES

Student Exercise 1: If one includes operating costs as part of the cost totals, these are the correct answers:

Project 1: Net Benefits = $4m Benefit/Cost Ratio = 1.36 rate of return 36.3 percent
Project 2: Net Benefits = $2m Benefit/Cost Ratio = 1.25 Rate of return 25 percent

If one included operating costs as negative operating revenues, Project 2 would have different rates of return and B/C ratios. Project 1 will have similar changes.

Project 2: Net Benefits = $2m Benefit/Cost Ratio = 1.33 Rate of Return = 33 percent

A policy analyst would generally recommend building wind farm Project 1, given the higher net benefits.

Student Exercise 2:

Table A1.1   Real estate alternatives

	Housing	Industrial Park	Outlet Mall	Vacant Lot
Benefits	$1,000,000	$1,250,000	$1,600,000	$1,000
Costs	$1,100,000	$900,000	$1,200,000	$1,000
Net Benefits	−$100,000	+$350,000	+$400,000	$0
B/C Ratio	0.909	1.389	1.333	1.000
Rate of Return	−9.09%	39%	33%	0%

Rankings:
Net Benefits: 1. Outlet Mall, 2. Industrial Park, 3. Vacant Lot, 4. Housing
B/C Ratio or Rate of Return: 1. Industrial Park, 2. Outlet Mall, 3. Vacant Lot, 4. Housing
The outlet mall would be recommended due to its higher net benefits.

Student Exercise 3: The optimal budget would be sufficient to fund the industrial park and the outlet mall. The total costs for the two projects equal $2,100,000.

Student Exercise 4:

Table A1.2   Project choices given a budget

	Housing	Industrial Park	Outlet Mall	Golf Course	Power Plant	Vacant Lot
Benefits	$1,000,000	$1,250,000	$1,600,000	$1,500,000	$4,200,000	$1,000
Costs	$1,100,000	$900,000	$1,200,000	$900,000	$3,000,000	$1,000
B/C Ratio	0.909	1.389	1.333	1.667	1.400	1.000
Net Benefits	−$100,000	+$350,000	+$400,000	+$600,000	+$1,200,000	$0

B/C Ratio Rankings:

1. Golf Course, 2. Power Plant, 3. Industrial Park, 4. Outlet Mall, 5. Vacant Lot, 6. Housing
Two alternative strategies could be chosen. First build the golf course, skip the power plant, which you could not afford, and build the industrial park and outlet mall, for a total cost of $3 million and $1,350,000 in net benefits. The second strategy would be to build the power plant, with net benefits of $1,200,000. The first strategy maximizes net benefits, and is the correct choice according to this decision rule.

Student Exercise 5: Strictly on the basis of benefit-cost analysis, it is not clear that any change in the arsenic standard should be made. Only for the 10 ppb and 20 ppb levels do the benefit and cost estimates overlap. The EPA chose the 10 ppb standard, in part based on other factors.
   The dollar benefits from lives saved equals $6 million times ½ (the death rate) times the number of cancer cases avoided. Using the high estimates of cancer cases avoided, the dollar values are $414 million for 3 PPB, $300 million for 5 PPB, $168 million for 10 PPB and $60 million for 20 PPB. If accurate, these benefits would account for a substantial majority of the total estimate for health benefits.

2.   Triangles and all that

Arnold C. Harberger

ABSTRACT

This chapter presents a simple exposition of general equilibrium applied welfare economics. It focuses first on the efficiency costs of a set of tax distortions on different goods, and then explores the efficiency effects of adding a new tax to a set of already existing ones. It next considers non-tax distortions such as pollution and traffic congestion, followed by a discussion of distributional weights and basic needs externalities. Finally, it deals briefly with several strategic issues involved in implementing a national system for the benefit-cost analysis (BCA) of public investments and other expenditures.

THE TRIANGLE THAT HARBERGER NEVER CLAIMED TO OWN

At the outset, let me pursue the question of how my name ever got attached to triangles that have been in the economics literature for close to 200 years, and were in textbooks long before I entered the profession. My best guess is that in the 1940s and 1950s consumer surplus was looked upon with suspicion, sometimes approaching scorn, to the point where hardly anybody used the surplus concept and those who did were largely ignored. Economists worried about the non-measurability of utility, and, about the "necessity" that consumer surplus requires the assumption of "constant marginal utility of income (or money), and so on".

So when I started writing on the subject, my contributions were something of a rarity. I also dealt with distortions in a general equilibrium framework. But even this was not new, having been amply set forth and used by Slutsky, Ramsey, Hotelling, Hicks and Meade, among others.

I do feel that my work probably helped to get the profession to once again take consumer surplus seriously. In addition, I was one of the first to derive empirical estimates of efficiency losses due to distortions. And finally, I did delve into some of the subtleties involved in working with consumer surplus.

In this chapter, I will take the reader step by step though my own thinking about the measurement of efficiency costs in a general equilibrium setting, and about some issues that arise as the analysis is broadened to cover stakeholders and distributional issues.

THE THREE BASIC POSTULATES—FOUNDATIONS OF APPLIED WELFARE ECONOMICS

To the best of my knowledge, the main contributions of historical applied welfare economics can all be derived from three basic postulates.

1. As one moves along a demand curve or function, the demand price of each successive unit measures the value of that unit to the demander.
2. As one moves along a supply curve or function, the supply price of each successive unit measures the value of that unit to the supplier.
3. To obtain benefits and costs to society, one simply takes the algebraic sum of the benefits $(+)$ and the costs $(-)$ to all relevant participants in the society.

The graph in Figure 2.1 shows a familiar application of the three postulates. A tax T_1 is imposed, shifting the equilibrium quantity from x_1^0 to x_1^1. The units "lost" as a result of the tax were valued by consumers as the area A + B + C (postulate I), and the resources released have an alternative value to suppliers equal to the area C (postulate II). Society's loss is obtained under postulate III by taking the difference between these two areas, giving us the familiar triangle A + B.

The lower panel of Figure 2.1 simply shows that the action of a monopolist is equivalent to a privately imposed, privately collected tax, equal to the optimizing monopoly markup $(p_2^m - MC_2^m)$. Of course, the monopolist has no supply curve—only the optimal point x_m.

A SIMPLE GENERAL EQUILIBRIUM TRIANGLE

In most applications of benefit-cost analysis, little and nothing is said about the assumptions underlying the demand and supply curves that are used. I feel it is essential to face this question head-on, in order to capture the general equilibrium nature of the problem. The assumption of standard consumer analysis (incomes and other prices all constant) fails to

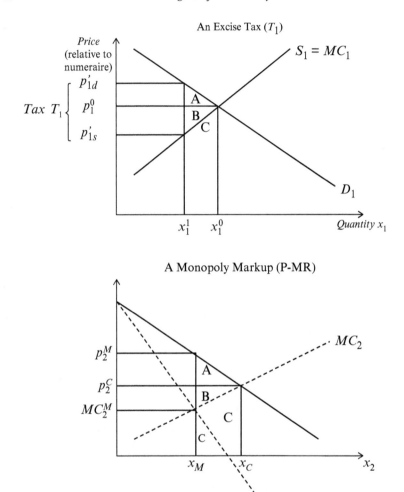

Figure 2.1   Welfare change: Applying the three postulates

fit many cases. What we want to hold fixed are: a) the tastes of consumers, and b) the conditions of supply of resources for the economy. With these elements taken as given, I used to tell my classes, we simply "let the economy be our computer".

This entails defining demand and supply curves "on the instruments", that is, on the tax or other policy instrument that we are analyzing. It is similar to what we do when we derive a reduced form in econometrics, expressing all endogenous variables (in our case supply price, demand price and equilibrium quantity) as functions only of exogenous and policy variables (in our simple case, a tax on x_1).

Student Exercise 1: Consider a tax T_1 on a good x_1 with no distortions in the rest of the economy and with the tax proceeds returned as lump-sum transfers (or—what amounts to the same thing—spent in such a way that the market demand curve in the presence of the tax matches the one that would prevail in its absence). This is simply a "canonical" assumption specifying what the government does with the tax proceeds. It defines a module (T_1 plus lump-sum transfers) which lets us answer the question "what are the effects of a tax on x_1?". If in the real world the proceeds will be spent on expenditures, say E_3, we would combine the T_1 module with an E_3 module showing the effects of E_3, financed by lump-sum taxes on its beneficiaries. Without such a convenient assumption, there would be an infinity of answers to any tax or expenditure questions, reflecting the infinite number of ways the tax proceeds might be spent.

We start **Student Exercise 2** in Figure 2.2 with a sheet of paper marked only with the quantity and relative price axes, and mark point A. This point shows the equilibrium price and quantity of x_i, when there is no tax. Then we perform similar exercises, each showing equilibrium quantity and equilibrium demand and supply prices for different levels of tax (T_{1i}) or subsidy (Z_{1i}) on x_1. To get general equilibrium supply and demand curves we simply connect these points (see also Chapter 5 on small versus large

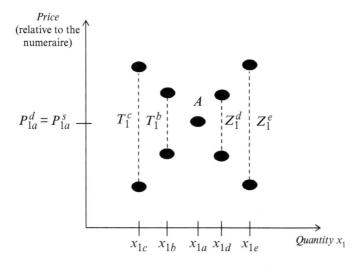

Figure 2.2   General equilibrium supply and demand

projects). To determine the efficiency cost we simply take the triangle $\frac{1}{2}T_1\Delta x_1$ for linear demands and supplies. This change in welfare is negative both for a tax ($T_1 > 0$, $\Delta x_1 < 0$) and for a subsidy Z_1 ($T_1 < 0$, $\Delta x_1 > 0$).

If the curves connecting the points are not linear, then we would take:

$$\Delta w = \int_{T_1=0}^{T_1^*} T_1 \frac{\partial x_1}{\partial T_1} dT_1, \tag{2.1}$$

where T_1^* is the specific level of T_1 for which we are calculating the triangle. The integral simply builds up the triangle, moving gradually from a tiny tax all the way up to T_1^*. Here Δw is the change in welfare from the undistorted optimum A to the equilibrium prevailing at T_1^*. It will always be negative, demander losses always exceeding supplier gains from taxes, and supplier costs always exceeding demander gains from subsidies. Recall that we are here assuming no distortions in the rest of the economy so that point A is part of an economy-wide optimum.

This is a good place to make a couple of very important points. First, the demand and supply curves that result from this exercise are in fact loci of potential equilibrium points. This should be clear from the derivation shown in Figure 2.2. Depending on the purpose of the analysis, they may reflect short-, medium- or long-term equilibria for different packages of fixed and variable factors. But any pair of D/S curves should reflect only one "term" of equilibrium. One is attracted by the analogy that generating triangles is like squeezing the toothpaste out of the tube, but one should never think of the equilibria for different levels of T_1 being sequential. Each quantity of x_1 defines an equilibrium which is alternative to the equilibria corresponding to other levels of T.

The second point is a general one, covering all market demand curves. We are measuring costs and benefits in terms of some numeraire, which should be chosen for our convenience. Sometimes this will be a general price index like the Consumer Price Index (CPI), but at other times (for example, conditions of flat supply prices for all goods) a unit level of costs is a simpler numeraire. At still other times, the world prices of tradable goods will be the most natural numeraire, with the country's real exchange rate being an endogenous variable, even under a fixed nominal exchange rate.

Now consider the demand curve of individual j for x_1. It is implicitly generated by the exercise of Figure 2.2. What happens here is that each individual j is translating his/her marginal utility of x_1 into numeraire units, using his/her marginal utility of the numeraire (our counterpart for the marginal utility of income or money that the early literature worried about). We can generate a demand curve for any product by measuring the demand prices of different individuals in a common unit. In this sense, we leave individual utility functions behind as we perform the very act of constructing a market demand (or supply) curve. Each individual makes the transition simply by having a demand price for each given unit.

The third point deals with the old question of the marginal utility of money. Formally, if efficiency cost in numeraire units is going to exactly reflect utility, the marginal utility of the numeraire has to remain unchanged as we go through the steps indicated in Figure 2.2, and must also be the same across individuals. But the triangles generated by those steps are still valid in numeraire units, even if the marginal utility of the numeraire changes along that path. And such changes, if they exist, would be very tiny, even for a big tax like a 20 percent tariff in all imports. If initially imports were 20 percent of gross domestic product (GDP), and if they fell all the way to 0.1 percent of GDP when this 20 percent tariff was imposed, the reduction in real income (Y), would be a triangle equal to ½ (0.2) (0.1Y), or 0.01Y. Thus, the marginal utility of the numeraire cannot change much as we go through the steps of generating this triangle, since what is involved reflects a change of only 1 percent in real income.

THREE TAXES IN A THREE-GOOD WORLD

This, **Student Exercise 3**, is a simple extension of the previous exercise, but now we have taxes on everything. For simplicity, we will assume that each of the three goods are produced at constant cost, and we will choose the quantity units so that this constant unit cost is equal to 1. Thus, we have $p_1^0 = p_2^0 = p_3^0 = 1$. And for any pattern of taxation $p_1^s = p_2^s = p_3^s = 1$. Under these assumptions, the resource constraint of the economy is $X_1 + X_2 + X_3 = K$, a constant.

The "demand" loci for the three goods are generated by a radial expansion of distortions hT_1^*, hT_2^* and hT_3^*, with h moving up from zero to 1.

With each step of h, we plot the equilibrium demand prices p_i^d and quantities (X_i), corresponding to the fraction h. Thus, when h is 0.2, the demand prices are $1 + 0.2T_1^*, 1 + 0.2T_2^*, 1 + 0.2T_3^*$; at h = 0.5 they are $1 + 0.5T_1^*, 1 + 0.5T_2^*, 1 + 0.5T_3^*$ and so on. The small circles in each market indicate four positions of full equilibrium as h is raised from zero to one. As drawn, in the top panel of Figure 2.3, the triangles for X_1 (A) and X_2 (B) are negative, representing consumer losses, while that for X_3 (C) is positive. This comes from people shifting their demand from the more highly taxed items to the one (X_3) with the lowest tax.

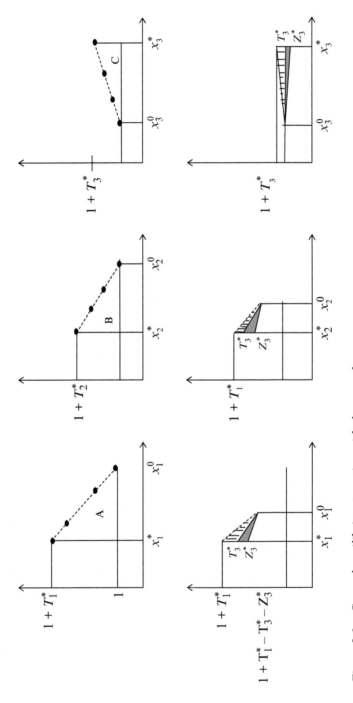

Figure 2.3 General equilibrium taxation with three goods

But the change in welfare Δw stemming from a particular pattern of taxes is not unique to that pattern. Algebraically, we have:

$$\Delta w = 0.5 \sum T_i^* \Delta x_i \tag{2.2}$$

But we get the same result for:

$$\Delta w = 0.5 \sum (T_i^* \mp \delta) \Delta x_i, \tag{2.3}$$

where δ is any constant amount. This stems from the resource constraint $X_1 + X_2 + X_3 = K$.

The bottom panel of Figure 2.3 shows the same loci as the top panel, but then makes two adjustments. First the tax on good three is eliminated so the positive triangle that arises with T_3^* is erased. But at the same time the taxes on T_1 and T_2 are reduced by T_3^*. So the original loss triangles there are reduced by $0.5 T_3^* \Delta x_1 + 0.5 T_3^* \Delta x_2$, where Δx_1 and Δx_2 are the same as before. The three triangles generated by eliminating T_3^* and reducing T_1^* and T_2^* by the same amount add up to zero. So Δw remains unchanged. The next step is to introduce an arbitrary subsidy Z_3^* on X_3, but at the same time reduce T_1 and T_2 by this same amount. With this step, we make the loss triangles on X_1 and X_2 still smaller, but we add a new loss triangle in the market for X_3 again leaving equilibrium quantities and the size of Δw unchanged.

Another way of visualizing these changes is to think of the original distortions T_1^*, T_2^* and T_3^* remaining in place, leaving consumers in exactly the same equilibrium as before. Then the first adjustment would be to introduce a subsidy equal to T_3^* on all three goods, payable to suppliers, and the second adjustment would entail a larger across-the-board subsidy $(T_3^* + Z_3^*)$ again payable to suppliers. In calculating the generalized triangle for these cases, we would of course have to use the net tax treatment of each item $(T_3^*, 0, Z_3^*)$ for X_3, and similarly for X_1 and X_2, as shown in Figure 2.3.

This exercise leaves consumers facing the exact same set of prices throughout, and underlines the fact that therefore the equilibrium solution will be the same in all the variants. Suppliers likewise will go to the same equilibrium, being subsidized across the board by T_3^* and Z_3^*, and paying the money back in lump-sum form.

THE GENERALIZED TRIANGLE

It is an easy step to add more commodities to the list. When we have n commodities the resource constraint becomes $\sum_{i=1}^{n} X_i = K$, with $P_i^s = 1$ for all i.

Then $\Delta w = 0.5 \sum_{i=1}^{n} T_i \Delta x_i$. In this case, as before, a uniform tax on all goods will have no efficiency costs. When we have constant costs, the Δx_i are generated solely by demand reactions,

$$\Delta x_i = \sum_{j=1}^{n} S_{ij} T_j \tag{2.4}$$

with $S_{ij} = \frac{\partial x_i^d}{\partial p_j^d}$, reflecting a purely "demand-story". Resources flow at constant cost as demanders respond to any pattern of taxes that might be imposed.

This gives us another expression for Δw, that is:

$$\Delta w = 0.5 \sum_{i=1}^{n} \sum_{j=1}^{n} S_{ij} T_i T_j \tag{2.5}$$

This quadratic form is useful in finding patterns of taxation that minimize the efficiency costs, given some assumed constraints. This is the way in which the famous "Ramsey rule" was derived. The problem to be solved was to minimize the efficiency cost involved in raising a desired amount of revenue by taxing a subset of commodities i = 1, 2, ..., k, out of a larger set of all commodities i = 1, ..., n. No generality is lost by treating all untaxed goods (k+1, k+2, ..., n) as a single commodity m, as their prices do not change. The Ramsey solution in this case involves taxing more heavily goods that are complements to m. Intuitively, we know that a uniform tax on all goods would be neutral, but we can't impose this because (under our problem) we cannot tax m. But if just one of the goods (g) in the taxable set were a perfect complement to m (fixed proportions), then we could simply have a uniform tax an all of the k goods except g, and load onto g all of the tax that would fall on g + m under a truly uniform tax. This solution would result in $\Delta w = 0$. But this case is not to be found in the real world, so the more relevant Ramsey solution has higher taxes on those goods that are the strongest complements (or weakest substitutes) for m, and lower taxes on the goods that are the strongest substitutes for m.

The next step is to abandon the assumption of constant costs. We already had this for the simplest of cases in Figure 2.1, where $\Delta w = 0.5 T_1 \Delta x_1$. This result generalizes to $0.5 \Sigma T_i \Delta x_i$, even in cases where costs are not constant. In that case, Δx_i becomes $\Sigma R_{ij} T_j$, where $R_{ij} = \frac{\partial x_i}{\partial T_j}$, reflecting how equilibrium quantity of x_i changes when T_j is changed. Also, the base from which Δx_i is measured is always the full undistorted optimum point (X_c in the lower panel of Figure 2.1). Obviously R_{ij} reflects the combined forces of supply and demand, and not just demand responses. But all the intuition that we get from studying demand carries over to the R_{ij}. $R_{ij} > 0$ indicates substitutability, while $R_{ij} < 0$ indicates complementarity in a general equilibrium sense. One can think of the R_{ij} as reduced form coefficients, even though one cannot hope to estimate more than at most a few of them econometrically. $\Delta w = 0.5 \sum_i T_i^* \Delta x_i$ stays unchanged as we drop the assumption of constant costs, and the expression,

$$\Delta w = 0.5 \sum_{j=1}^{n} \sum_{i=1}^{n} S_{ij} T_i T_j, \tag{2.6}$$

becomes

$$\Delta w = 0.5 \sum_{j=1}^{n} \sum_{i=1}^{n} R_{ij} T_i T_j, \tag{2.7}$$

the former being a special case of the latter. It holds for linear loci, and for linear approximations.

CHANGING ONE TAX, GIVEN THE EXISTENCE OF OTHER TAXES

I hope I have made clear that the expression $\Delta w = 0.5 \sum T_i^* \Delta x_i$ measures the change in welfare starting from an undistorted optimum. Most real-world problems concern changes in policy, given the existence of a whole set of pre-existing or likely future taxes. Our policy changes consist of changing one or more of those existing taxes and/or introducing new ones.

Thus, we take the existing

$$\Delta w = 0.5 \sum_{j=1}^{n} \sum_{i=1}^{n} R_{ij} T_i T_j, \tag{2.8}$$

and ask how this changes when a new tax is introduced.

Figure 2.4 introduces a new tax on X_3 in the presence of existing taxes on X_1 and X_2. As in Figures 2.2 and 2.3, we start with a blank sheet of paper, and first insert a starting point A.

Here X_1, X_2 and X_3 are not the only goods. X_1 and X_2 are both general equilibrium substitutes ($R_{ij} > 0$) for X_3. In the linear case, adding T_3^* to the tax package generates a triangle of loss $0.5 R_{33} T_3^2$ ($=$D) plus two trapezoids of gain—$T_1^* R_{13} T_3^*$ and $T_2^* R_{23} T_3^*$ ($= E + F$). This story is different from that of Figure 2.3. There, as T_3 was reduced, T_1 and T_2 were also reduced by the same amount. Here T_1^* and T_2^* remain fixed as T_3^* is imposed, and x_1 and x_2 increase as a result of the introduction of T_3^*.

As shown, the increase (H + J) in resource use in markets 1 and 2 is

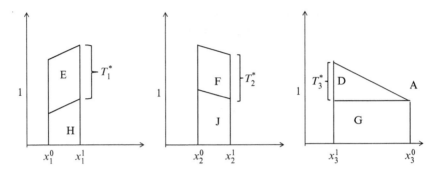

Figure 2.4   Welfare change with prior distortions

smaller than the reduction (G) in the resource use in market 3, because some resources are also shifted from X_3 to undistorted markets (m), not shown because T_m^* is zero. Yet, in spite of this fact, the efficiency gains (E + F) taken together outweigh the loss triangle (C) in market 3. This illustrates the uncertainty of results, when pre-existing distortions are taken into account. If there are no other distortions, even the smallest new tax or subsidy gives rise to a loss in efficiency. But if finite taxes or subsidies exist in the related markets, anything can happen. In most cases the dominant distortions are taxes on substitutes ($T_i R_{ij} dT_j > 0$), generating indirect efficiency gains as T_j increases, as shown by areas E and F in Figure 2.4.

NON-TAX DISTORTIONS

When a new tax is imposed on good j, its welfare effects may extend beyond items subject to existing taxes. Thus, it may affect traffic on existing roads, creating induced congestion costs, or add to the levels of air and water contamination, creating induced pollution costs. These external effects can be accounted for by the analysis already presented; simply by substituting the expression

$$\Delta w = 0.5 \sum_{i=1}^{n} D_i \Delta x_i, \qquad (2.9)$$

in place of

$$\Delta w = 0.5 \sum_{i=1}^{n} T_i \Delta x_i \qquad (2.10)$$

In this case D_i covers both taxes and distortions like congestion and pollution costs. The analysis thus created is relevant for all cases in which the external distortion is tied to some activity level, such as traffic on a road or the output of a power plant or a chemical factory.

Just as congestion and pollution costs enter as existing distortions so also do the privately levied taxes stemming from the exercise of private monopoly or monopsony power. To deal with such phenomena, we simply count monopoly markups and monopsony markdowns as existing taxes in the analysis. For generalized triangle analysis, however, we have to define the undistorted equilibrium as the point where demand price equals the monopolist's marginal cost for the case of private monopoly and also the point where the monopsonist's demand price equals supply price (along the excess supply curve from which his marginal cost is derived). With these adjustments, the private monopoly markups and monopsony markdowns are treated as taxes in the generalized triangle formulation. That is, the undistorted equilibrium from which we start the generalized triangle measurement is the non-monopolistic, non-monopsonistic optimum.

A still further complication arises when a country possesses some degree of monopoly or monopsony power in world markets. Brazil has such power in the world market for coffee, Bolivia has it for tin, Chile may have it for copper and so on. The classical cases on this problem deal with situations in which the actual production takes place under competitive conditions (for example, coffee growing in Brazil), but the volume of exports is sufficiently large to give this country a degree of influence on the world market price. This gives rise to the optimum export tax, by which the country exploits its monopoly position.

The case illustrated in Figure 2.5 has interesting implications. If we are performing a generalized triangle exercise, the no-distortion starting point is x_m (with the optimal tariff) when we are measuring Δw for Brazil, but it is x_c (the competitive equilibrium) when we seek Δw for the world as a whole. Similarly, if we are measuring the sum of external effects of any new tax T_j^*

$$\sum_{i \neq j} D_i R_{ij} T_j^*, \tag{2.11}$$

for Brazil, the existing distortion for coffee exports is D_c when the existing situation is at X_c, and zero when it is at X_m. It is the other way around when we are doing the same exercise from the point of view of the world as a whole.

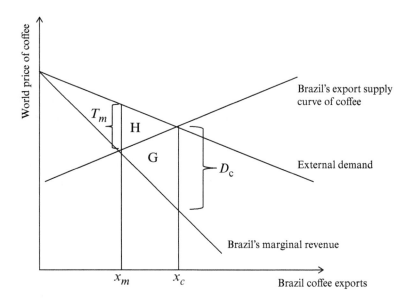

Notes: G = Triangle of gains for Brazil from imposing its optimum T_m (also part of the loss to RoW).
H+G = Total loss to the rest of the world due to Brazil's imposing T_m.
H = Overall world loss due to T_m.

Figure 2.5   Welfare and international trade with market power

INTRODUCING DISTRIBUTIONAL WEIGHTS

Of the three postulates, the one that has been most subject to doubt and attack is the third—"adding up". If you ask people, "Does an extra dollar mean more to a poor person than to a rich one?", over 90 percent will probably answer yes. We know that it is practically beyond our reach to measure the utilities of different people and quantify them for analysis. What we can do, however, is measure the benefits and costs accruing to different groups, and assign weights that differ between rich and poor, friend and foe, deserving and underserving and so on. This may occur as a result of the government instituting a formal system of distributional weights. Or it might simply be a way to help convince an audience of the wisdom of a given policy proposal.

I undertook my first step in this direction in a 1978 paper explaining how to implement a scheme of distributional weights in social cost-benefit analysis (Harberger, 1978). In that paper, I assigned a weight of one to government inflows and outflows and also assumed that some relevant average of the weights assigned to people was also one. In general, this meant that dollars of benefits would count as more than a dollar if they accrued to the poor and less than a dollar if they accrued to the rich.

We will explore distributional weights mainly in the context of the earlier sections of this paper—that is, as a modification of the third postulate. We start in the top panel of Figure 2.6 with a simple stakeholder analysis of the case of a single excise tax, assuming no distortions elsewhere in the economy. Here, rather than measuring effects along the quantity axis, we

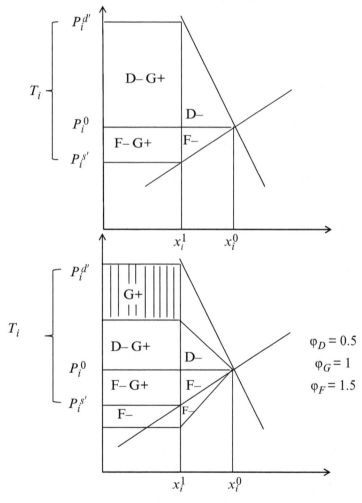

Figure 2.6   Stakeholder (top) and distributional weights (lower) analysis

look at them from the perspective of the price axis, thus identifying who gains and who loses. In the diagram, D represents demanders, F refers to factors of production, and G refers to the government (see also Chapter 17 in this volume on distributional accounting).

In the lower panel of Figure 2.6 we apply distributional weights (φ_i) of 0.5 for demanders and 1.5 for suppliers, keeping the government's weight at 1.0. These changes cause the D-rectangle to be cut in half, and the F-rectangle to be augmented by 50 percent. The reduction of D- leaves the top half of the former rectangle as an unalloyed gain to G, and hence to society. The opposite happens in the bottom rectangle, with F- increasing by 50 percent and G+ staying the same. We also have changes in the traditional deadweight loss triangle with D- being cut in half and F- being augmented by half. The bottom line in this weighted case is that the deadweight loss triangles and the F-loss rectangle are outweighed by the G+ gain rectangle, resulting in the tax generating a net social gain.

TWO COMMON ERRORS IN STAKEHOLDER DISTRIBUTIONAL ANALYSIS

The first common error is the assumption that an increment of project demand for a good or a factor of production will be met solely through an expansion of the quantity supplied of that good or factor. Similarly, its common counterpart is the assumption that items supplied as a result of a program or project will be fully absorbed via incremental demand. It is easy to find the source of these errors. Economics students are taught very early that competitive demanders and suppliers have little influence on the market prices of the things they buy and sell, and thus take market prices as given. This assertion is basically sound as a descriptor of their behavior, but it is totally misleading if it is interpreted to say that the sole ultimate source to meet a competitor's new demand is an increase in market quantity supplied or that the sole ultimate destination of a competitor's new supply is a corresponding increase in market quantity demanded.

The actual ultimate sourcing of supply to meet a new demand or of demand to absorb a new supply depends on the relative elasticities of market demand and supply. If these are equal, the ultimate sources to meet a project's new demand arise half from displacing other demanders and half from stimulating a new supply. If supply is twice as elastic as demand, the sourcing arises two-thirds from new supply and one-third from displaced demand. The sourcing of demand to absorb new supply is likewise split between increments of market demand and displacements of market supply, as dictated by the elasticities.

Figure 2.7 shows how the adjustments to a new source of demand (top

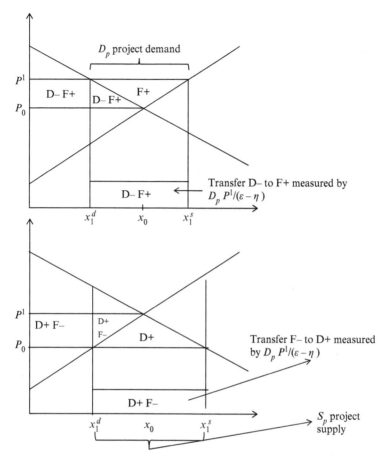

Figure 2.7   Adjustments to new demand or supply

panel) or supply (bottom panel) take place. Readers should recall that we are dealing with situations of full market adjustments to whatever disturbances we are analyzing. For projects, we are considering where the market would be in years 1, 2, 3, . . . n of the project's life, in the event the project is implemented compared with where the same market would be in the absence of the project. What we see in both panels of Figure 2.7 is a significant transfer taking place, demanders losing and factors gaining in the top panel and factors losing and demanders gaining in the bottom panel. There are also small triangles F+ in the top panel and D+ in the bottom panel. In real-world examples, these are small enough to be neglected in nearly every case. When this is done, it is easy to express the transfer as a fraction $1/(\varepsilon - \eta)$ of project demand or supply, where ε is the elasticity of market supply and η (<0) is that of market demand.

Figure 2.7 automatically disposes of the first common error. New demand is met completely by new supply only when $\varepsilon = \infty$. Similarly, new supply is fully absorbed by an equal increment of total demand only when $\eta = -\infty$.

The second common mistake entails an over-attribution of the benefits that accrue to labor as a result of a program or project. Most economic impact studies simply assign a project's entire wage bill as a benefit to the labor it employs. This would be true only if all the labor newly hired as a consequence of the project would otherwise have been unemployed, and moreover would have had a supply price of zero!! (see also Chapter 10 of this volume on labor markets and BCA).

The actual gain to labor as a consequence of a project accrues only minimally to the project's own labor force, and instead goes mainly to infra-marginal workers as they benefit from the project's impact on wages. Moreover, this benefit is simultaneously reflected in a loss to demanders, as shown in Figure 2.7, so there are at least two reasons—$(\varepsilon - \eta)$ higher than one, and $(\varphi_f - \varphi_d)$ likely to be well below one—why it is wrong to attribute a project's entire wages bill as a benefit to labor.

A PITFALL IN THE USE OF DISTRIBUTIONAL WEIGHTS

The literature on optimal taxation abounds with applications using exponential weighting functions. For an elasticity of one, a person's weight is cut in half with each doubling of income. With an elasticity $\partial \log MU_x / \partial \log(x)$ of one half (a flatter marginal utility curve) the weight is halved when income is multiplied by four. With an elasticity of two, a person's weight is cut to one fourth when income is doubled. I mention these specific elasticities because they are the ones most often found in published numerical examples.

I believe that the use of functions with elasticities in this range is a huge mistake. I can only understand its prevalence because it happens to lead to results which are certainly interesting and to a degree plausible, in work on optimal income tax schedules.

These results typically involve optimal tax structures which are progressive in average tax rates but regressive in marginal tax rates. All start with an exempt level of income (Y_e), and have the highest marginal tax rate in the first bracket. Marginal tax rates fall after that, as brackets increase, but average tax rates τ (represented by rays from the origin in a graph showing tax liability as a function of income) rise.

The source for regressiveness in the marginal rate was that raising τ_1, the first bracket rate by $d\tau_1$, caused all higher brackets to sustain an extra infra-marginal tax $(Y_1 - Y_e)d\tau_1$ producing distributional benefits of $\Sigma_j(\varphi_g - \varphi_j)(Y_1 - Y_e)d\tau_1$.

As these distributional benefits only applied to higher brackets, the second bracket had one fewer of them than the first, the third had one fewer than the second and so on, until finally the top bracket had no higher bracket at all producing "external" distributional benefits.

I feel that this somewhat surprising (to most people) result sort of lulled the profession into an unwarranted degree of comfort with respect to exponential weighting schemes with elasticities in the range of 0.5 to 2.

The problem is that it is not at all acceptable to use such a weighting scheme for the optimal income tax problem, and then reject its use for a huge range of other problems. What's sauce for the goose should be sauce for the gander!

The problem lies in the fact that the use of distributional weights leads to marginal conditions of an optimum being characterized by marginal deadweight loss being equal to marginal distributional benefit. Thus, with an elasticity of one and a weight of one for average income Y_a, one would have to barely accept a project which took $1000 away from a person with income of $2Y_a$ and gave only $250 to a person with an income of $0.5Y_a$, even when all of the remaining $750 was deadweight loss. The marginally acceptable efficiency loss reaches 15/16 when, using an elasticity of one, we look at the span between $0.25Y_a$ and $4Y_a$.

The above examples get squeezed as we consider lower elasticities (such as 1/3), and get stretched as we consider higher elasticities such as 3. But there is no doubt that these elasticity assumptions, if applied to real-world cases, call for redistributions to be carried to the point when marginal efficiency costs are large multiples of the benefits received by the deserving recipients.

In speaking with many audiences on these issues over many years, I have encountered no voices expressing loyalty to such weighting schemes. No logical flaw would be involved if a person really was willing to accept their full implications. But not many people appear to fall into that category.

BASIC NEEDS EXTERNALITIES

A very natural reaction to the previous section is to say "if not this, then what?". I struggled with this question in my 1978 paper, but was not satisfied with any answer until 1985, when the full implications of basic needs externalities occurred to me. Around that time, many benefit-cost discussions used the terms distributional weights and basic needs externalities quite interchangeably. But they seemed quite different to me, as I explained in a paper on "Basic needs versus distributional weights" (Harberger, 1984).

I take as my starting point the fact that most of the exponential-weight literature has operated with a single utility function thought to represent average utility-consumption or utility-income trade-off, but applied equally to all relevant income strata. I characterized this scheme as altruistic, the extra utility of the poor being the justification for transferring resources to them. In contrast, I justified basic needs externalities as generating improvements not necessarily in the utility of the recipients but in their welfare as defined by "society" (voters/taxpayers/government). I thus labeled basic needs externalities as "paternalistic" rather than altruistic.

To support my point, I called attention to the facts that most transfers from governments to citizens come in kind rather than in cash. Free public education can be obtained only by attending schools; free medical care can occur only by visiting medical institutions and/or professionals; free or subsidized housing comes only when you live there; and food subsidies are typically also contingent.

I support my argument with the hypothetical case of distributional weights for handling free public education. Maximizing the utility of recipients would favor giving each family money equal to the cost of sending their kids to school, and letting them spend it on other things if that will better reflect their utility functions. At the other extreme most voters are distressed to learn of cases in which food stamps are used to buy cigarettes, or sold on the black market.

Thus, we justify basic needs externalities as reflecting donors' tastes— that is, taxpayers' or the government's willingness to pay. This fits neatly into the framework of the three postulates and reflects a positive external-ity that can easily stand side by side with the negative externalities of congestion and pollution.

Who determines the size and coverage of basic needs externalities? The same people who would otherwise determine distributional weights. In my 1984 paper I introduced a "social demand curve", say for food, which lay above the demand curve of each poor household, joining it at the point of "adequacy" (Harberger, 1984).

Since then I have come to prefer a social "demand curve" applying not to food, but to an index of the family's nutritional level. This curve would display a society's willingness to pay more to move the family from index 80 to 81 than to move it from index 85 to 86, and to pay nothing at all once the family reached, say, an index of 90. Society's willingness to pay could be summarized by a straight line starting from a premium of 50 percent over market value at some lower level (say 70) of the index, and going to zero at some cut-off point. The result could be generous (an 80 percent premium to start, cut-off at index 100), or miserly (a 30 percent premium to start, cut-off at index 85).

The actual implementation of basic needs externalities could take the form of tax credits or income subsidies. I am told that the UK has instituted an externality premium of 20 percent on increments to income for families in the lowest income brackets. This could be considered a simple non-exponential distributional weighting scheme or a portmanteau way of generating basic needs externalities. Note that in either case, the highly extreme implications of exponential weights are avoided.

A SHADOW PRICE OF GOVERNMENT FUNDS?

The standard assumption in most real-world (and also theoretical) benefit-cost analysis has been that the marginal dollars of public spending are drawn from the capital market and that marginal inflows of funds spill into the capital market. This is a reasonable assumption because this is the way budgetary deficits and surpluses are in fact handled.

Capital-market sourcing is also convenient in helping to establish the economic opportunity cost of public funds, since the capital market reacts to inflows in much the same way regardless of their source, and similarly to outflows regardless of the use to which they are put. If we were to try to use taxes as the canonical source and absorber of funds we would be hard put to find anything resembling a "standard" tax source. Also, we must bear in mind that the release of resources for the great bulk of real-world projects and programs takes place via the capital markets.

But we cannot completely exclude taxation from our calculus, because increased public debt involves an increased opportunity cost which must be accounted for. This year's increment to borrowing ΔB generates a future flow of liabilities, whose present value, discounted at the same opportunity cost, is ΔB. Considering future economic costs to be paid by taxes, we must recognize that incremental taxation incurs an excess burden of deadweight loss. The role of the shadow price of government funds (SPGF) is to reflect this excess burden.

The calculation of the excess burden attaching to a marginal dollar of a tax finance is a simple extension of the standard deadweight loss triangle. In Figure 2.8, H represents the increment of deadweight loss associated with an increment to the excise tax ΔT_i. The incremental tax revenue generated by ΔT_i is J + K − H. So the excess burden per dollar of added revenue is H/(J + K − H) = δ_i and the shadow price of government funds from this source would be $(1 + \delta_i)$.

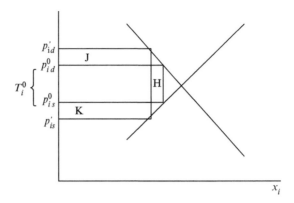

Notes: Δdeadweight loss $\sim$ H
Δ Tax revenue = J+K-H
Tax externality per dollar = H/(J+K-H) = δ
Shadow price of government funds if T_i were the only tax $x_i = (1+\delta_i)$

Figure 2.8   Shadow price of government funds

Given the utter simplicity of the concept, it is somewhat surprising that it has not become a component of standard real-world benefit-cost analysis. My only explanation for this is the fact that empirical estimates of δ_i range from lower levels between 10 and 15 percent, up to levels well in excess of 100 percent. A lone analyst of a new bridge or airport can probably be forgiven for failing to break new ground by introducing his or her own guess as to what the right δ_i should be.

But I don't think that the economics profession at large deserves equal pity, for we know with virtual certainty that $\delta_i = 0$ is not the right answer. Yet that is what we implicitly accept when we fail to include a shadow price of government funds in our analyses. If we as individuals are understandably reluctant to insert our own estimates, I feel that we as a profession have a duty to fight for the adoption of the SPGF concept by the government agencies that do and/or sponsor benefit-cost studies, and also by the World Bank and the regional development banks that have played a leading role in the history of benefit-cost work. These entities should be pressed to adopt a figure for δ that they ask to be used in the benefit-cost (BC) studies that they undertake or sponsor.

In my opinion, this task is easy, at least now and for a quite extended future. No such agency is likely to push for a shadow price of government funds of 1.3 or 1.4 or 1.5, simply because of the political firestorm that such a figure would create. A figure like 1.5 would imply that all public employees should, on economic grounds, have a marginal product of at least 1.5 times their salaries. The only mitigation of the 1.5 factor would come into play as the same factor would also apply to any cash inflows generated (directly or indirectly) by a program or project. But this would not be a big factor for many public projects. The increment of cash inflows generated by a new or improved road is not the gas tax on its traffic. Rather it is the net increment to gas tax receipts—taking into account that most of the increment of the traffic on a new or improved road is not really new, but simply diverted from other roads.

So we should recognize that political realities will dictate starting with low and easily defended values of δ. Ten or 15 percent makes sense to me, as these figures are very unlikely to be too high, and are at the same time low enough (I hope) to avoid a political firestorm.

ON PROFESSIONALISM IN BENEFIT-COST ANALYSIS

The preceding section is a natural trampoline for a broader discussion of professionalism in our field. A good start at defining what this means is to have as a goal that there should be a distinct central tendency in the results obtained when a number of different professionals analyze the same problem. If there is to be such a "consensus" among us, there must also be a central methodological core from which to work. Historically, this core for welfare economics as a whole has consisted of the three basic postulates set out previously. These postulates are easy to apply to cases involving prices set in the open market—regardless of whether or not they are distorted by taxes or monopolies. But the three postulates require some outside assistance in one large category of other cases and may simply be unhelpful in another large category.

I like to divide our cases into three categories. In the first category, where the three postulates reign supreme, we can do our professional task without any outside help. In the second set we have to turn to some outside source, or make some arbitrary assumptions in order to complete our job. In distributional weights, somebody has to give us the weights, or we have to simply assume certain values. No basis exists for a professional consensus based on scientific principles. This is equally true for basic needs externalities, for the shadow price of government funds, for the economic price of carbon emissions, and last but far from least, for the statistical cost of premature death (see Chapter 8 of this volume for more on this cost).

In a well-organized system of evaluation of public projects and programs, there should usually be authorities that would give us the authorized numbers for the above elusive externalities. In the absence of such an authority, our best hope is to explore what seem to be plausible ranges for the externality values that we seek. But we must always make clear the distinction between our professional core methodology on the one hand and these assumed externalities on the other.

The third and final category consists of cases where we should simply recuse ourselves, because of our inability to handle these cases in a professional way, using our professional tools. Nearly all problems in the national security and defense arena fall into this category. So also do most issues in the foreign aid arena. We might be able to assess the value to Sudan of an aid-financed irrigation scheme, but that is at best a precondition for it to be financed by a national foreign aid program. So too do programs of special assistance to victims of disease epidemics and natural disasters. In some of these cases we can help to identify inefficiencies in the delivery of benefits, but our professional methodology will not help us place a value on these benefits.

I think the rule is simple. Just as an orthopedist does not claim expertise in problems of the heart, ear, eye or liver, we should limit our professional claims to the areas where our tools work, and we should openly seek help when that is needed before our tools can be properly brought into play. In other areas, we can voice personal opinions, but should not cloak them as professional pronouncements.

This discussion is not just idle ramblings. In more than 50 years of work in this field, much of it in a hands-on practical context, I have many times witnessed a particular scenario. It starts with me and others trying to convince some agency of the usefulness of benefit-cost analysis. This effort meets resistance, due partly to inertia and partly to vested interests. But with persistence and with the demonstration effects of successful BCAs, the top authorities become converts to the BC cause. But when they make this shift, they often go too far. They see BCA as a way of being relieved of the difficult burden of choice—in short, a way of making their lives easier. The end result is all too often a mandate to do BC analyses of *all* the projects and programs under their control. This happens without their recognizing the important role they have to play in setting the key parameters in category 2 cases, and without their realizing the limits to our professional competence in category 3 cases.

This all too often leads to routinized BCAs. In Colombia in 2006 we encountered a situation where there were more than 200 BC analysts, most of them with less than a month of training done at institutions of little merit. In Peru, a few years later, the authorities pointed with pride to having evaluated over 4000 projects the previous year. But in both these cases the authorities were embarrassed when asked how many important projects they had successfully stopped or been able to modify in important ways. But routine acceptance of projects—going through the motions, filling out detailed dossiers on each of them, but finally giving nearly all the stamp of approval—seems to be the end result much of the time, once the net is extended too far.

There is another sensitive issue that has received far too little attention. It can go under the label "the benefit-cost analysis of benefit-cost analyses". To put it simply, it makes no sense to spend $100 000 to analyze an investment whose total cost is $100 000, but it could well pay to spend $10 million to analyze a project whose cost was $2 billion. This example makes it clear that the format of analysis has to vary with the size of the project or program. Further, BC analysts should pursue the same principle as sequential sampling—do not carry your work beyond the point at which you already have enough evidence to say yes or no.

These are some of the challenges that must be faced as we seek to expand the role of professionalism in real-world benefit-cost analysis.

Why do we care so much about professionalism? It is because it is quite rare in the real world for a BC analysis to be paid by an agency interested only in maximizing net social benefits. Most funding entities are either themselves interested parties, or have a preferred outcome for other reasons. It is all too easy for them to hire mendacious "experts" who will find ways to reach their sponsor's desired decision. To me, our professionalism is the only weapon that we can rely on to resist such pressures, and to fulfill the true purpose of benefit-cost analysis.

REFERENCES AND RECOMMENDATIONS FOR FURTHER READING

Chetty, R. (2009). "Sufficient statistics for welfare analysis: A bridge between structural and reduced form methods", in K. Arrow and T. Bresnahan (eds), *Annual Review of Economics*, Volume 1, Palo Alto, CA: Annuals Reviews.

Goulder, L. and R. Williams III (2003). "The substantial bias from ignoring general equilibrium effects in estimating excess burden and a practical solution", *Journal of Political Economy*, **111**(4), 898–927.

Harberger, A. (1964). "The measurement of waste", *American Economic Review*, **54**(3), 58–76.

Harberger, A. (1971). "Three basic postulates for applied welfare economics: An interpretive essay", *Journal of Economic Literature*, **9**(3), 785–97.

Harberger, A. (1978). "On the use of distributional weights in social cost-benefit analysis", *Journal of Political Economy*, **86**(2, part 2), S87–S120.

Harberger, A. (1984). "Basic needs versus distributional weights in social cost-benefit analysis", *Economic Development and Cultural Change*, **32**(3), 455–74.

Harberger, A. (1993). "The search for relevance in economics" (Richard T. Ely Lecture), *American Economic Review*, **83**(2), 1–16.

3. Defining the baseline

Charles Griffiths* and Chris Dockins*

ABSTRACT

Evaluating the benefits and costs of any action is fundamentally determined by the baseline, which determines the basis of comparison for the action. However, the topic of a baseline is often given limited attention in benefit-cost analysis (BCA) textbooks and journal articles, despite the fact that this is one of the first issues economists confront when doing applied analysis. This paper addresses this gap by discussing some of the nuances of defining and constructing a defensible baseline and illustrates these nuances with examples from the US Environmental Protection Agency (EPA). Core materials for BCA teachers include the narrative as well as links to documents, websites and regulatory impact analyses illustrating these baseline nuances.

BACKGROUND

Evaluating benefits and costs of any action is fundamentally determined by the state of the world that will be used as a basis of comparison. For example, suppose a regulation were proposed to require every car to have a backup camera installed but, due to consumer demand, the auto manufacturers would install these cameras anyway. How should we assess the benefits and costs of this regulation? In this case, the benefits and costs of the regulation would only be associated with how the regulation accelerated the manufacturers' actions. If the pace at which manufacturers would install these cameras is unchanged by the regulation, both the benefits and costs of the regulation would be zero. It might even be the case – albeit unlikely – that the regulatory timeline might induce manufacturers to move more slowly, and net benefits could be negative. Ultimately, the benefits and costs of an action are a direct consequence of the baseline conditions that one estimates or assumes will hold if the action is not taken. Properly defining and modeling of the baseline is a crucial component of benefit-cost analysis (BCA) that often deserves more attention than it gets.

The Federal Government notes the importance of an accurate and transparent baseline in several contexts. The Congressional Budget Office (CBO) provides ten years of projected annual baseline information for many Federal Government programs as part of its budget projections (CBO, 2017a), data critical for CBO scoring of the effect of legislation. The Office of Management and Budget's (OMB) Circular A-4 (US OMB, 2003) on regulatory analysis includes identifying a baseline as part of the key elements of a regulatory analysis and the OMB primer on regulatory impact analysis (RIA) (US OMB, 2011) lists defining the baseline as one of the nine steps required for a complete RIA. Perhaps the most complete treatment of baseline issues in BCA is contained in the Environmental Protection Agency's (EPA) *Guidelines for Preparing Economic Analyses* (US EPA, 2010) which devotes an entire chapter to baseline issues.

Recently added requirements for regulatory analysis have heightened the importance of rigorous and consistent baselines. For example, President Trump's Executive Order 13,771 (2017) on reducing regulation and controlling regulatory costs requires that at least two regulations be eliminated for every new regulation issued and that each federal agency must not exceed an annual "total incremental cost of all new regulations." For fiscal year 2017, the EPA's regulatory budget is zero – that is, the cost of all regulation must be fully offset by deregulatory cost savings. Meeting this regulatory budget requires an explicit calculation of the incremental costs of both regulatory and deregulatory action and, as a consequence, a determination of a consistent baseline. Another example is a bill introduced by Senator Thune of South Dakota in April 2017 that would require federal agencies to include a scenario in which proposed rules and not yet implemented final rules be excluded from the baseline of RIAs (Skibell, 2017).

While the importance of defining a proper baseline is well understood by experienced practicing economists, the topic is generally given limited attention in BCA textbooks and journal articles.[1] This is despite the fact that this is one of the first issues economists confront when doing applied analysis. This paper attempts to address this gap by discussing some of the nuances in defining and constructing a baseline that should be part of proper benefit-cost analysis, with an emphasis on how key issues have arisen in regulatory analyses at the US EPA. The final section offers some recommendations for appropriate baseline specifications.

DEFINITIONS OF A BASELINE

According to US EPA (2010)

> A baseline is defined as the best assessment of the world absent the proposed regulation or policy action ... The baseline serves as a primary point of comparison for an analysis of a proposed policy action. An economic analysis of a policy or regulation compares the current state of the world, the baseline scenario, to the expected state of the world with the proposed policy or regulation in effect, the policy scenario. Economic and other impacts of policies or regulations are measured as the differences between these two scenarios.

In other words, the baseline is the assumed evolution of the world if the policy under consideration is not undertaken. Cost or benefits in the policy scenario are the incremental effects compared to this baseline.

The Best Assessment of the World Absent the Proposed Action

For regulatory policy, a "no action" baseline is usually the best choice. This is the state of the world assuming that there is no change in the current regulatory regime. That is, the regulatory burden on the regulated industry is assumed to remain constant and in place. However, this may not always be an accurate representation of the baseline. If a regulatory program is set to expire or dramatically change in the absence of the proposed action, then the baseline specification should be the best representation of the state of the world assuming this change. In general, a baseline should represent the regulatory environment that will most likely manifest, not necessarily the regulatory environment that currently exists.

Consider this example from the Renewable Fuel Standard (RFS) program where the baseline must consider a changing regulatory regime.[2] The 2007 law statutorily sets specific volumes of renewable fuel to replace or reduce the quantity of petroleum-based fuel. However, the statute also grants EPA a general waiver authority to reduce the RFS volumes if the program is causing severe economic or environmental harm or if there is inadequate domestic supply of renewable fuel. Since 2010, EPA has determined that cellulosic fuels are not being produced in sufficient quantities to meet the statutory standards so it has reduced the required volume of cellulosic biofuel through this waiver authority. Table 3.1 lists the volume standard for the various types of renewable fuel as were specified in the 2007 statute and the volume requirements established by EPA for 2014–17.

The statutory volume for cellulosic biofuel in 2007 is 5.5 billion gallons (US EPA, 2017b) but EPA set the 2017 obligation at 311 million gallons (US EPA, 2017a). In 2016, the cellulosic biofuel obligation was 230 million

Table 3.1 Renewable Fuel Standard volume requirements (billions of gallons)

	Set Forth in EISA				Required by EPA			
	2014	2015	2016	2017	2014	2015	2016	2017
Cellulosic Biofuel	1.75	3.00	4.25	5.50	0.03	0.12	0.23	0.31
Biomass-Based Diesel	1.00*	1.00*	1.00*	1.00*	1.63	1.73	1.90	2.00
Advanced Biofuel	3.75	5.50	7.25	9.00	2.67	2.88	3.61	4.28
Total Renewable Fuel	18.15	20.50	22.25	24.00	16.28	16.93	18.11	19.28

* The statute sets a 1 billion gallon minimum but EPA may raise requirement

Source: EPA (2017a, 2017b).

gallons. This creates a question of the appropriate baseline to use to assess costs. Is EPA's 2017 cellulosic biofuel standard an increase from 230 million gallons or a decrease from 5.5 billion gallons? Rather than relying on the static state of the world as specified by the statute, EPA used the revised, current state of the world in 2016. This was addressed in the final rule establishing the 2017 volume requirements (US EPA, 2015c; p. 77,487):

> a number of different scenarios could be considered the "baseline" for the assessment of the costs of this rule. One scenario would be the statutory volumes in which case this final rule would be reducing volumes, and reducing costs. For the purposes of showing illustrative overall costs of this rulemaking, we use the preceding year's standard as the baseline.

With vs. Without, Not Just Before vs. After

It is important to note that the incremental benefits and costs are a comparison of the state of the world *with* the action – the policy scenario – to the world *without* the action – the baseline. This may be distinct, and quite different, from a comparison of the state of the world *before* the action to the state of the world *after* the action (unless the baseline future is unchanging). EPA's benefits assessment of the Clean Water Act (CWA) since 1972 for conventional pollutants in rivers and streams provides a useful illustration of this point (US EPA, 2000).

In Figure 3.1, water quality with the CWA is shown as the upper solid line and depicts improvement since 1972 due to pollutant reductions mandated by the CWA. One approach for a baseline against which to compare these improvements is to look at conditions in 1972. This is appealing

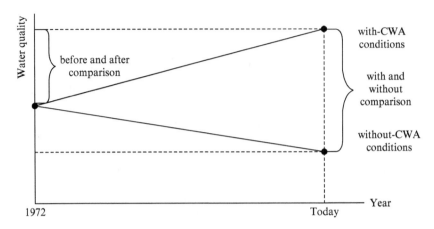

Source: EPA (2000).

Figure 3.1   Proper baseline comparison: with vs. without the action

because we have data on water quality conditions in both time periods, so
we can measure the actual change. However, this "before vs after" perspective most likely would understate the actual benefits because many factors
that affect water quality have changed since 1972. In particular, economic
production and population both increased and, absent the CWA, would
likely have resulted in a deterioration of the nation's water quality, shown
in Figure 3.1 as the lower solid line. The correct calculation of the benefits
of the CWA is obtained using this as the baseline: comparing the best
estimate of the world "with vs without" the CWA and not just the world
before vs. after. As the US EPA report (2000, p. 1–4) states:

> The challenge in such analyses is to develop a consistent, accurate characteriza-
> tion of the without-CWA conditions. That characterization must link estimates
> of pollutant discharges (i.e., loadings) without the CWA to their impacts on
> surface water quality, on the services provided by water resources, and on the
> social value of these services. Those metrics are then compared to the ones
> developed similarly under with-CWA conditions.

Considerations for Retrospective vs. Prospective BCA

The choice of the starting point for the baseline also depends on whether
the analysis is a retrospective or a prospective analysis. For regulatory
policy, the majority of BCA are forward-looking (that is, prospective),
evaluating the anticipated effectiveness of a policy compared to the world
without that policy. In this case, the baseline is the world without the

policy action being considered and is, arguably, easier to model since it is most likely a business-as-usual scenario. Demographic and economic activity projections are generally available and the resulting environmental conditions can be modeled from those projections. The policy scenario requires additional assumptions about the effectiveness of the policy and behavioral and market responses to the policy. In contrast, a retrospective analysis of a policy compares the effectiveness of an existing policy to the world if the policy had never been enacted. In this case, the policy scenario is easier to model, because it is the evolution of the world that actually occurred, and the baseline is the "counterfactual" scenario that requires additional behavioral and economic assumptions.

The EPA's report on the benefits and costs of the Clean Air Act (CAA) from 1990 to 2020 (US EPA, 2011) provides a useful illustration of using different baselines for a retrospective and prospective study. Section 812 of the Clean Air Act Amendments (CAAA) (1990) require EPA to conduct scientifically reviewed studies of the costs, benefits and other impacts of the CAA. To date, EPA has conducted three studies under this authority: one retrospective study from 1970 to 1990 (US EPA, 1997) and two prospective studies, both beginning in 1990 (US EPA, 1999; US EPA, 2011).

The retrospective study assessed the benefits and costs of the 1970 CAA and the 1977 Amendments, up to the passage of the CAA Amendments of 1990. The baseline in this case is the modeled evolution of air emissions beginning with the state of the world in 1970 and proceeding as if the Clean Air Act had not been enacted. This is the solid line labeled "Pre-CAA" in Figure 3.2.[3] The costs and benefits of the CAA up to 1990 is the impact of the difference in emissions with the CAA (labeled "Post-CAA") compared to without the CAA (labeled "Pre-CAA"), and is the wedge labeled "A" in the graph. The policy scenario for the retrospective study ends with emissions as they actually existed in 1990.

The two prospective studies evaluated the impact of the 1990 CAA Amendments. Those amendments went beyond the requirements of the original 1970 CAA and the 1977 Amendments by tightening implementation goals and introducing new control programs. The baseline for both prospective analyses began in 1990 and was the state of the world without the 1990 Amendments. This is the line labeled "Without-CAAA" in Figure 3.2. The costs and benefits of the 1990 Amendments is the impact of the difference in emissions in the wedges labeled "B" and "C." As the second retrospective report (US EPA, 2011, p. 1–2) states:

> Because the 1990 Amendments represented an additional improvement to the nation's existing clean air program, the analysis summarized in this report was designed to estimate the costs and benefits of the 1990 CAAA incremental to those costs and benefits assessed in the Retrospective analysis. In economic

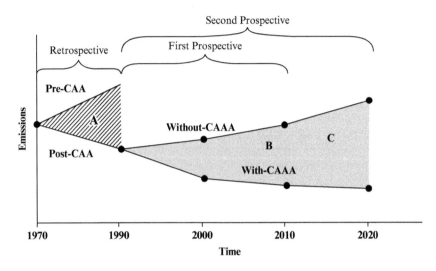

Figure 3.2   Policy and baseline emissions for EPA reports to Congress on the benefits and costs of the Clean Air Act

terminology, this report addresses the marginal costs and benefits of the 1990 CAAA.

It is important to realize that the two prospective analyses do not represent the costs and benefits of the entire Clean Air Act because they do not use a baseline associated with a world without the CAA, something made clear by graphically illustrating the baselines and policy cases in Figure 3.2. An analysis of the entire CAA would require modeling the emission trajectory continuing from the "Pre-CAA" line into the future.

MODELING THE BASELINE

While the definition of a baseline – the best assessment of the world absent the proposed regulation or policy action – sounds deceptively simple, it involves nuanced modeling questions. Modeling the world without a policy requires a number of basic input variables. US EPA's guidelines (2010), for example, list demographic change, future economic activity, changes in consumer behavior and technological change as four broad categories of "basic variables" that should be considered when modeling both the baseline and the policy scenario.

Some of these variables are modeled by government agencies and can generally be used as baseline assumptions. For example, the US Census Bureau (2017) projects the size and composition of the US population. The Congressional Budget Office (2017b) produces projections of the government budget, economic activity and government spending and revenue. Other variables, such as changes in consumer behavior and technological change, are more difficult to predict but can have substantial influence on the estimate of benefits and costs of a policy. If changes in population, economic growth and other basic variables are incorrectly modeled in the baseline then the estimated incremental costs and benefit of an action will be inaccurate.

It may be tempting to assume that the levels and changes in these basic variables should be the same for both the baseline and the policy scenario, but this is inappropriate in many cases. Environmental policy actions are unlikely to affect broader demographic and macroeconomic variables, but they might reasonably affect consumer behavior and technological change. In fact, many environmental policies are specifically designed to affect these variables. As a consequence, changes in the basic variables may differ significantly between the baseline and the policy scenario. A general guideline is that the basic variables should be *consistent*, arising from common logic, across the two scenarios. This means that the levels and changes of the variables should be explicitly reported and the assumptions of how and why they change in the scenarios should be reported.

Additionally, a consistent baseline should be used to evaluate both the *costs* and the *benefits* of a policy action as well as different policy options. In this case, a consistent baseline means the same baseline. However, since the cost analysis and the benefits analysis are often done independently of each other, the more practical interpretation of a consistent baseline is that they should use the same assumptions or estimates of basic variables. For example, the Total Maximum Daily Load (TMDL) for the Chesapeake Bay requires that jurisdictions in the Bay find offsets for any new or increased pollution loads that are not included in the TMDL, and that this can be accomplished through a pollution credit trading program. EPA recognizes two approaches for determining the baseline for generating credits: a practice-based and a performance-based baseline. A practice-based baseline identifies the practices required to be implemented before credits can be generated. A performance-based baseline specifies the numeric target or percentage reduction required but leaves the decision of which practices to implement up to the individual credit generator (US EPA, 2016). The existence of two baseline methodologies raises the possibility of an inconsistent baseline for any given analysis. It would be inappropriate in benefit-cost analysis to have the costs based on one baseline approach and the benefits based on the other, unless the practices of the two approaches were shown to be the same.

In some cases, the modeling assumptions for the baseline are so uncertain that multiple baselines are required. That is, more than one baseline is estimated to evaluate costs and benefits. For example, EPA's 2006 analysis of revisions to oil pollution prevention regulation faced considerable uncertainty about compliance with prior oil pollution prevention regulations (US EPA, 2006). Because the 2006 revision was primarily deregulatory this brought into question what actual cost savings might result from the rule: regulated facilities who were not complying with the prior regulation would not experience cost savings from deregulatory provisions of the new rule. EPA did not have reliable empirical evidence on the extent of non-compliance, but developed and presented an alternative baseline scenario in an appendix based on a non-compliance rate of 50 percent.

It should be noted that alternative baselines may be considered in studies designed to support a specific policy analysis. For example, EPA recently conducted a stated preference study to examine households' marginal willingness to pay for incremental water quality improvements in the Chesapeake Bay from the TMDL (Moore et al., 2015). Because of uncertainty in predicting the future water quality of the Bay in the absence of pollution reductions from the TMDL – the baseline scenario for the analysis – three possible baselines were used: a "constant baseline," in which environmental conditions remain unchanged, a "declining baseline," in which future baseline conditions were assumed to be worse than current conditions, and an "improving baseline," in which future baseline conditions were assumed to be better than current conditions. In this case, multiple baselines for the analysis must be matched with the benefits analysis results specific to each baseline.

OBLIGATIONS FROM OTHER REGULATIONS

In addition to the basic modeling variables, OMB recognizes other potential factors that may affect the baseline (US OMB, 2003, p. 15).

> The choice of an appropriate baseline may require consideration of a wide range of potential factors, including:
>
> - evolution of the market,
> - changes in external factors affecting expected benefits and costs,
> - changes in regulations promulgated by the agency or other government entities and
> - the degree of compliance by regulated entities with other regulations.
>
> It may be reasonable to forecast that the world absent the regulation will resemble the present. If this is the case, however, your baseline should reflect the future effect of current government programs and policies.

Including Finalized Regulation

While the first two factors relate to modeling issues described in the last section, the last two factors relate to the future effect of current government programs and policies. In general, the baseline needs to reflect actions that have already been taken or committed to. This means that the effect of rules and actions that have already been promulgated should be included, even if those effects have not yet occurred but will occur in the future. Note that these future effects are affected by the anticipated level of compliance with the regulations: the less businesses comply with promulgated regulation, the less the effect that regulation will have.

Consider this example. On March 10, 2005, EPA finalized the Clean Air Interstate Rule (CAIR) designed to reduce sulfur dioxide and nitrogen oxides emissions in 28 eastern states and the District of Columbia (US EPA, 2005b). However, the control technology that EPA assumed would be used also reduced mercury emission. Five days after issuing CAIR, EPA finalized the Clean Air Mercury Rule (CAMR) to cap and reduce mercury emissions from coal-fired power plants (US EPA, 2005c).[4] Table 3.2, adapted from the CAMR RIA (US EPA, 2005a), lists the total US mercury emission in 2001 and the baseline emissions in 2020, including estimated reductions from CAIR in the baseline.

In 2001, total mercury emissions from power plants (EGUs, or electric power generating units) were 48.57 tons. EPA estimated that after CAMR, EGU mercury emissions would decline by 72 percent to 13.59 tons by 2020. However, this decline includes the effects of CAIR. As Table 3.2 shows, the estimated baseline emissions in 2020, with CAIR but without CAMR, were 34.4 tons. So the actual estimated incremental effect of CAMR was a 20-ton reduction, from 34.42 tons to 13.59 tons, a 39.5 percent decline. If the EPA has not included CAIR in the baseline, then it would appear that

Table 3.2   Mercury emissions in 2001 and the estimated 2020 (with CAIR) baseline

Emissions Source	Total Mercury Emissions (tons)	
	2001 Base Year	2020 (with CAIR) Baseline
EGUs	48.57	34.42
Non-EGU Point	58.78	45.01
Non-point	7.54	7.76
Total, All Sources	114.89	87.19

Source: Adapted from EPA (2005a, p. 8–3).

CAMR would generate a 35-ton reduction in mercury emissions, which would overstate both the benefits and the costs of complying with CAMR.

Non-final Regulations and Related Complications

The incorporation of CAIR into the CAMR baseline illustrates the correct inclusion of the future effects of a previously promulgated rule, consistent with EPA's guidelines (2010) which state that "All final rules promulgated prior to the rule under consideration should be included in the baseline." What is less clear is the extent to which *anticipated* rules should be included. While a proposed rule may signal the intention of an agency to enact new regulation, the effect of proposed rules is generally not included in the baselines because the rule has not been formally promulgated. A recent exception to this practice was the RIA for the 2015 National Ambient Air Quality Standards (NAAQS) for ozone (US EPA, 2015b). The baseline for the rule included current state and federal programs, but it also included "adjustments" for the proposed Clean Power Plan (CPP). The CPP is an EPA action to reduce carbon emissions from fossil fuel-fired and natural gas-fired EGUs by setting CO_2 emission rates and then allowing states to develop plans to meet those rates (US EPA, 2014a). The 2015 ozone NAAQS assumed in its baseline that some ozone precursors, particularly NOx, would be reduced because of the CPP, even though the CPP had not yet been finalized. Similarly, the 2015 Steam Electric rules (US EPA, 2015a) included the effect of the proposed CPP in its baseline. EPA recognized the uncertainty surrounding this decision and included a footnote to the ozone NAAQS (US EPA, 2015b) that reads:

> The impact of these forecast changes in NOx emissions between the proposed and final CPP on ozone concentrations in specific locations is uncertain. There is no clear spatial pattern of where emissions are forecast to be higher or lower in the final CPP relative to the proposed CPP. Furthermore, states have flexibility in the form of their plans that implement the CPP and therefore the specific impact of the CPP on NOx emissions in any state is uncertain.

The inclusion of proposed rules in a baseline is problematic for a number of reasons. First, while a proposed rule signals the intent to issue a final rule and the agency maintains a schedule to do so, there is no guarantee that it will issue that final rule nor that it will follow the planned schedule.[5] The CPP is a case in point. The CPP was finalized in August 2015, but was stayed by the Supreme Court in February 2016 pending judicial review. In March 2017, President Trump issued Executive Order 13,783 (2017) directing the EPA Administrator to review the CPP and many anticipate that the rule will be rescinded. In effect, the CPP was never actually implemented and may never be implemented and so any rule that included a baseline with the effects from the proposed CPP will have inaccurate benefits and cost estimates. Second, a final rule may differ significantly from the proposed rule which means that the assumptions embedded in a baseline using the proposed rule will not accurately reflect the future effects of the final rule.

This decision to include the proposed CPP may have induced Senator Thune to introduce Bill S.971, the Real EPA Impact Reviews Act (2017). The summary of this bill reads:

> To require the Administrator of the Environmental Protection Agency to include in each regulatory impact analysis for a proposed or final rule an analysis that does not include any other proposed or unimplemented rule.

In other words, the bill requires EPA to include an analysis that does not include proposed rules. It also requires an analysis that does not include "unimplemented rules," and this has caused some concern (Skibell, 2017). An unimplemented rule is defined in the bill as "any other rule that, as of the date of the analysis – (a) has been finalized by the Administrator; but (b) has not been implemented" (Real EPA Impact Reviews Act, 2017). This most likely refers to rules like the CPP that have not been implemented because of court or the Congressional Review Act action. However, for proper benefit-cost analysis, it should *not* suggest that the future effects of final rules should not be included in the baseline. Often, in fact, implementation dates and schedules span years, if not decades, for environmental regulations. The best characterization of the world should, in general, consider the changes associated with future implementation as given.

Regulatory Actions of Other Actors

To be fully comprehensive, the final regulatory actions of *all* other actors – other offices in the same agency, other regulatory agencies, and states – should be considered in the baseline. However, dealing with the decision of outside actors can cause complications about what to include in the baseline and how to measure incremental costs and benefits. For example, in December of 2012, EPA issued a proposed rule with numeric water quality standards for certain estuaries, coastal and inland waters in Florida (US EPA, 2012b). This was done because Florida had not yet issued its own numeric standards and EPA was required to comply with a consent decree with a number of environmental groups that established a schedule for promulgating these numeric criteria. Earlier in 2012, the Florida Department of Environmental Protection had submitted a set of narrative water quality standards but did not actually provide numeric values. As such, EPA provided the numeric water quality standards.

EPA estimated that there would be \$239 million to \$634 million in incremental annual costs and \$39 million to \$53.4 million incremental annual benefits associated with meeting these numeric standards. However, EPA argued that because the numeric criteria were simply enumerating Florida's narrative criteria and did not add additional requirements, the costs and benefits of EPA's proposed rule were actually close to zero. In other words, EPA effectively assumed that the costs and benefits of meeting the water quality criteria were incurred by Florida's action and were in its baseline. Specifically, EPA (2012b, p. 74,927) said:

> Although the proposed rule does not establish any requirements directly applicable to regulated entities or other sources of nutrient pollution, EPA developed an economic analysis to provide information on potential costs and benefits that may be associated with the State implementation requirements that may be necessary to ensure attainment of WQS . . . It is important to note that the costs and benefits of pollution controls needed to attain water quality standards for nutrients for waters already identified as impaired by the State (including waters with TMDLs in place and without TMDLs in place) are not included in EPA estimates of the cost of the rule. EPA believes that these costs and benefits would be incurred in the absence of the current proposed rule and are therefore part of the baseline against which the costs and benefits of this rule are measured

Another example occurred in June 2012 when EPA issued NOx emission standards for gas turbine engines used on commercial passenger and freight aircraft (US EPA, 2012a). These standards were the same as those adopted in 2010 by the International Civil Aviation Organization (ICAO) and EPA was part of the US representative team at the ICAO meetings. When EPA issued its rule, it did not estimate the costs and benefits of the more expensive aircraft engines. Rather, it argued that because the standards had been adopted by ICAO and because aircraft engines are an international commodity, EPA was simply codifying the standards that would be met anyway rather than imposing any additional burden. While US manufacturers were not obliged to make compliant engines, EPA believed that they would do so in the absence of the rule. Specifically, EPA (2012a, p. 36,377) said:

> we do not attribute any costs to the compliance with today's regulations that conform to ICAO standards and recommended practices. Aircraft turbofan engines are international commodities. As a result, engine manufacturers respond to this market reality by designing and building engines that conform to ICAO international standards and practices. Therefore, engine manufacturers are compelled to make the necessary business decisions and investments to

maximize their international markets even in the absence of U.S. action . . . Therefore, EPA believes that today's requirements that conform with ICAO standards and practices will impose no real additional burden on engine manufacturers.

While the general rule for benefit-cost analysis is that actions that have previously been implemented or enacted should be included in the baseline, deciding what to include becomes more difficult when evaluating a regulation or action that another party has already taken or is "obligated" to take but has not done so. For both the Florida water quality standards and the NOx standards for aircraft engines, EPA assumed a baseline that suggested that its actions imposed no costs or benefits on society. While EPA's approach did not violate any standards of BCA, the decision to include the actions of other parties in the baseline was, to some degree, a policy call.

RECOMMENDATIONS FOR APPROPRIATE BASELINE SPECIFICATIONS

A baseline is "the best assessment of the world absent the proposed regulation or policy action" (US EPA, 2010) and is a fundamental component of BCA. For the incremental benefits and costs of a BCA to be relevant and understood, it is important to specify an accurate and transparent baseline to indicate what the benefits and costs are incremental to. This chapter addresses some of the nuances of defining and constructing a defensible baseline and illustrates these issues with examples from the EPA.

A number of important recommendations can be drawn from this discussion.

- For regulatory policy, a "no action" baseline, assuming no change in the regulatory regime, is a common choice for regulatory policy, but it may not always be the best choice if a regulatory program is set to expire or dramatically change in the absence of the proposed action.
- The benefits and costs in a BCA are a comparison of the incremental effect on the state of the world with the action (the policy scenario) to the world without the action (the baseline). It is not a comparison of the state of the world before the action to the state of the world after the action.
- For prospective, forward-looking analyses, the baseline is the world without the policy action being considered and is, often, a business-as-usual scenario. For retrospective, backward-looking analyses, the

baseline is the "counterfactual" scenario of the world if the policy had never been enacted and may require behavioral and economic assumptions to be modeled.

- Some of the basic variables used to estimate the baseline, such as demographics and future government and economic activity, are available from government agencies like the Census Bureau and the Congressional Budget Office. Other variables, such as changes in consumer behavior and technological change, are more difficult to predict. In general, the levels and changes of the variables used to model the baseline should be explicitly reported and the assumptions of how and why they change in the scenarios should be reported.
- Changes in the basic variables may differ between the baseline and the policy scenario but they should be consistent across the two scenarios. Important differences should be transparently reported.
- A consistent baseline should be used for both the cost and the benefit analysis; this almost always means that they should use the same baseline.
- When the modeling assumptions for the baseline are particularly uncertain, multiple baselines can be used to evaluate the effect of a policy action. When this occurs, analysts should be careful not to combine the cost and the benefits using two different baseline scenarios and the results of the benefit-cost analysis should clearly refer to the specific baseline scenario being used.
- The baseline should reflect actions that have already been taken and should include the effect of rules and actions that have already been promulgated, even if those effects will occur in the future.
- In general, proposed or anticipated rules should *not* be included in the baseline because they have not been formally promulgated. Proposed rules may not accurately reflect the effect of a final rule.
- In some cases, a baseline might include the effect of an action taken by another actor (for example, another agency, state or international organization). Similarly, a baseline might include the effect of another actor if that actor is "obligated" to take but has not done so. However, including these effects in the baseline can have a dramatic effect on the estimated costs and benefits and so all assumptions should be transparently reported.

NOTES

*   The views expressed in this paper are those of the authors and do not necessarily represent those of the US Environmental Protection Agency (EPA). This work has not been

subjected to the agency's required peer and policy review. No official agency endorsement should be inferred.

1. A notable exception is Farrow (2013).
2. RFS requirements are specified in the Energy Policy Act (2005) and the Energy Independence and Security Act (EISA) (2007).
3. Note that while the x-axis here is similar to that in Figure 3.1, the y-axis is the inverse. In Figure 3.1 the y-axis depicted increasing water quality while in Figure 3.2 the y-axis depicts increasing emissions of pollutants, and therefore diminished air quality. In either case, the benefits and costs are driven by the difference between the baseline and policy scenarios.
4. In 2008, the DC Circuit Court vacated CAMR and remanded CAIR, so neither ultimately went into effect, but the inclusion of CAIR in the CAMR RIA baseline is still illustrative.
5. There are many cases where an agency must issue a rule by some judicially or statutorily mandated date and so a final rule can more reasonably be expected. But, absent legal or statutory constraints, an agency is not required to issue a final rule simply because it issued a proposed rule.

REFERENCES AND RECOMMENDATIONS FOR FURTHER READING

Clean Air Act Amendments (1990), *Public Law 101-549*, accessed 12 July 2017 at https://www.gpo.gov/fdsys/pkg/STATUTE-104/pdf/STATUTE-104-Pg2399.pdf.

Congressional Budget Office (CBO) (2017a), *Baseline Projections for Selected Programs*, accessed 14 June 2017 at https://www.cbo.gov/about/products/baseline-projections-selected-programs.

Congressional Budget Office (CBO) (2017b), *Outlook for the Budget and the Economy*, accessed 14 June 2017 at https://www.cbo.gov/topics/budget/outlook-budget-and-economy.

Energy Independence and Security Act (2007), *Public Law 110-140*, accessed 12 July 2017 at https://www.gpo.gov/fdsys/pkg/PLAW-110publ140/pdf/PLAW-110publ140.pdf.

Energy Policy Act (2005), *Public Law 109-58*, accessed 12 July 2017 at https://www.gpo.gov/fdsys/pkg/PLAW-109publ58/pdf/PLAW-109publ58.pdf.

Executive Order 13,771 (2017), "Reducing regulation and controlling regulatory costs", *Federal Register*, **82** (22), 9339–41, accessed 3 May 2017 at https://www.gpo.gov/fdsys/pkg/FR-2017-02-03/pdf/2017-02451.pdf.

Executive Order 13,783 (2017), *Promoting Energy Independence and Economic Growth*, accessed 31 August 2017 at https://www.gpo.gov/fdsys/pkg/DCPD-201700204/pdf/DCPD-201700204.pdf.

Farrow, S. (2013), "How (not) to lie with benefit-cost analysis", *The Economists' Voice*, **10** (1), 45–50.

Moore, C., D. Guignet, K. Maguire, C. Dockins and N. Simon (2015), "A stated preference study of the Chesapeake Bay and Watershed Lakes", *NCEE Working Paper # 15-06*, accessed 3 May 2017 at https://www.epa.gov/sites/production/files/2016-03/documents/2015-06.pdf.

Real EPA Impact Reviews Act (2017), *S. 971, 115th Cong.*, accessed 20 June 2017 at https://billcam.dailyclout.io/bill-texts/iMSpedGgOw.

Skibell, A. (2017), "Thune bill would revamp regulatory cost-benefit analysis", *E&E*

News, accessed 8 May 2017 at https://www.eenews.net/eenewspm/2017/04/28/
stories/1060053781.

US Census Bureau (2017), *Population Projections*, accessed 14 June 2017 at https://
www.census.gov/topics/population/population-projections.html.

US Environmental Protection Agency (EPA) (1997), *The Benefits and Costs of the
Clean Air Act, 1970 to 1990*, accessed 3 May 2017 at https://www.epa.gov/sites/
production/files/2015-06/documents/contsetc.pdf.

US Environmental Protection Agency (EPA) (1999), *The Benefits and Costs of the
Clean Air Act, 1990 to 2010*, accessed 3 May 2017 at https://www.epa.gov/sites/
production/files/2015-07/documents/fullrept.pdf.

US Environmental Protection Agency (EPA) (2000), *A Benefits Assessment of
Water Pollution Control Programs Since 1972: Part 1, The Benefits of Point
Source Controls for Conventional Pollutants in Rivers and Streams*, accessed 2
February 2017 at https://yosemite.epa.gov/ee/epa/eerm.nsf/vwAN/EE-0429-01.
pdf/$file/EE-0429-01.pdf.

US Environmental Protection Agency (EPA) (2005a), *Regulatory Impact Analysis
of the Final Clean Air Mercury Rule*, accessed 3 May 2017 at https://www3.epa.
gov/ttnecas1/regdata/RIAs/mercury_ria_final.pdf.

US Environmental Protection Agency (EPA) (2005b), "Rule to reduce interstate
transport of fine particulate matter and ozone (clean air interstate rule); revisions to acid rain program; revisions to the NOx SIP call; final rule", *Federal
Register*, **70** (91), 25162405, accessed 19 June 2017 at https://www.gpo.gov/fdsys/
pkg/FR-2005-05-12/pdf/05-5723.pdf.

US Environmental Protection Agency (EPA) (2005c), "Standards of performance
for new and existing stationary sources: Electric utility steam generating units;
final rule", *Federal Register*, **70** (95), 28606–700, accessed 20 June 2017 at https://
www.gpo.gov/fdsys/pkg/FR-2005-05-18/pdf/05-8447.pdf.

US Environmental Protection Agency (EPA) (2006), *Regulatory Impact Analysis
for the Final Revisions to the Oil Pollution Prevention Regulations*, accessed 5
September 2017 at https://www.regulations.gov/document?D=EPA-HQ-OPA-20
05-0001-0171.

US Environmental Protection Agency (EPA) (2010), *Guidelines for Preparing
Economic Analyses*. Washington, DC, US Environmental Protection Agency,
accessed 3 May 2017 at https://www.epa.gov/environmental-economics/guideli
nes-preparing-economic-analyses.

US Environmental Protection Agency (EPA) (2011), *The Benefits and Costs of the
Clean Air Act from 1990 to 2020*, accessed 3 May 2017 at https://www.epa.gov/
sites/production/files/2015-07/documents/fullreport_rev_a.pdf.

US Environmental Protection Agency (EPA) (2012a), "Control of air pollution
from aircraft and aircraft engines; emission standards and test proceduress",
Federal Register, **77** (117), 36342–86, accessed 23 June 2017 at https://www.gpo.
gov/fdsys/pkg/FR-2012-06-18/pdf/2012-13828.pdf.

US Environmental Protection Agency (EPA) (2012b), "Water quality standards for
the state of Florida's estuaries, coastal waters, and South Florida inland flowing
waters", *Federal Register*, **77** (243), 74924–85, accessed 23 June 2017 at https://
www.gpo.gov/fdsys/pkg/FR-2012-12-18/pdf/2012-30117.pdf.

US Environmental Protection Agency (EPA) (2014a), "Carbon pollution emission
guidelines for existing stationary sources: Electric utility generating units",
Federal Register, **79** (117), 34830–958, accessed 5 September 2017 at https://www.
gpo.gov/fdsys/pkg/FR-2014-06-18/pdf/2014-13726.pdf.

US Environmental Protection Agency (EPA) (2014b), *Regulatory Impact Analysis (RIA) for EPA's 2015 Coal Combustion Residuals (CCR) Final Rule*, accessed 20 June 2017 at https://www.regulations.gov/document?D=EPA-HQ-RCRA-20 09-0640-12034.

US Environmental Protection Agency (EPA) (2015a), *Benefit and Cost Analysis for the Effluent Limitations Guidelines and Standards for the Steam Electric Power Generating Point Source Category*, accessed 20 June 2017 at https://www.epa.gov/ sites/production/files/2015-10/documents/steam-electric_benefit-cost-analysis_09-29-2015.pdf.

US Environmental Protection Agency (EPA) (2015b), *Regulatory Impact Analysis of the Final Revisions to the National Ambient Air Quality Standards for Ground-Level Ozone*, accessed 3 May 2017 at https://www3.epa.gov/ttn/naaqs/standards/ ozone/data/20151001ria.pdf.

US Environmental Protection Agency (EPA) (2015c), "Renewable fuel standard program: Standards for 2014, 2015, and 2016 and biomass-based diesel volume for 2017", *Federal Register*, **80** (239), 77420–518, accessed 5 September 2017 at https://www.gpo.gov/fdsys/pkg/FR-2015-12-14/pdf/2015-30893.pdf.

US Environmental Protection Agency (EPA) (2016), *Establishing Offset and Trading Baselines in the Chesapeake Bay Watershed*, accessed 14 June 2017 at https://www. epa.gov/sites/production/files/2016-12/documents/baseline_technical_memorand um.pdf.

US Environmental Protection Agency (EPA) (2017a), *Final Renewable Fuel Standards for 2017, and the Biomass-Based Diesel Volume for 2018*, accessed 5 September 2017 at https://www.epa.gov/renewable-fuel-standard-program/fin al-renewable-fuel-standards-2017-and-biomass-based-diesel-volume.

US Environmental Protection Agency (EPA) (2017b), *Overview for Renewable Fuel Standard*, accessed 5 September 2017 at https://www.epa.gov/renewable-fue l-standard-program/overview-renewable-fuel-standard.

US Office of Management and Budget (OMB) (2003), *Regulatory Analysis Circular A-4*, accessed 3 May 2017 at http://purl.access.gpo.gov/GPO/LPS45563.

US Office of Management and Budget (OMB) (2011), *Regulatory Impact Analysis: A Primer*, accessed 3 May 2017 at https://obamawhitehouse.archives.gov/sites/ default/files/omb/inforeg/regpol/circular-a-4_regulatory-impact-analysis-a-prime r.pdf.

4. The concept of standing in benefit-cost analysis

Richard O. Zerbe

ABSTRACT

It is sometimes said that benefit-cost analysis adds up impacts "to whomsoever they accrue". But in practice that general guidance is more complex and it is the issue of "standing" that defines more precisely whose benefits and costs are to be counted. As in law, where to bring a suit one must have "standing" before the court; so too in benefit-cost analysis conditions must be described for what and whose benefits and costs count. Key issues involve not only whose preferences count (should "foreigners'"?), but also which preferences (should criminal activity count?) and over what period of time? As with law, some answers are not clear-cut but can create useful and informative class discussion on sensitive topics.

INTRODUCTION[1]

Just as in law there is a concept of standing to bring suit so in economics there is the concept of standing to have values counted in a welfare analysis. The question immediately arises why shouldn't all values count? The short answer is that they do count but have been overwhelmed by other values or constraints; more mundanely it is not practical to count all values.

In 1975, Nash, Pearce and Stanley raised issues of standing in the context of benefit-cost analysis (BCA). They asked the following questions:

1. Whose preferences count?
2. Which preferences count?
3. When should preferences count?
4. How should individual preferences be aggregated?[2]

These questions form the major questions of standing. They are all normative questions as each can be phrased in a "should" form, and each raise interesting sub-questions.[3] The first three questions were revisited by Whittington and MacRae (1986). They note that, since President Reagan's Executive Order 12291 expanded use of BCA, issues of standing have become increasingly controversial and important. They give examples in which the following questions arise: Should costs to fetuses be counted? Should the educational benefits of the children of illegal aliens be counted? Should the gains of the criminal from theft be counted? One can add to these an almost interminable list of similar further questions: for example, should effects on citizens of foreign countries be counted? What about the imputed preferences of future generations? Should the willingness to pay (WTP) to avoid or induce envy be counted? Should the costs of psychological stress that a project induces be counted and so forth?

One can devote a great deal of thought and effort to providing separate answers to each of these specific questions without arriving at a general principle. Nash et al. (1975) maintain that the analyst should (normative statement) impose his or her own norms and morals to decide these questions. They note:

> if results are presented in a disaggregated format ... with incidence of effects and methods of valuation clear. Then it is likely that the reader will be able to adjust the results to conform to his own moral notions, and thus to reach an informed opinion on the desirability of the scheme.

This approach is unsatisfactory. If followed, both the use and usefulness of BCA will rapidly decline, decision making will degenerate into foundational discussions not likely to be quickly resolved, and the opportunity to compare BCAs will be lost. What then is to be done with standing issues? Justice is reached by cultivating virtue and reasoning together about the common good. The same is the case for economic efficiency so that we can get to this for purposes of BCA analysis through looking at rights as embodied in law.[4]

STANDING AND THE LAW

Zerbe (1991) suggests that the correct approach to these issues lies in law, noting that the issue of standing in BCA is not different from the issue of rights and wrongs. Imagine for example that everyone agrees on the proper norms for resolving standing questions. This would of course make BCA much easier, more replicable, more comparable in results across projects, in accord with the foundations of BCA, and consistent with its role of providing relevant information. The BCA analysts would then avoid the pitfall of imposing their own values on issues better left to group processes.

The way to achieve something like this is to recognize that BCA is itself rooted in public rights and duties, in short, in the law. In BCA, gains and losses are to be measured from a status quo starting point in which rights are determined by law. Thus, if I own a good, the value ascribed to my loss of it is to be measured by my willingness to accept payment (WTA) for the loss. If I do not own a good, the value of it is determined by my willingness to pay for it. Since these measures normally differ, the law helps determine valuation in BCA by indicating where rights lie. For economists, an initial question is "what is an economic good?" An economic good is one for which there is a WTP.[5] This is tricky, however, because people are also willing to pay for a good to not exist or to pay for others not to have it.

In determining where rights lie, the law embodies society's moral sentiments about right and wrong. In a society that is both democratic and abides by the rule of law, law is the best measure to be had and is reasonably consistent with a recognition of societies' mores and norms. In using the law, the analyst properly removes himself or herself from the too subjectively attractive role of philosopher king, avoids the uncertainty of diverse moral sentiments and, to a significant degree, relies on societies' determination of morality. As this legal determination itself represents the outcome of willingness to pay and to accept consideration, such use of law is consistent with BCA foundations.

WHICH PREFERENCES COUNT?

Criminal Activity

It should be clear that preferences for criminal activity do not count. In considering a good such as criminal activity, the economic good is the legality of criminal activity.[6] There will be a WTP for such activity and a WTP to avoid it. The fact of illegality expresses a social norm that may be reasonably said to embody the social judgment that the WTP to avoid such activity is greater than the WTP to have it. A taste for murder is reasonably assumed to be overwhelmed by society's taste against it and the sentiments of society are indicated by laws against murder. Thus, in general BCA does not count the value of the goods in the hands of the criminal. Only in a situation where a legal change is either making criminal or decriminalizing an activity, is it reasonable to consider criminal preferences.

Envy and Status

More difficult is the treatment for goods such as envy or status. Envy is not illegal. A project that increases the envy of others could count the WTP to avoid envy, just as a project that increased one's status would be desirable. A more reasonable or practical stance, however, would not focus on individual envy or status, as this sentiment can be invidious, but to consider envy and status as part of inequality and thus to consider societies' WTP to reduce inequality. Such a consideration would be part of a reasonable BCA and is one for which data can be available. This would maintain the logic of BCA in using WTP or WTA measures but avoid the analyst using his or her own preferences.

Avoidance of Stress

There are, I suspect, few BCAs that consider stress in calculating costs, which could be valued in observing costs of treatment (European Agency for Safety and Health at Work, 2014). Yet psychological stress is a cost, and affects both work productivity and individual well-being. There is no good reason to not count the costs of such stress. It is worth noting that the Office of Management and Budget (OMB, 2003) suggests that inconvenience costs be counted and I here note that inconvenience causes stress. Osuna (1985, p. 82) notes that:

> [T]he study of any problem involving waiting situations invariably assumes that people dislike having to wait. The analysis of queueing problems usually prescribes that some costs should be associated with the time people spend waiting to be served. These are usually considered to be of an economic nature. It is proved that, under very general conditions, the resulting psychological stress accumulated during the process is a marginal increasing function of the waiting time, and some strategies to minimise (sic) it are developed.

When Illegal Goods or Activities Have Standing

In general, gains from illegal goods or activities do not count. Some goods are illegal, such as heroin, cocaine, crystal meth, rape and privately owned tanks with operating guns. Such goods would not generally count as values in a BCA, unless the question was their legalization. When the issue to be decided is, however, whether or not the good or activity *should be illegal* then it is proper to count the value of stolen goods to the thief and the value of addictive drugs to the addicts.

WHOSE PREFERENCES COUNT?

Criminal Preferences

The thief's criminal activity speaks to the issue of whose preference counts. The very fact that an activity is criminal removes the fruits of such activity from having standing. Thus, in considering whether or not stolen goods should be returned to the owner, even if the thief values them more than the owner, the value to the thief is to be ignored.

WHEN DO THEY COUNT?

The question of when preferences count is a time-related version of whose preferences count. This question is primarily one of time. The BCA answer is that preferences and costs are to be counted when they are expected to occur and are to be discounted to a present time. There are instances, however, when future benefits or costs become quite speculative and should be treated with a recognition of this as one treats uncertainty. An example of bad policy with respect to time is to be found in OMB's recognition of a low 3 percent discount rate in considering projects that contain intergenerational equity. This is supposedly justified on the basis that future generations will be richer. This well may be the case but does not justify the lower discount rate. This is because it has generally been the case that projects are available that yield 7 percent or higher so that the 3 percent rule could substitute a lower performing project for a superior one. (Burgess and Zerbe, 2013).

Where the Law is Unclear or Contentious

Where the law is silent, the use of social norms serves as a substitute. When there is neither law nor norms, the logic of BCA is that there is no WTA to give up a right so that value is measured by the WTP to obtain the good; that is a putative auction format holds. Complicated situations can, however, arise.

Suppose that one is conducting a BCA considering benefits and costs for a country with a different legal structure than your own. Suppose for example, that slavery is legal in the country in question but not in your own. Are slaves to be given standing in your analysis when they do not have it in the foreign country? Or, suppose slavery is legal in your country but not in the foreign country. Or suppose your country is considering eliminating slavery and you are considering the costs and benefits of the legal change. In these sorts of cases the best that one can do is to make your calculations both with and without the location of the right, as Nash et al. (1975) recommend.

Where the law is unclear, there are two ways to address standing. One is to follow norms. The other is to prepare alternative analyses contingent on whom is assumed to have the right.

Norms

The great medieval jurist Henry de Bracton noted that in England legal right is based on an unwritten law that usage had approved. Where the law and norms differ, that which best expresses psychological preferences should be followed. The fashionable statement is that norms should be followed when they are stable and uncontentious. Ellickson (1991) tells of a case in which the law was changed but the standard practice continued nevertheless. In such a case, it is the law that should be changed and the norm that determines standing. In Shasta County, California, the norm was that ranchers were liable for damages caused by straying cattle. A change in the law to remove rancher liability and substitute farmer liability, however, did not change the de facto liability of ranchers. An additional example of using a norm is found in Plessy v. Ferguson (1896). In Plessy the US Supreme Court upheld a Louisiana statute that provided for separate but equal accommodations for white and African American train passengers and provided fines and imprisonment for violators. The Court held that a racially discriminatory law is constitutional if it is "reasonable" in light of the "established usages, customs, and traditions of the people." But in doing this they relied on Louisiana customs not on those of the US. The Plessy decision is clearly norm seeking but, as Justice Harlan argued, it is not Louisiana's norms that are relevant, but those of the United States.[7]

A Contingent Analysis

Where both law and norms are unclear or highly contentious, and in cases in which the legality of the good is in question, the recommended approach is to perform a contingent analysis, an analysis that calculates benefits and costs under alternative assumptions about the location of rights. For example, consider a law to prevent the blocking of sunlight by another proposed building where the law is uncertain or contentious. The analysis could proceed by first supposing the prior building had a right to sunlight and second by supposing instead that the second building had a right to build and block light.

In many of these cases, and especially where the right is important, the putative assignment of the right is fully determinative of the result because the WTA required to give up the right is overwhelming. For example, suppose you have been asked to do a BCA on the right to an abortion. If you start with the assumption that abortion is legal, you will find the BCA supportive of its legality. If instead, you start with the assumption that it is illegal, your BCA will support its illegality. (I leave it to the reader to explicate this result). Similar issues arise when there are important and contentious issues. This simply shows that BCA is not the appropriate tool for such questions.

Where the law is unclear or non-existent, the analyst must consider alternative specifications of rights and present data showing benefits and costs under the alternative specification. For example, suppose the project being considered is reducing noise from airplanes. If residents affected by noise have a right to a certain level of quiet, then the measure of their losses from excess noise is measured by the WTA. If no such right exists, the valuation measure is their WTP to gain the right, a much smaller amount.

In contentious cases of great moment, the actual right or the putative right will determine the outcome. In considering questions such as the right to own slaves or abortion rights, the BCA answer is completely determined by the initial assignment of right. The most the analyst can do in such cases is to point out the indeterminacy and its legal foundation.

THE ISSUE OF DATA

The above discussion has taken place without reference to the costs, the uncertainty or even the possibility of data collection. Since data must be limited by the resources available to collect them, there will always be those individuals and those sentiments who de facto do not have standing. The analyst can only choose data that are likely to yield the most and most relevant information. This issue bears also on that of whether a partial or general equilibrium analysis should be chosen, but this is not a subject of this essay.

CURRENT GOVERNMENT STANDARDS

The Federal OMB and the Congressional Research Service (CRS) along with Presidential Executive Orders offer some guidance on standing issues (see also Chapters 6 and 18 in this volume). In Carey (2014) writing for the CRS it is noted: "[C]ost-benefit analysis, involves the systematic identification of all of the costs and benefits associated with a forthcoming regulation, including non-quantitative and indirect costs and benefits, and how those costs and benefits are distributed across different groups in society." Both CRS and OMB and President Reagan and Carter Executive Order stress the importance of inclusivity. OMB Circular A-4 (Office of Management and Budget, 2003, p. 10) for example states that benefit-cost analysis that ignores benefits or costs or even has unquantified benefit or costs "is less useful, and it can even be misleading, because the calculation of net benefits in such cases does not provide a full evaluation of all relevant benefits and costs." Analysts should therefore attempt to quantify benefits or costs as much as possible (for example, tons of pollution avoided, or the number of children who will not suffer discrimination), and "exercise professional judgment" in determining whether non-quantified factors are important enough to justify consideration of the regulation.

As stated in OMB (2003, p. 3) Presidential Executive Order 12286 (Clinton) requires that covered agencies (executive agencies):

> should assess all costs and benefits of available regulatory alternatives" and that "costs and benefits shall be understood to include both quantifiable measures (to the fullest extent these can be usefully estimated) and qualitative measures of costs and benefits that are difficult to quantify, but nevertheless essential to consider.

These statements appear to imply that all people and sentiments have standing to the extent feasible. However, restrictions arise, such as per OMB (2003), where BCA analysis of government regulations based on Executive Order 12286 is restricted to rules that:

> have an annual effect on the economy of 100 million or more or adversely affect in a material way the economy, a sector of the economy, productivity, competition, job, the environment, public health or safety, or State, local or tribal governments or communities.

These are referred to by OMB (2003, p. 15) as economically significant or major regulatory actions. An additional restriction is that: "The analysis should focus on benefits and costs that accrue to citizens and residents of the United States. Where the agency chooses to evaluate a regulation that is likely to have effects beyond the borders of the United States, these effects should be reported separately."

A time requirement is referenced in several places by OMB (2003). When choosing the appropriate time horizon for estimating benefits and costs, agencies should consider how long the regulation being analyzed is likely to have economic effects. The guidance further states that the time frame for the analysis should cover a period long enough to encompass all the important benefits and costs likely to result from the rule. However, the agency should also consider for how long it can reasonably predict the future and should limit its analysis to that time period. Thus, if a regulation has no predetermined sunset provision, the agency will need to choose the endpoint of its analysis based on the foreseeable future or the agency's ability to forecast reliably. For rules that require large upfront capital investments, the life of the capital is also an option.

CONCLUSION: STANDING TYPE QUESTIONS FOR THE READER

A number of standing type questions involve issues of making choices on behalf of those unable to express their own preferences. For example, consider the following:

1. How should the preferences of children be counted? Are their WTPs so low they should be disregarded? If counted, from what age? Does a fetus then have no standing? What are the rights of a fetus?
2. Do the mentally ill have standing to have their preferences counted? Does this depend on circumstances and the type of mental illness? What about the preferences of those with dementia?
3. Should existence (non-use) values be counted? Aren't these preferences similar to charitable ones? Should charitable preferences be counted?
4. Should poorly informed preferences be counted? Should any survey of valuations related to BCA contain material to ensure the respondent is well informed? Should the analyst suggest an information approach prior to conducting any analysis in which attitudes are to be determined outside of market values? In considering market values should allowances be made for people's poor choices? Do you agree with an early giant of BCA, Mishan (1971, p. 695), who says:

   > People's imperfect knowledge of economic opportunities, their imprudence and unworldliness have never prevented economists from accepting as basic data the amounts people choose at given prices. Such imperfections cannot, therefore consistently be invoked to qualify people's choices when, instead, their preferences are exercised in placing on some increment of a good or bad?

5. Are people's ethical preferences expressed as impersonal social preferences rather than their subjective preferences that count? People's opinions about issues of public policy may differ from their prefer-

ences for themselves. Isn't the relevant issue simply their WTP (or accept) for an outcome?

6. Who should provide the answer to these questions for the profession?

I have my own answers to these questions but am interested in yours. Feel free to contact me with your answers or to request mine. I may be reached at: richardozerbe@gmail.com.

NOTES

1. I thank Monika Foltzyn-Zarychta and William Talbott for useful comments. This chapter is not meant to be a complete discussion of standing issues. For more complete treatment see Zerbe (1991).
2. This issue is the subject of debates about social welfare functions and not addressed here. My own view is that using weights for different persons or preferences is not appropriate, but that the aggregate WTP to achieve greater equity or some moral result is appropriate.
3. Normative questions concern what should be, such as what data should be collected, how data should be used to make decisions and what should be the justification for the decisions. Normative component involves "should" questions and their answers. Positive components are those that speak to factual issues including prediction. They consist of definitions, data collection and their predictions, and, in short, any issues that speak about what is or what will be. The question "should I sweep the sidewalk?" is a normative question. The statement, "I will feel guilty if I don't clean it now" is a positive prediction. The statement "the sidewalk is clean now" is likewise a positive one.
4. An extensive discussion of these sorts of issues is found in Sandel (2009).
5. There are many of goods or activities, for example stolen goods or theft, for which there is a WTP but law suggests that the WTP to count those goods or activities is much less than the WTP or WTA to not give standing to those goods or activities. That is, there is a standing issue about what values to count and goods and activities that are not given standing as they fail a BCA test for acceptance.
6. Monika Foltyn-Zarychta notes that this issue comes up in GDP counting the product of illegal immigrants working *sub rosa* (Personal communication, 2017).
7. For more on this see Zerbe (2006).

REFERENCES AND RECOMMENDATIONS FOR FURTHER READING

Burgess, D. and R.O. Zerbe (2013), "The most appropriate discount rate", *Journal of Benefit-Cost Analysis*, **4**(3): 391–400.

Carey, M. (2014), "Cost-benefit and other analysis requirements in the rulemaking process", Congressional Research Service, Washington, DC.

Ellickson, R. (1991), *Order Without Law: How Neighbors Settle Disputes*, Cambridge: Harvard University Press.

European Agency for Safety and Health at Work (2014), *Calculating the Cost of Work-related Stress and Psychosocial Risk*, Luxembourg.

Mishan, E. (1971), *Cost-Benefit Analysis: An Informal Introduction*, London: Allen & Unwin.

Nash, C., D. Pearce and J. Stanley (1975), "An evaluation of cost-benefit analysis criteria", *Scottish Journal of Political Economy*, **22**(2): 121–34.
Office of Management and Budget (OMB) (2003), "Regulatory analysis", OMB Circular A-4, Washington, DC.
Osuna, E. (1985), "The psychological cost of waiting", *Journal of Mathematical Psychology*, **29**(1): 82–105.
Sandel, M. (2009), *Justice: What's the Right Thing to Do?*, New York: Farrar, Straus and Giroux.
US Supreme Court (1896), *Plessy v. Ferguson*, 163 U.S. 537, 16 S. Ct. 1138, p. 9.
Whittington, D. and D. MacRae (1986), "The issue of standing in benefit-cost analysis", *Journal of Policy Analysis and Management*, **5**(4): 665–82.
Zerbe, R.O. (1991), "Comment: Does benefit cost analysis stand alone? Rights and standing", *Journal of Policy Analysis and Management*, **10**(1): 96–105.
Zerbe, R.O. (2006), "Justice and the evolution of the common law", *The Journal of Law, Economics & Policy*, **3**(1): 81–122.

5. Partial equilibrium versus general equilibrium evaluations or small versus large projects

Per-Olov Johansson and Bengt Kriström

ABSTRACT

The typical approach in benefit-cost analysis is partial equilibrium. Thus, a policy's impacts on other markets are ignored. We discuss partial equilibrium evaluation versus general equilibrium ones. It is shown that the rules coincide when markets are perfect and the considered policy is (infinitesimally) small. If changes in some parameters are discrete, the approaches produce different outcomes, in general. In particular, market-based (Marshallian) demand curves no longer reflect the willingness-to-pay for, say, a change in a price. Therefore, income-compensated (Hicksian) tools must be employed.

Many students are exposed first to partial equilibrium benefit-cost analysis as project or policy appraisal where only one primary market is analyzed using consumer surplus. As is demonstrated below the difference between partial and general equilibrium evaluations vanish as the project becomes infinitesimally small and markets are perfectly competitive. However, greater theoretical and empirical complexity often results for the large projects and real world complications that often receive the most attention. Refer to Farrow and Rose (2018) for a fine discussion of these issues while greater technical detail is provided here that may be more familiar to graduate students in economics.

THE SMALL PROJECT

Let us consider an infinitesimally small project producing a commodity supplied on a perfectly competitive market. The project has an impact on the output price. By the envelope theorem and Roy's identity, the loss of consumer surplus of a marginal increase in the own-price of a commodity equals the negative of the quantity demanded, say $-x^d$. By the envelope theorem[1] (Hotelling's lemma), the gain in producer surplus equals the quantity supplied, say x^s. If the price clears the market, supply equals demand, implying that the sum of changes in consumer surplus and producer surplus sum to zero.

These envelope properties imply that for the marginal project we can focus on $p^* \cdot \Delta x - \Delta C$, where p^* is the initial equilibrium price, Δx is the change in production by the small project under consideration, and ΔC is the change in the project's costs. Thus, we can ignore any price changes. In an intertemporal setting, p^* and Δx can be interpreted as a column vector of present value prices and a row vector of quantity changes, respectively, while ΔC is the present value of investment costs plus the present value sum of operational costs evaluated at initial equilibrium prices (less any present value scrap value).

This approach is seemingly partial equilibrium because we ignore any induced price changes in other markets. However, once again, by the envelope theorem, changes in consumer surpluses plus changes in producer surpluses in other markets also sum to zero, just as earlier. Hence the benefit-cost rule (BCR) $p^* \cdot \Delta x - \Delta C$ is a general equilibrium rule (ignoring here any distortions). In particular, note that we do not have to worry about the distinction between market or Marshallian concepts and income-compensated or Hicksian concepts, because we evaluate at a "point". This latter fact means that the marginal utility of income, which acts as the exchange rate between units of utility and monetary units, is a constant. Thus, $\Delta V / V_m = \text{BCR} = p^* \cdot \Delta x - \Delta C$, where ΔV is the change in (indirect) utility of the representative household, and V_m is the marginal utility of income.[2] Note that our benefit-cost expression is proportional to the underlying and unobservable change in utility. Thus, our rule is a sign-preserving metric of what we would like to measure, that is, the change in welfare caused by a project.

THE LARGE PROJECT

The crucial assumption underlying the above result is that the project is infinitesimally small with no distortions. This may or may not be a realistic assumption. Let us now turn to a discrete project, that is, a project having a significant impact on p; for the moment any other discrete price changes are ignored. A first complication is that the Marshallian demand curve no longer reflects the willingness-to pay (WTP) or the willingness-to-accept compensation (WTA), in general.[3] In terms of the above benefit-cost rule, the marginal utility of income V_m is not constant when p changes more than marginally; hence the relationship between ΔV and BCR becomes foggy.[4] Therefore, we must turn to a Hicksian demand function. Then, the household's income is reduced (increased) so as to keep utility constant as the price decreases (increases). If the project causes p to change from p^0 to p^1, the household pays or receives compensation for this change. Note that this approach implies that the actual price change is valued, not a hypothetical price change derived from a Hicksian demand function (with a slope typically differing from the slope of the market demand curve) and a market supply function.

SEVERAL PARAMETERS CHANGE

Let us now turn to the case where more than a single parameter undergo non-marginal changes. For example, the project may cause large changes in a commodity price as well as in income. One problem that is faced in using the Marshallian demand functions to assess the project was addressed previously: the slope of the function differs from the slope of a Hicksian demand function. The other problem is known as the path dependency problem. The value of the combined (Marshallian) change depends on the order in which the price and income are changed, in general. In principle, the value could run from plus infinity to minus infinity. Hence, in the non-marginal case, an evaluation based on Marshallian concepts is generally not unique. An illustration is found in the Appendix. There are exceptions, a homothetic utility function provides path independency if prices are changed, holding income constant, as is further discussed in the Appendix. However, because the slope of a (homothetic) Marshallian demand curve differs from the slope of a Hicksian demand curve, an area to the left of a Marshallian curve does not reflect the WTP/WTA for a discrete price change. The only exception occurs if preferences are quasi-linear. Then, all additional income is spent on the numeraire commodity, hence the Marshallian and Hicksian demand curves coincide for the remaining commodities.

The benefit-cost rule (BCR) accordingly must be modified. If the household is kept at its initial level of utility, the rule may be stated as BCR $=$ $CV^p + \Delta\pi = CV$, where CV^p is the compensating variation associated with the actual change in the equilibrium price p caused by the project, $\Delta\pi$ is the change in profit of the representative firm producing the commodity; recall that the representative household must be the owner of the representative firm(s). The change in profit is equal to $(p^1 \cdot x^1 - p^0 \cdot x^0 - \Delta C)$, and also equals the household's WTP for this change in income. Hence, the total WTP (CV) equals the sum of the WTP for the price change from

p^0 to p^1 plus the WTP for the change in its profit. The BCR may seem to be a partial equilibrium rule, but as long as any other price changes are infinitesimally small, it can also be interpreted as a general equilibrium rule. Is CV a sign-preserving measure of the change in utility? The answer is affirmative, because one can find a marginal utility of income evaluated at an intermediate income between the initial income, say m^0, and the final income, $m^1 = m^0 - CV$, such that $\Delta V / \bar{V}_m = CV$, where $\bar{V}_m$ is the marginal utility of income evaluated at some intermediate income.

A NUMERICAL ILLUSTRATION

In order to provide further illustration, let us turn to a simple numerical example of partial versus general equilibrium evaluation. The project under evaluation is a large increase in the provision of a single public good. The good is produced using a single private good, denoted x_1, as input. The utility function, that is the social welfare function, is assumed to be log-linear. Hence, the second private good, acting as the numeraire, can be suppressed (because its price is unity so that $\ln(1) = 0$). Suppressing constant terms, the indirect utility function is written as:

$$V(.) = \ln(1000 + \pi_1 - T) - 0.5 \cdot \ln(p_1) + 0.5 \cdot \ln(z), \qquad (5.1)$$

where $\pi_1 = (1/2) \cdot p_1^2$ denotes the profit of the single firm producing x_1, exogenous other (profit) income is set equal to 1000, T denotes a lump-sum tax covering the cost of providing the public good, and z denotes the public good. Initially, one unit of the public good is provided using one unit of x_1 as sole input. In the final situation 20 units are provided requiring ten units of the input. Output of x_1 is equal to p_1, assuming that the firm acts as a price taker; $\partial \pi_1(.) / \partial p_1 = x_1^s(.) = p_1$ (and to avoid having to solve a system of equations ignore how private goods are produced). Consumer demand equals $0.5 \cdot m/p_1$, where m is total disposable income. Equilibrium in the market for the commodity is obtained when the price is such that supply equals the sum of consumer demand plus public sector demand:

$$p_1^0 = 0.5 \cdot [1000 + (1/2) \cdot (p_1^0)^2 - 1 \cdot p_1^0]/p_1^0 + 1$$
$$p_1^1 = 0.5 \cdot [1000 + (1/2) \cdot (p_1^1)^2 - 10 \cdot p_1^1]/p_1^1 + 10, \qquad (5.2)$$

where a superscript 0 (1) refers to the initial (final) equilibrium price, and the first term on the right-hand side of each line is the (Cobb-Douglas) consumer demand function for the commodity. Solving one obtains

$p_1^0 \approx 26.1554$ and $p_1^1 \approx 29.3675$, that is, the public sector project has more than a marginal impact on the market for the commodity.

Next, let us calculate the WTP for the increase in z, holding income m as well as p_1 constant at their initial levels:

$$\ln(1315.9 - CV^z) + 0.5 \cdot \ln(z^1) = \ln(1315.9), \qquad (5.3)$$

where $\ln(z^0)$ is suppressed because it equals zero. CV^z now is a measure of the WTP for the increase in the provision of the public good. CV^z corresponds to the area below an income-compensated inverse demand curve for the public good $(\text{MWTP} = \partial CV^z(z)/\partial z = e^{V^0} \cdot \sqrt{p_1^0}/z^{3/2})$ between initial and final levels of provision, and is around 1021.65. Deducting the cost of producing the additional goods at initial prices, around 235.4, the partial equilibrium surplus of the project is around 786.25.

Next, let us account for the price adjustment. This causes a loss of compensated consumer surplus and makes the provision of the public good more expensive. However, profit income increases. Consider first the loss of compensated consumer surplus caused by the price increase:

$$\ln(1315.9 - 1021.65 - CV^{p_1}) + 0.5 \cdot \ln(p_1^1) + 0.5 \cdot \ln(z^1)$$
$$= \ln(1315.9) + 0.5 \cdot \ln(p_1^0). \qquad (5.4)$$

Note that CV^{p_1} is evaluated conditional on what was paid in exchange for the increase in the provision of the public good. The loss in compensated consumer surplus is around 17.54. The loss of disposable income is valued as:

$$\ln(1137.55 - 1021.65 + 17.54 - CV^m) + 0.5 \cdot \ln(p_1^1) + 0.5 \cdot \ln(z^1)$$
$$= \ln(1315.9) + 0.5 \cdot \ln(p_1^0), \qquad (5.5)$$

where CV^m is evaluated conditional on CV^z and CV^{p_1}. Thus, CV^m is around -178.35, that is, equals the loss of income itself (1137.55–1315.9).

Even though LeChatelier's principle, see, for example, Milgrom and Roberts (1996), suggests that the general equilibrium outcome is smaller than the partial equilibrium outcome, the reverse holds true here:

$$\ln(1137.55 - CV) - 0.5 \cdot \ln(p_1^1) + 0.5 \cdot \ln(z^1) = \ln(1315.9) - 0.5 \cdot \ln(p_1^0), \quad (5.6)$$

where $CV = CV^z + CV^{p_1} + CV^m$. The net WTP for the project is around 825.76, that is, exceeds the partial equilibrium outcome of 786.25. The reason for this outcome is that profit increases so as to counteract the increase in the cost of providing the public good and the loss of compensated consumer surplus. These results illustrate that we cannot rule out that a general equilibrium benefit-cost analysis produces a larger surplus than a partial equilibrium one; recall that even if all other prices adjust marginally, we can ignore these induced effects in a general equilibrium context with no distortions.

Note that we could take other paths and arrive at the same total net WTP. However, the magnitudes of CV^z and CV^{p_1} will depend on where in the sequence they are evaluated (while the WTP for a change in income always equals change itself). To see why, evaluate the change in compensated consumer surplus first using $x_1^H(.) = e^{V^0}/(\sqrt{p_1} \cdot \sqrt{z})$, where the price of the second private good is set equal to unity and hence is suppressed. Then the Hicksian demand curve is drawn given $z = z^0$. Next, assume that the compensated consumer surplus is evaluated after the change in z. Now, the Hicksian demand curve for x_1 is drawn for $z = z^1$, that is, shifts to the left in comparison to the initial demand curve. The deeper in a sequence a change is evaluated, the smaller its CV will be (unless commodities are perfect complements). This assumes that each policy measure is associated with a positive WTP. In contrast, the WTP for the public good is higher for p_1^1 than for p_1^0 because the household is income-compensated for the increase in the commodity price. To further illustrate, consider the WTP for a BMW when there is a second choice, say, a Volvo. Suppose that the household is asked for its maximal WTP for the Volvo. Given this payment, the WTP for the BMW is lower than the unconditional WTP for the same car. For more general discussion focusing on public goods the reader is referred to Hoehn and Randall (1989) and Carson et al. (1998).

NOTES

1. According to the envelope theorem, the change in the maximal value of a function (whether constrained, such as an indirect utility function, or unconstrained, such as a profit function) as a parameter changes marginally is the change caused by the direct impact of the parameter on the function, holding the value of x fixed at its optimal value; the indirect effect, resulting from the change in the optimal value of x caused by a change in the parameter, is zero. Refer to Johansson and Kriström (2016, Ch. 2).
2. In order to set aside distributional issues, we focus on a representative household. This household must be the owner of all firms and also the only agent having transactions with the government.
3. The only exception occurs when preferences are quasi-linear.
4. If the utility function is homothetic (for example, Cobb-Douglas), one can make a monotonous transformation (for example, by taking logarithms) such that V_m becomes independent of prices. Nevertheless, the slope of the demand curve is different from the slope of the Hicksian demand curve. Hence the area to the left of the Marshallian demand curve between initial and final price does not reflect WTP/WTA.

REFERENCES AND RECOMMENDATIONS FOR FURTHER READING

Carson, R.T., N.E. Flores and M.W. Hanemann (1998), "Sequencing and valuing public goods," *Journal of Environmental Economics and Management*, 36, 314–23.

Farrow, S. and A. Rose (forthcoming, 2018), "Welfare analysis: Bridging the partial and general equilibrium divide for policy analysis," *Journal of Benefit-Cost Analysis*.

Hoehn, J.P. and A. Randall (1989), "Too many proposals pass the benefit cost test," *American Economic Review*, 79, 544–51.

Johansson, P.-O. and B. Kriström (2016), *Cost–Benefit Analysis for Project Appraisal*, Cambridge: Cambridge University Press.

Milgrom, P. and J. Roberts (1996), "The LeChatelier Principle," *American Economic Review*, 86, 173–9.

APPENDIX

Consider once again a simple log-linear utility function generating a demand function $x_1(.) = 0.5 \cdot m/p_1$. Income is increased from 100 to 110 and the own-price is increased from 2 to 3. Differentiating the indirect utility function with respect to m (to obtain $V_m dm$) and p (to obtain $-V_m \cdot x_1(.) dp_1$), dividing by V_m, and integrating, one obtains:

$$\int_{100}^{110} dm - \int_{2}^{3} (0.5 \cdot 110/p_1) dp_1 \approx -12.3 \neq -\int_{2}^{3} (0.5 \cdot 100/p_1) dp_1 + \int_{100}^{110} d_m \approx -10.3,$$
$$(A.1)$$

where the second parameter change is evaluated conditional on the first parameter change. Thus, the order in which the parameters are changed matters, that is, the line integral is not path independent. If there are just two commodities with identical demand functions, but with the price of the second commodity, acting as numeraire, equal to unity, the compensating variation is about -12.5, that is, differs from the Marshallian estimates. The CV is easily obtained as the solution to:

$$0.5 \cdot (\ln[0.5 \cdot (110 - CV)/3] + \ln[0.5 \cdot (110 - CV)/1]) =$$
$$0.5 \cdot (\ln[0.5 \cdot 100/2] + \ln[0.5 \cdot 100/1]). \qquad (A.2)$$

Note that the WTP for a change in income equals the change in income. Here the evaluation is based on the indirect utility function. Alternatively, and equivalently, the assessment may be based on the Hicksian expenditure function. If the price of the second commodity, acting as numeraire, is set equal to 1, the Hicksian demand function for the commodity under evaluation is $x_1^H(\cdot) = e^{v^0}\sqrt{1}/\sqrt{p_1}$, where initial utility V^0 equals about 3.57. Integrating the function between initial and final p-values, one obtains around -22.5. Adding the WTP for the change in income, one arrives at -12.5, just as when basing the assessment on the indirect utility function.

However, changing both prices holding income fixed, that is, using m as numeraire, then path independency applies.[1] Recall that both cross-derivatives are equal to zero, $\partial x_1/\partial p_2 = \partial x_2/\partial p_1 = 0$, hence the order in which prices are changed does not affect the total value; this result generalizes to any number of commodity-price changes. (This is why indirect utility functions and expenditure functions work: their cross-derivatives are symmetric). However, because the slope of a Marshallian demand curve differs from the slope of a Hicksian curve, an area to the left of a

Marshallian curve cannot be interpreted as reflecting the WTP/WTA for a price change, in general.

Note

1. This property holds for any homothetic utility function, that is, a monotonic transformation of a homogeneous function. The considered equally weighted Cobb-Douglas utility function is both homothetic and homogeneous (of degree 1). The log-linear utility function is homothetic (but not homogeneous) because it is a monotonic transformation of the homogeneous Cobb-Douglas function.

6. Benefit-cost analysis and US regulatory review: Finding a market failure

Susan E. Dudley

ABSTRACT

In this chapter, students learn how benefit-cost analysis (BCA) is applied to US regulation. Students gain an overview of the federal regulatory process and the important role BCA plays in making regulatory policy. The chapter reviews how markets work in order to introduce the concept of "market failure," which agencies are required to identify to justify government regulation. Students should gain an appreciation of possible government failures as well.

US REGULATORY PRACTICES

When issuing new regulations, federal agencies are constrained by their enabling legislation, by the Administrative Procedure Act, which requires them to provide public notice and seek comment before issuing new regulations, and by executive requirements for regulatory impact analysis (RIA) (primarily BCA). Presidents of both parties for more than 40 years have called for *ex ante* RIA to make agencies weigh the likely positive and negative consequences of regulations before they are issued.

Executive Order 12866 (Clinton 1993) issued by President Bill Clinton in 1993, and reinforced by both George W. Bush (OMB 2003) and Barack Obama (Obama 2011), currently guides the development and review of regulations. It expresses the philosophy that regulations should (1) address a "compelling public need, such as material failures of private markets"; (2) be based on an assessment of "all costs and benefits of available regulatory alternatives, including the alternative of not regulating" and (3) "maximize net benefits" to society unless otherwise constrained by law.

It also assigns the Office of Information and Regulatory Affairs (OIRA) within the Office of Management and Budget (OMB) responsibility for reviewing executive branch agency proposed and final regulations before they are issued, along with supporting analysis. President Trump has called on agencies to offset the costs of new regulations by removing or modifying existing regulations, but has retained these E.O. 12866 requirements and procedures.

ROLE OF BCA IN REGULATORY DEVELOPMENT

In the US and most developed countries, BCA is considered an important aspect of *ex ante* regulatory impact analysis. OIRA explains that the purpose of the RIA is to provide the public with a "careful and transparent analysis" of the effects of regulatory actions (OMB 2011b). In general, the level of analysis should reflect the importance of the decision in question. OIRA reviews hundreds of draft regulations each year, most of which are accompanied by some form of analysis, and, on average, 80 or more per year are deemed "economically significant" (with likely impacts of $100 million or more in a year) and thus require a quantitative BCA. For regulations expected to have impacts of $1 billion or more, agencies often conduct quantitative uncertainty analysis (OMB 2011a).

Default Presumption of Efficient Markets

Executive Order 12866 directs that as a first step in deciding whether and how to regulate:

> Each agency shall identify the problem that it intends to address (including, where applicable, the failures of private markets or public institutions that warrant new agency action) as well as assess the significance of that problem (Clinton 1993).

The concept of "market failure" is an important one in regulation and students should understand why analysis of regulation starts with the default presumption that market processes are efficient at allocating scarce resources. In a market economy disciplined by competition, the exchange of goods and services between willing buyers and sellers uses price signals to allocate scarce resources to their most valued use, to encourage innovation and to meet consumer needs. Regulation and other forms of government intervention can disrupt those signals, make the market less efficient and ultimately harm social welfare.

Student Exercise: A double oral auction "experiment" is useful for illustrating that markets are efficient, even with a handful of participants and imperfect information. The Economic Science Institute at Chapman University (founded by Nobel Laureate Vernon Smith) has developed free software for teachers interested in using economic experiments in their classrooms (Chapman Economic Science Institute n.d.). In the double auction experiment, students are assigned roles of buyers and sellers of an unidentified commodity. Sellers are given cards that show the number of units they can sell and the marginal cost of producing each unit; buyers are given similar cards showing the value they would receive from purchasing each unit. Sellers' marginal costs are increasing and buyers' marginal values are decreasing with more units, and you can use this opportunity to discuss why that might be. Students then engage in a double oral auction to exchange one unit at a time through you – the central clearing house. Sellers can raise their hand and offer a unit, and buyers can raise their hand to bid to buy one. When the bid and offer prices match, that buyer-seller pair has successfully traded a unit. This double auction market goes on until there is no more interest in buying or selling. Participants do not have to buy or sell all their units; their only goal is to maximize profits.

After the first round, you might ask buyers if they thought the sellers were charging too much or "price gouging." If so, you could regulate the price through a price cap and run the experiment again (perhaps with different cost-value information). After a few rounds (perhaps with and without price controls), you can reveal the results. The cost-value information for each of their individual units sums to form supply and demand curves, and in the unconstrained rounds, you will likely see very efficient outcomes, with the quantity of units exchanged equal to that predicted by the intersection of the curves, and the final price close to that marginal price. Imposition of the price controls, on the other hand, will reveal an inefficient outcome; not only will sellers be harmed relative to the unconstrained case, but also buyers who could have "profited" from purchasing at a price above the cap are also harmed.
(See: http://www.chapman.edu/research/institutes-and-centers/economic-science-institute/academics-research/software.aspx.)

WHEN MARKETS DON'T ALLOCATE RESOURCES EFFICIENTLY

After they understand how markets function, you can explain that markets may not efficiently allocate resources for several reasons. Michael Munger does a nice job of explaining this (Munger 2000). First, efficient markets need an adequate infrastructure, including the rule of law, well-defined property rights and a system of exchange. You might ask students to identify the infrastructure and rules in the experiment (that is, they worked through you, they couldn't steal each other's cards, each bid or offer had to improve upon the previous one and so on). Second, existing policies that were poorly designed may impede the functioning of markets. The price constraint could illustrate this; you could discuss how economic regulation of private sector prices, entry and exit tends to distort market signals and has historically kept prices of some goods and services higher than necessary, harming consumers rather than protecting them.

Munger argues that to blame markets for the first problem is like blaming your car because there are no roads to drive it on. Blaming markets for the second problem is like blaming your car because you put maple syrup in the gas tank (Munger 2000).

The third reason markets may not perform efficiently is due to classic "market failures" or deficiencies inherent in the market itself. OMB Circular A-4 breaks these into three categories: (1) externalities, public goods and common property resources, (2) market power and (3) inadequate or asymmetric information (OMB 2003).

Externalities occur when one party's actions impose uncompensated costs or benefits on another party. For example, if a factory disposes of its waste in a nearby stream, it may reduce the value of the water for downstream uses (for example, fishing, swimming, drinking). Those are real costs, but they are borne by downstream users so neither the factory owner nor the consumers of its products factor them into their decisions. This could be an opportunity to talk with students about the Coase Theorem; if property rights to the stream were clearly defined and the upstream and downstream users could bargain with each other, they could reach an agreement that "internalizes" those external costs. But, if there are many upstream and downstream users, they face what economists call "transaction costs," which make such bargaining complicated so resources are not allocated efficiently (Coase 1960).

Common property resources and public goods occur where it is costly or impossible to exclude users. Common property resources tend to be overused (people would overfish a common fishery, for example). Public goods can be under-provided (new discoveries might not be made if not for patents granting the discoverer rights to profit).

According to OMB, "firms exercise market power when they reduce output below what would be offered in a competitive industry in order to obtain higher prices" (OMB 2003). Some industries may be considered "natural monopolies" because economies of scale are so great that a market can be served at lowest cost only if production is limited to a single producer. For example, once a railroad track is laid between two cities, the marginal costs of running trains along that track are very low. But, since laying rail tracks is very costly, the established railroad operator has a natural monopoly and its prices are not disciplined by competition. In this case, it could charge higher prices (and serve less traffic) than under competitive conditions. Students should keep in mind, though, that monopolies are often short lived; technological advances (motivated by the prospect of profits), can provide competition that will lower prices for consumers. For example, railroads may have once had monopoly power, but trucks and other forms of transportation emerged to compete with them, dissipating any excess profits. Also, as OMB warns, "government action can be a source of market power, such as when regulatory actions exclude low-cost imports" (OMB 2003).

When market participants have asymmetric information, markets may not allocate resources efficiently; however, you should note that perfect information is neither necessary nor optimal. Referring to the experiment, you can point out that neither buyers nor sellers had perfect information on the commodity or each other's characteristics, yet the market allocated resources very efficiently. As OMB advises agencies:

> Because information, like other goods, is costly to produce and disseminate, your evaluation will need to do more than demonstrate the possible existence of incomplete or asymmetric information. Even though the market may supply less than the full amount of information, the amount it does supply may be reasonably adequate and therefore not require government regulation. Sellers have an incentive to provide information through advertising that can increase sales by highlighting distinctive characteristics of their products. Buyers may also obtain reasonably adequate information about product characteristics through other channels, such as a seller offering a warranty or a third party providing information (OMB 2003).

OTHER "COMPELLING PUBLIC NEED"

In some cases, a regulation may be initiated not in response to a failure of private markets, but to improve the efficiency of government programs, or to implement a legislative mandate of one kind or another where the underlying objective is something other than improving efficiency as such, for example, to redistribute incomes or provide for "universal" access to services deemed important (Dudley et al. 2017). In this case, BCA is still important for identifying which alternative can achieve the regulatory goal in the most efficient or cost-effective way.

GOVERNMENT SOLUTIONS DON'T ALWAYS WORK AS PLANNED

Students should recognize that markets will always fall short of the perfectly competitive market conditions in textbooks, so simply identifying a market failure will not be sufficient to justify a "compelling public need" for regulation. Regulatory guidance refers to "material" or "significant" failures of private markets and you might ask students what they would consider significant. Does a classmate who ate a garlic bagel for breakfast impose externalities on others? Would that require a regulation? If so, should the federal government ban garlic bagels, or would a more localized solution work better?

They should also be aware of government failure. Imagine an *American Idol*-like singing competition between two contestants. What if the judges heard the first contestant and because she was so horrible they immediately awarded the prize to the second without hearing him? In examining the need for regulation, students should recognize that comparing imperfect market conditions against an assumed perfect government response is unrealistic. This is an opportunity to talk about the theories of regulation, and that regulations often confer concentrated benefits on a few citizens while the costs are dispersed (Stigler 1971). Special interests work to gain a competitive advantage through regulation, at the expense of competitors and consumers (rent seeking) (Tullock et al. 2002). Also, political time horizons may lead to short-term regulatory fixes rather than long-term solutions. Further, regulatory officials don't face the same feedback loop that individuals do, so they are less likely to learn from their mistakes and make corrections.

CONCLUSION

At the end of this module, students should appreciate the role for markets in allocating resources efficiently, encouraging innovation and meeting social needs and understand why the concept of market failure has been key to regulatory principles adopted by presidents of both parties for decades. They should be skeptical of the "there oughta be a law" approach that justifies the need for regulation on anecdotal observations that may illustrate *symptoms* of a problem without articulating the underlying *cause* of those symptoms. Regulatory actions that do not explicitly point to a failure of private markets or public institutions underlying the need for action are likely to produce lower net benefits than those that correctly identify and seek to remedy the fundamental problem.

REFERENCES AND RECOMMENDATIONS FOR FURTHER READING

Chapman Economic Science Institute (n.d.), *Software Economic Science Institute Chapman University*. Chapman University, accessed June 20, 2017 at https://www.chapman.edu/research/institutes-and-centers/economic-science-institute/academics-research/software.aspx.

Clinton, W.J. (1993), Executive Order No. 12,866, 3 C.F.R. 638, accessed June 19, 2017 at https://www.whitehouse.gov/omb/inforeg_regmatters#eo12866.

Coase, R.H. (1960), "The problem of social cost", *The Journal of Law and Economics* **3**(3), 1–44.

Dudley, S.E. and J. Brito (2012), *Regulation: A Primer.* 2nd ed. The George Washington University Regulatory Studies Center and Mercatus Center at George Mason University. Accessed January 3, 2018 at https://regulatorystudies.columbian.gwu.edu/sites/regulatorystudies.columbian.gwu.edu/files/downloads/RegulatoryPrimer_DudleyBrito.pdf.

Dudley, S.E., R. Belzer, G. Blomquist, T. Brennan, C. Carrigan, J. Cordes, L.A. Cox, A. Fraas, J. Graham, G. Gray, J. Hammitt, K. Krutilla, P. Linquiti, R. Lutter, B. Mannix, S. Shapiro, A. Smith, W.K. Viscusi and R. Zerbe (2017), "Consumer's guide to regulatory impact analysis: Ten tips for being an informed consumer", *Journal of Benefit-Cost Analysis* **8**(2), 187–204. Accessed January 3, 2018 at https://www.cambridge.org/core/journals/journal-of-benefit-cost-analysis/article/consumers-guide-to-regulatory-impact-analysis-ten-tips-for-being-an-informed-policymaker/FAF984595B822A70495621AEA7EF7DEB/core-reader.

Mannix, B.F. and S.E. Dudley (2015), "The limits of irrationality as a rationale for regulation", *Journal of Policy Analysis and Management* **34**(3), 705–12. Accessed January 16, 2017 at http://onlinelibrary.wiley.com/doi/10.1002/pam.21841/full.

Munger, M.C. (2000), *Analyzing Policy: Choices, Conflicts, and Practices.* New York: Norton.

Obama, B.H. (2011), Executive Order No. 13,563, 3 C.F.R. 215, accessed January 3, 2018 at https://obamawhitehouse.archives.gov/the-press-office/2011/01/18/executive-order-13563-improving-regulation-and-regulatory-review.

Office of Management and Budget (OMB) (2003), "Circular A-4, regulatory analysis", last modified September 17, 2003. Accessed on January 3, 2018 at https://www.whitehouse.gov/sites/default/files/omb/assets/omb/circulars/a004/a-4.pdf.

Office of Management and Budget (OMB) (2010), "Agency checklist: Regulatory impact analysis", last modified October 28, 2010. Accessed January 3, 2018 at https://www.whitehouse.gov/sites/default/files/omb/inforeg/regpol/RIA_Checklist.pdf.

Office of Management and Budget (OMB) (2011a), "Circular A-4, regulatory impact analysis: Frequently asked questions (FAQs)", last modified February 7, 2011. Accessed January 3, 2018 at https://www.whitehouse.gov/sites/default/files/omb/assets/OMB/circulars/a004/a-4_FAQ.pdf.

Office of Management and Budget (OMB) (2011b), "Circular A-4, regulatory impact analysis: A primer", last modified August 15, 2011. Accessed January 3, 2018 at https://www.whitehouse.gov/sites/default/files/omb/inforeg/regpol/circular-a-4_regulatory-impact-analysis-a-primer.pdf.

Stigler, G.J. (1971), "The theory of economic regulation", *The Bell Journal of*

Economics and Management Science **2**(1), 3–21. Accessed January 3, 2018 at www.jstor.org/stable/3003160.

Tullock, G., A. Seldon and G.L. Brady (2002), *Government Failure: A Primer in Public Choice*. Washington, DC: Cato Institute.

7. The essentials: A short course for young professionals

Gelsomina Catalano and Massimo Florio

ABSTRACT

In the contest of the European Regional Policy, benefit-cost analysis (BCA) is explicitly required, amongst other elements, as a basis for decision making on the co-financing of major projects by the European Structural and Investment Funds (ESI Funds). How to teach the principles and applications of BCA in an intensive short course (one week) targeted to an audience of civil servants and young professionals with a range of backgrounds (economics, public administration and others) from different countries? The content of this chapter is motivated by the experience gathered by the team of the University of Milan and Centre for Industrial Studies (CSIL) in seven editions of a summer school on BCA and other training courses. The objective is to distill some lessons learned from this experience.

INTRODUCTION

The role of benefit-cost analysis (BCA) of investment projects expanded in the framework of the EU Regional Policy. Since the 1990s, BCA is a mandatory requirement for major projects applying for co-financing from the ESI Funds, namely for those investment projects whose eligible cost is higher than EUR 50 million (Articles 100–103 of EU Regulation 1303/2013). Guidelines on how to properly carry out the BCA as well as appraise its quality have been fine-tuned and become binding over time, with the aim to assure more rigor and homogeneity in investment decisions. In 2014, an updated and expanded Guide was adopted by the European Commission, including a reinforced operational approach to investment appraisal in the framework of the EU Regional Policy.

The call for better project evaluation has led to an increasing need for training initiatives among public authorities called to implement large investment projects, especially for those using ESI Funds. This chapter draws from the experience – gathered at the University of Milan and the CSIL – of BCA training courses targeting civil servants acting at different levels of governance (international, EU, national and regional level), practitioners in European and non-European countries as well as students with different backgrounds.

The objective of this chapter is specifically to report the lessons learned by the University of Milan and CSIL teams from carrying out seven editions of the Milan Summer School on BCA of investment projects.[1] The first edition of this school dates back to 2011 and builds on own experiences of training and seminars on BCA. Some examples include *inter alia* training courses (lasting maximum four days) carried out for Word Bank country economists working in countries of Eastern Europe and Central Asia (in 2007), European Commission officials (for example, DG REGIO desk officers in 2009) in charge of reviewing BCA and taking the decision on co-financing of major projects, staff from several National Ministries of the EU Member States – such as Skopje (in 2010 and 2017), Lithuania (in 2010), Romania (2012), Poland (in 2015), Slovenia (2017) – involved, on the other side, in the preparation of major project applications for co-funding under ESI Funds (particularly ERDF, Cohesion Fund and IPA). Such training experiences have shown that a comprehensive training course could be effectively concentrated in one week, starting from the principles and methods of BCA and then moving on to cover different sectoral applications. The Milan BCA Summer School has attracted (over the past seven editions) around 300 participants – 37 years old on average – mostly from public administrations and in particular from national governments and ministries of the EU Member States (Figure 7.1).

Over the several editions of the school, lessons have been learned on the main ingredients for delivering an effective and comprehensive short BCA course, that can be broadly grouped into two main items, namely the 'setting-scene' and the 'content' items. These ingredients are briefly presented and discussed in the following sections. In particular, the next section focuses on the 'setting-scene' items, namely those ingredients affecting the structure and the design of the course while later sections deal with the 'content' items which are related to the topics addressed during the lectures.

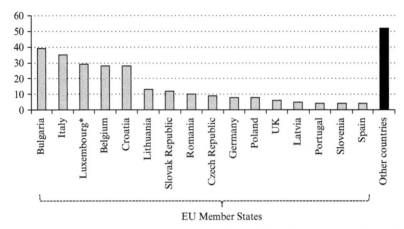

EU Member States

Note: * Mostly from the European Investment Bank

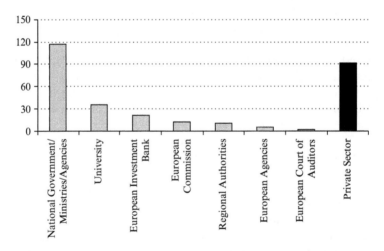

Notes: Other EU countries: Hungary, Greece, Malta, Sweden, Denmark, Estonia, France, Ireland.
Other countries: Afghanistan, Albania, Armenia, India, Indonesia, Iran, Jordan, Kenya, Nepal, Nigeria, Norway, Pakistan, Saudi Arabia, Serbia, South Africa, Turkey, Ukraine.

Figure 7.1   Participation in the Milan BCA Summer School by countries and affiliations (2011–17)

THE ESSENTIALS FOR SETTING THE SCENE

A first ingredient for setting the scene of an effective and comprehensive short BCA course concerns its structure. The course should be able to

provide a comprehensive picture to trainees with different academic backgrounds and levels of knowledge and practice with BCA. Seven editions
of the Milan Summer School suggest that the most effective solution to
address this objective is to structure the course into two training modules:
the first module should focus on the key principles and key steps on how
to perform a BCA (including financial, economic and risk analysis) while
the second module should concern the peculiarities of BCA application
across different sectors of investment. Depending on the number of sectors covered, parallel sessions can be held during the second module thus
enabling trainees to attend the sessions that are most relevant for them.

This course structure may be combined with a second ingredient that
proved to be very successful over the past training experiences, namely the
interactive and practical approach of the lectures. Apart from traditional
training methods – face-to-face presentations delivered by the lecturers
on the main topics of the BCA – the course should provide room for
interactions and active participation of trainees. From our experience
with seven editions of the Milan Summer School, this can be encouraged
in different ways. First, the course might include hands-on sessions where
trainees, under the guidance of a tutor, are encouraged to work individually or divided in small groups (5–6 people at most) on practicing analytical
skills in BCA. These hands-on sessions should reflect the structure of the
course into two modules. This means that during the first module, trainees
are asked to develop – through the use of spreadsheets – a fully-fledged
financial and economic analysis and calculation of performance indicators
starting from basic assumptions and key input data. During the second
module, trainees are instead asked to perform a critical review of a real
sectoral project example including the overall design and rationale of the
project, the calculation of economic benefits and performance indicators,
and so on. A final plenary discussion with a brief presentation delivered
(individually or in groups) by trainees on the results of their assignments
concludes each module. In order to further foster the active participation,
during the experience of summer school we triggered a sort of competition
amongst participants by awarding the best presentation delivered. Another
way to encourage interaction among participants is that the course provides the opportunity to raise questions and share thoughts and enquiries
during the face-to-face presentations. Trainees might be invited to bring
their personal experiences with the use of BCA they may have come across
in their professional experience. Also, they can be invited to get prepared
for the course in advance by having access to a reading list and didactical
material before the start of the lectures so that they are already engaged in
the content of the course and can contribute with constructive comments.
Finally, a debate can be raised during the last day of the school by inviting

both lecturers and trainees to reflect on how to feed BCA analysis into the decision making process and how to improve the quality of BCA (for example, common mistakes and practices).

A further ingredient belonging to the 'setting-scene' items is the appropriate selection of participants. Previous training experiences in BCA have taught that around 40 trainees is the maximum acceptable size for a short course in BCA. A higher number would make difficult the interactions during the courses and the active participation of the trainees during practical hands-on sessions. An aspect brought about by the Milan Summer School is to welcome different categories of participants acting at different levels of governance (such as international and EU institutions, national and regional governments, academic, private sector) in different countries and using BCA in different sectors and for different purposes (such as, for taking decisions on co-financing of investments or on the other side preparing applications for asking for the co-financing from ESI Funds.). This varied composition represents a positive asset of a course since it allows a sharing and transfer of experiences and lessons learned in the use of BCA from different contests and perspectives. A good and balanced composition of the class can be achieved by admitting trainees through a selection procedure based on the assessment of their background and previous working experience. Moreover, for the purpose of the practical sessions, they can be divided in groups according to their past exposure to BCA.

A final ingredient which is needed for setting the scene of an effective course is the composition of the faculty. A mix of academics, practitioners and public administrators has proved to be welcome and particularly effective since it offers different perspectives to trainees, from the theoretical framework of BCA to its practical applications and use in decision making processes. Of course, there are further ingredients which might contribute to setting the scene for an effective course on BCA. These are less essentials than the ones discussed above but likewise worth considering. These include the location of the course (it should be easily reachable), the dissemination channels (such as website, newsletter and email) in order to make the course as visible as possible, asking for an evaluation of the training after its completion in order to learn about possible aspects to improve, designing an online platform for the sharing of materials with selected trainees (for example full set of slides used, spreadsheet for the production of financial and economic analysis, bibliography and so on).

Finally, it is an obvious advantage if each lecturer has a blend of academic and professional background in order to find the right balance between teaching theory and lessons learned by experience.

The above structure is illustrated in Table 7.1.

Table 7.1 A short BCA course structured in two modules: An example based on the Milan Summer School

	Day 1	Day 2	Day 3		Day 4		Day 5
			Parallel Session. Part I				
			TRANSPORT	ENVIRONMENT	RESEARCH	URBAN DEVELOPMENT & MOBILITY	
Morning sessions	Key principles and steps of the CBA	Economic Analysis	1) Investment priorities, EU strategic framework, project typologies, typical economic benefits	1) Investment priorities, EU strategic framework, project typologies, typical economic benefits	1) Investment priorities, EU strategic framework, project typologies, typical economic benefits	1) Investment priorities, EU strategic framework, project typologies, typical economic benefits	Presentations of groups' results and discussion with experts. Part I
		Focus I: Shadow Wage					
	Financial Analysis Part I	Focus II: Social Discount Rate	2) Evaluation methods and tools	2) Evaluation methods and tools	2) Evaluation methods and tools	2) Evaluation methods and tools	
	Financial Analyses Part II	Focus III: Willingness to pay	Parallel Session. Part II				
			TRANSPORT	ENVIRONMENT	RESEARCH	URBAN DEVELOPMENT & MOBILITY	
		Risk Assessment	3) Presentation of a case history	3) Presentation of a case history	3) Presentation of a case history	3) Presentation of a case history	Presentations of groups' results and discussion with experts. Part II
	Q&A session	Q&A session	Q&A session	Q&A session	Q&A session	Q&A session	Concluding Remarks
Afternoon	Hands-on workshop on Financial Analysis	Hands-on workshop on Economic Analysis	Hands-on workshop on sectoral case histories		Hands-on workshop on sectoral case histories		

THE ESSENTIAL TOPICS OF A BCA COURSE: FIRST MODULE ON ANALYTICAL CONCEPTS

Beyond the 'setting-scene' element, the 'content' ingredients of the course are the essential topics of BCA to be covered during the course. As mentioned, the Milan Summer School is divided in two modules, held in sequence: in the first module trainees learn the general principles, methods and techniques of BCA, such as the rules and techniques to perform financial analysis, economic analysis, sensitivity and risk analysis; the second module focuses on sectoral applications of BCA (such as transport, environment, research and urban development).

The course starts by providing a broad and general understanding of the BCA rationale before entering into the details of financial analysis, economic analysis and risk analysis. During this introduction session, the theory and the key principles in applied BCA are illustrated, by focusing on the following topics:

- Objectives and scope of BCA
- The role of BCA in the decision making
- Long-term perspective
- Incremental technique (counterfactual)
- Option and demand analysis
- Monetary evaluation (performance indicators)
- Opportunity costs of goods and services (shadow prices)
- Microeconomic approach of BCA

There is no guarantee that participants, although using BCA during their daily work, are fully aware of BCA origins and scope. Therefore, we found it to be essential to start any course by reminding that the purpose of BCA is simply 'to provide a consistent procedure for evaluating decisions in terms of their consequences'[2] and also provide some historical background from *inter alia* Dupuit (1844), Little and Mirrlees (1974), Squire and Van der Tak (1975), UK *Green Book* (HM Treasury 2003), or as summarized in Florio (2014).

While illustrating the role of BCA in decision making process, attention should be paid to the relevant institutional contest for the trainees. Focusing on the EU contest for instance, it would be useful to draw the attention of trainees to the EU regulation (Article 101 of Reg. 1303/2013) explicitly requiring BCA for co-financing of major projects as well as to show how the methodology has been evolved and fine-tuned over five editions of the BCA Guide (the first in 1994) adopted by the European Commission and that became binding for the EU Member States.

After having clarified the objectives and role of BCA, the key principles of performing a good BCA should be explained. The first principle concerns the long-term perspective of the analysis, which briefly means to set a proper time horizon for carrying out the BCA and forecasting future costs and benefits on a long time span (looking forward). The time horizon may, of course, be different according to the sector of intervention. Attention should be drawn on the importance of adopting appropriate discount rates (discount cash flow method) to calculate the present value of future costs and benefits. It is worth clarifying that these rates should be different for the financial and economic analysis. Financial discount rate reflects indeed the opportunity cost of capital while social discount rate is the rate at which society is willing to postpone a unit of current consumption in exchange for more future consumption. Examples of recommended discount rates according to the relevant institutional contest should be provided. For instance, in the EU Regional contest, a financial discount rate of 4 per cent for all the EU Member States while a social discount rate of 5 per cent is recommended for major projects in Cohesion countries and 3 per cent for the other Member States.

To better explain and illustrate some issues, such as the incremental approach of the BCA, performance indicators and opportunity costs of goods and services, simple tests and figures may be helpful to explain these concepts. We show some examples we have used during the Milan Summer School (see Table 7.2 below on the choice of the counterfactual and Figure 7.2 on Financial versus Economic Performance).

The course moves on with the first step of BCA according to the European Commission (2014) Guide, namely the financial analysis. Starting from the principles introduced above, such as the discounted cash flow method and the choice of a time horizon, discussion about financial analysis should focus on the following topics:

- *Scope and relevance of the financial analysis.*
- *Tricks for carrying out the analysis:* such as net of VAT (if this is recoverable by the project promoter), use of constant prices (no inflation), use of a financial discount rate and so on.
- *Structure of the financial analysis:* differences between financial return on investment, financial sustainability and financial return on capital.
- *Investment costs and replacement costs:* which items to consider, how to estimate them and so on.
- *Residual value:* definition, how to estimate it, how to consider it in the analysis (last year of the time horizon) and so on.
- *Operating costs:* definition (difference to investment costs), how to estimate them and so on.

Table 7.2   Incremental approach: The choice of the counterfactual

	Scenarios		EUROm	NPV
1	Proposed project		Net benefit	1058
			Investment	435
2	Do-minimum		Net benefit	661
			Investment	29
3	Business as Usual		Net benefit	442
			Investment	0
		Results		
1–2	Proposed project net of Do-minimum		Net flows	−9
			ERR	3%
1–3	Proposed project net of Business as Usual		Net flows	181
			ERR	6%
2–3	Do minimum net of Business as Usual		Net flows	219
			ERR	5%

Note: BCA compares a scenario with-the-project with a counterfactual baseline scenario without-the-project. The financial and economic performance indicators are calculated on the incremental cash flows only, namely the difference between the cash flows in the with-the-project and the counterfactual scenarios.

Source: Milan Summer School.

- *Revenues (if any):* tariffs setting (polluter-pays principle and the full-cost recovery principles).
- *Identification of the sources of financing and calculation of the financial sustainability:* rules and techniques of the EU grant calculation (if the course is targeting the EU Regional Policy).
- *Calculation of financial performance indicators:* how to estimate these indicators, which items to consider in the case of financial return on investment and return on capital.
- *Common mistakes and errors in carrying out financial analysis.*

Some of these concepts may be introduced with the support of practical examples of calculation and spreadsheets.

Moving to the second step of the BCA, namely the economic analysis, the course should focus on the following essentials:

- *Scope and relevance of the economic analysis (differences to the financial).*
- *Key steps to move from the financial analysis to economic analysis,* including (1) fiscal corrections (prices net of VAT and other taxes),

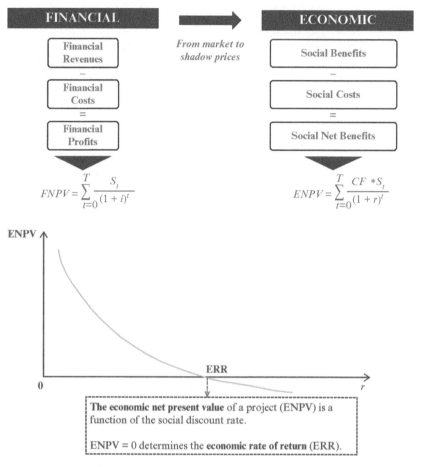

$$FNPV = \sum_{t=0}^{T} \frac{S_t}{(1+i)^t}$$

$$ENPV = \sum_{t=0}^{T} \frac{CF * S_t}{(1+r)^t}$$

The **economic net present value** of a project (ENPV) is a function of the social discount rate.

ENPV = 0 determines the **economic rate of return** (ERR).

Source: Milan Summer School.

Figure 7.2 Project performance in a nutshell

(2) transforming market prices into shadow prices, adding externalities (not captured by observed market prices in financial analysis) and (3) calculation of economic indicators. While explaining these steps, focus is needed on the following relevant topics:

- *Different approaches for estimating shadow prices for tradeable and non-tradeable goods,* namely border prices rules, shadow wages, standard conversion factors, long-run marginal cost, willingness to pay (**WTP**) or willingness to accept (**WTA**).

- *Shadow Wages:* how they can be estimated for different countries.
- *Techniques to estimate the WTP and WTA,* namely stated preferences (contingent valuation), revealed preferences (travel costs, hedonic prices, cost of illness, defensive behavior methods) and benefit transfer.
- *Social Discount Rate:* how it can be estimated for different countries.

Similar to the financial analysis, these concepts may be illustrated through practical examples.

To conclude the first module as well as the steps of the BCA, the courses should focus on the *risk assessment* of a project and more specifically encompass the following topics:

- *Sensitivity analysis;*
- *Scenario analysis and switching values;*
- *Risk analysis;*
- *Monte Carlo simulation;*
- *Qualitative risk analysis; risk prevention and mitigation measures.*

The hands-on sessions – we hold them in the afternoon – should be structured in order to enable the trainees to practice these concepts and specifically, to perform a fully-fledged financial and economic analysis. For a comprehensive practice on BCA, it would be helpful to illustrate also a simulation of the risk analysis with a dedicated software.

Our experience is that contrasting the assumptions and results of economic versus financial analysis is key in conveying the core function of BCA in decision making. That is, to address market failures and policy objectives that are not revealed by the financial performance of the project.

THE ESSENTIAL TOPICS OF A BCA COURSE: SECOND MODULE ON CONTEXT AND CASES

The essential ingredients of the second module mostly depend on the sectors of investment covered by the course. Investigating the interest of potential trainees during the selection process may be helpful in this regard, particularly in selecting those sectors and sub-sectors which are mostly relevant for them and, moreover, in tailoring the materials to their needs and expectations.

A widespread interest in BCA teaching focusing on transport, environment, urban development and research and development (RDI) sectors has been observed amongst trainees of the Milan Summer School. Previous editions of this school have proved that a maximum of four different sectors of investment can be addressed in a short, effective and comprehensive BCA course. These can be held, for instance, through parallel sessions by leaving the trainees the possibility to attend the session which is most relevant for them.

Drawing from the experience of the Milan Summer School, for each sector of investment, the course should include at least the following four sessions:

- Session 1: *Investment priorities of the sector.*
- Session 2: *Typologies of projects financed.*
- Session 3: *Typical economic benefits.*
- Session 4: *Evaluation methods and tools*

A concluding 'case history' session may be helpful to provide real life examples of projects the trainers are familiar with. Such sessions should be aimed to show how the results of a BCA have to be interpreted and discussed in order to support the prioritization and financing of investment projects. During the hands-on sessions, an interactive discussion can be encouraged by dividing trainees in sectoral group and assigning them a real project to discuss and critically review.

Of course, the topics addressed during the aforementioned sessions may be different depending on the sector. Let us use the Milan BCA Summer School to provide some examples for transport, environment and urban development sectors. A detailed discussion on the RDI sector is provided in Chapter 15.

Focusing on the classical example of the transport sector, an effective BCA teaching should deal, amongst others, with the following specific issues:

- *How to properly carry out the demand analysis of the transport project,* thus meaning adopting a suitable and credible traffic forecast method (for example, network analysis method using computer modelling or simple modelling method – elasticity co-efficient and so on) and preparing traffic forecasts for competitive modes of transport.
- *How to monetize typical costs and benefits of transport projects,* thus meaning estimating (for example, through rule of half approach) the savings of travel time in passenger transport, savings of time in freight transport, savings in vehicle operating and also computing the savings in costs of accidents, environmental impacts (air, noise pollution), costs of climate changes and so on.

- *How to estimate the value of time* (the most significant benefit in the case of transport projects) for different typologies of travellers (such as businesses, commuting and other travellers) through different methodologies (for example, survey and/or empirical approach, cost saving approach, available government guidelines).

As for the environment sector, the following specific issues of the sector should be certainly addressed and are summarized in Table 7.3:

- *How to identify a suitable counterfactual scenario,* that is, assessing whether it is legally compliant with the National regulation/EU

Table 7.3   Environment sector (water supply): Different benefits and evaluation tools

Impacts	Type	Valuation method
Increased availability of drinking water supply and/or sewer services	Direct	WTP estimated as the avoided cost for self-provision
Improved reliability of water sources and water supply service	Direct	WTP estimated as the avoided cost for self-provision
Improved quality of drinking water	Direct	WTP estimated as the avoided cost to purchase water on the market
Improved quality of surface water bodies	Direct	WTP for water bodies with a use value (for example, market value of concessions, avoided cost of shellfish purification, travel cost method or benefit transfer) WTP for water bodies with a non-use (for example, contingent evaluation or benefit transfer)
Resource cost savings (water preserved for other uses)	Direct	Long run marginal cost for water production
Health impacts	Externality	Cost of illness approach
Congestion savings due to improved rainwater drainage	Externality	Time savings
Variation in GHG emissions	Externality	Shadow price of GHG emissions

Source: Milan Summer School.

directives concerning the sector (such as quality standards of the water treatment).

● *How to set the tariff for the services provided,* that is, ensuring compliance with the cost recovery and pay-polluter principles and taking into account results of the affordability analysis.

● *Identifying barriers to implement the cost recovery principle* (for example, opposition of stakeholders and users to tariffs increase, significant price differences between local communities which are politically motivated) and *trade-off between cost recovery and affordability.*

● *Identifying the typical benefits* in the case of water supply, waste water and solid waste projects (see, for instance, Table 7.3) as well as the different *evaluation tools and approaches* for their estimation.

A cross-sectoral approach should be adopted while dealing with the urban development sector as summarized in Table 7.4. Projects in this field, indeed, usually include benefits which are common to other sectors

Table 7.4   Urban development sector: Typical projects, benefits and methodologies

Type of project	Type of benefits	Methodologies
Natural environment / urban spaces (that is, parks, requalification)	● Environmental improvement ● Recreational value ● Real estate requalification	● Travel cost method ● Hedonic prices ● Contingent evaluation
Urban transport	● Improve connections ● Reduce traffic	● Value of time ● Shadow prices of polluting agents ● Avoided costs for accidents
Cultural heritage	● Safeguard cultural heritage ● Increase of tourism	● Contingent evaluation ● Travel cost method
Public security	● Reduction of injuries and fatalities ● Reduction of damages to property ● Decrease of public expenditure for crime management	● Avoided costs for medical costs and loss of income ● Insurance payments received for the loss or damages to a property ● Avoided costs for public expenditure in crime management

(such as transport, environment, cultural heritage, among others). A BCA course on the urban development sector should, first of all, clarify the typologies of projects which can be classified as urban development projects and identify the typologies of benefits which may occur. The essentials of the course should include, amongst others, a lecture on the methodological approaches which are usually adopted for the estimation of benefits related to these projects, such as travel cost method (for example, to estimate the the value of recreational infrastructures by looking at the costs to access them), hedonic prices method (for example, to estimate the value of environmental amenities) and contingent valuation method (for example, to estimate the willingness to pay for changes in the quantity or quality of a non-market good or service by directly asking citizens).

CONCLUSION

While the design and implementation of a successful short course on BCA should be a case-by-case exercise, we believe that our experience may be of some interest for other teams. Among the different lessons learned we would suggest that the most critical are the following ones. First, in terms of 'setting the scene' there is the structure. It happens very frequently outside a regular university curriculum, where homogeneity of the students may be 'built-in', that participants have a very wide range of backgrounds. Thus, it is of essence to offer a first part where a common set of tools is firmly made available, and then move to a second part where applications are presented. Second, the composition of the faculty and the classroom should ideally blend academic and practical experience.

In terms of content, we have noticed that starting from financial analysis is far from being a waste of time. In fact, it makes evident what is the key role of BCA in project appraisal. Moreover, adding risk analysis, even in a very simplified form, suggests to students that – even in an uncertain world – BCA can be based on something more than a best guess.

NOTES

1. https://www.csilmilano.com/Summer-School/Summer-School.html, accessed June 11, 2017.
2. As defined by Dréze and Stern (1987).

REFERENCES AND RECOMMENDATIONS FOR FURTHER READING

Dréze, J. and N. Stern (1987). 'The theory of cost-benefit analysis', in A. Auerbach and M. Feldstein, *Handbook of Public Economics*, Amsterdam: North Holland.

Dupuit, J. (1844). 'De la mesure de l'utilité des travaux publics', *Annales des Ponts et Chaussées*, 2 (116).

European Commission (2014). *Guide to Cost-Benefit Analysis of Investment Projects* (fifth edition), Luxembourg: Publications Office of the European Union.

Florio, M. (2014). *Applied Welfare Economics: Cost-Benefit Analysis of Projects and Policies*, New York: Routledge.

HM Treasury (2003). *The Green Book – Appraisal and Evaluation in Central Government*, UK Government. Available at www.gov.uk/government/publications/the-green-book-appraisal-and-evaluation-in-central-governent, accessed June 11, 2017.

Little, I.M.D. and J.A. Mirrlees (1974). *Project Appraisal and Planning for Developing Countries*, London: Heinemann.

Squire, L. and H.G. Van der Tak (1975). *Economic Analysis of Projects*, Baltimore: World Bank/Johns Hopkins Press.

PART II

Challenging concepts and examples

8. Valuing statistical lives

Lisa A. Robinson

ABSTRACT

The value of small changes in mortality risks, conventionally expressed as the value per statistical life (VSL), is an important parameter in benefit-cost analysis. These risk reductions often dominate the benefit estimates for environmental, health and safety policies and regulations. As a result, their value has been extensively studied, raising questions about how to best synthesize the resulting research and to adjust it for different contexts. The VSL terminology has led to substantial confusion about what is being measured, however. The VSL reflects individuals' willingness to pay (WTP) for small reductions in their own mortality risks within a defined time period. It is not the value of preventing certain death.

INTRODUCTION[1]

Reducing premature mortality is a major goal of many interventions and accounts for a substantial share of the benefits estimates for numerous policies and regulations.[2] The value of these risk reductions has been extensively studied and several government agencies have developed related guidance. Inconsistencies in the results and research gaps raise a number of questions, however, about how to best synthesize and apply this research given the diversity of risks and populations addressed. In addition, these values are conventionally expressed as the value per statistical life (VSL), which is often misunderstood. The VSL reflects individuals' willingness to pay for small reductions in their own mortality risks within a defined time period. It is not a value that others place on preventing their death.

CONCEPTUAL FRAMEWORK AND DEFINITIONS[3]

In benefit-cost analysis, the starting point for valuing mortality risk reductions is typically an estimate of the change in the likelihood of death in a defined time period for those individuals affected by the policy. This risk change can be aggregated over the affected population to calculate the number of statistical cases averted.

The term "statistical" is used to emphasize the role of probability; most policies reduce the risk incurred by the affected population rather than preventing identifiable deaths with certainty. The specific individuals who would have died without the policy generally cannot be identified, either before or after the policy is implemented. In addition, because death can be delayed but not prevented, reducing deaths in one year necessarily increases deaths in future years; the policy increases the life expectancy of these affected.

For example, it is not unusual for a policy to decrease the risk of dying by perhaps 1 in 10 000 or 1 in 100 000 per year. A statistical life involves aggregating these small risk changes across individuals. If 10 000 individuals each experience a risk reduction of 1 in 10 000 in a given year, then one statistical life is "saved" ($10\,000 * 1/10\,000 = 1$). This means that, if in the absence of the policy, three out of 10 000 people are expected to die in that year, with the policy two of these 10 000 people are expected to die.

Consistent with the benefit-cost analysis framework, the value of these risk reductions is generally based on individuals' willingness to trade-off their spending on other goods and services for reductions in their own risks. Money is not important per se, rather it reflects the resources available to spend on risk reductions and other things. For mortality risk reductions, individual WTP is typically expressed as the VSL.[4] More precisely, VSL is an individual's marginal rate of substitution between wealth and the risk of dying in a defined time period. Presumably, individual WTP accounts for both the pecuniary effects of the risk change (including avoided out-of-pocket medical expenses and losses in future earnings) and the non-pecuniary effects (including experiencing the joys of life itself and averting pain and suffering). These values are likely to vary across individuals and also across different types of risk: for example, a risk that is viewed as voluntary and controllable may be valued very differently than a risk that is not.

For small changes in risk, VSL can be approximated by dividing WTP for a risk reduction by the risk change. For example, if an individual is willing to pay $900 for a 1 in 10 000 reduction in his or her risk of dying in the current year, his or her VSL is $9 000 000 ($900 WTP ÷ 1/10 000 risk change). These estimates are often aggregated throughout the population, in which case the total value of the risk reduction is equal to the sum of each individual's WTP for the risk reduction he or she is likely to experience. This sum can be divided by the number of expected deaths averted to estimate the average VSL within that population. For example, if a population of 10 000 persons is willing to pay, in the aggregate, $27 million in a given year for a risk reduction that is expected to result in three fewer deaths in that year, the VSL would average $9 million ($27 million divided by three cases).

The VSL terminology is often misunderstood.[5] VSL is not the amount that the government, the analyst or an individual places on saving a life with certainty. Rather, it represents the values we each place on small changes in our own risks. We demonstrate these values almost every day; for example, in deciding whether to buy protective equipment, to drive more safely or to use less polluting fuels.

PRIMARY RESEARCH METHODS

Estimates of individual WTP are generally derived using stated or revealed preference methods. Stated preference methods typically employ survey techniques to ask respondents about their WTP for an outcome under a hypothetical scenario. Such methods are attractive because researchers can tailor them to directly value the outcome(s) of concern; surveys can describe particular health risks from specific causes and also target respondents with particular characteristics (such as geographic location, health status, age or income). A key concern is that respondents may have little incentive to respond accurately because the payment is hypothetical. Conducting a study that yields valid and reliable results thus requires careful design and implementation.[6]

Revealed preference methods infer the value of nonmarket goods from observed behaviors and prices for related market goods. For example, wage-risk studies examine the additional compensation associated with jobs that involve higher risks of fatal injuries, using statistical methods to separate the effects of these risks on wages from the effects of other job and personal characteristics.[7, 8] While this use of market data has the advantage of relying on behavior with real consequences, it may be difficult to find a market good that can be used to estimate the value of the outcome of concern. For example, wage-risk studies address deaths resulting from job-related injuries among workers, while many policies affect illness-related deaths and may disproportionately affect the very young or the very old.

An alternative measure of the value of reducing mortality risks is the human capital approach. This approach was widely used in older analysis, but is not fully consistent with the benefit-cost analysis framework. It estimates the value of a change in mortality risk based solely on the value of lost production rather than individual WTP. This approach does not include the value that individuals are likely to place on survival other than the loss in income (and the associated consumption), such as the joy of living more generally, and is not recommended for use in benefit-cost analysis.[9]

BENEFIT TRANSFER AND RESEARCH SYNTHESIS

Because conducting new primary research requires substantial time and expense, typically analysts rely on existing valuation studies. This approach is referenced as "benefit transfer" to indicate that the populations and policies studied are not necessarily identical to the population and policy considered in the benefit-cost analysis. Similar to the approaches used to estimate other parameters in policy analysis, such transfers involve carefully reviewing the literature to identify high-quality studies that are suitable for use in a particular context, and determining whether and how to combine and adjust the results prior to application. "Quality" is evaluated by considering the likely accuracy and reliability of the data and methods used; "suitability" involves exploring the similarity of the risks and the populations affected. There are no firm guidelines; benefit transfer relies heavily on the informed judgment of the analyst and requires clear disclosure and discussion of related uncertainties and their implications.

The VSL is relatively well studied; recent reviews suggest that over 200 studies have now been completed globally. Because of the importance of these estimates, substantial attention has been paid to developing criteria for evaluating study quality and applicability. In particular, many government agencies (particularly in high-income countries) have published guidance for estimating VSL in analyses of regulatory and other policies.[10]

For example, in the US, recommended values are generally derived by reviewing the literature and identifying a range of values and a central estimate from selected studies (see US Department of Health and Human Services 2016, US Department of Transportation 2016 and US Environmental Protection Agency 2010).[11] The US Environmental Protection Agency is currently working on an update of its estimates, based on meta-analysis of selected studies. The resulting values are generally between $9 million and $10 million (2015 dollars), and rely largely on wage-risk studies.

The Organisation for Economic Co-operation and Development (OECD) has taken a somewhat different approach, focusing on stated preference studies and using meta-analysis to combine the results. For example, in OECD (2012), the authors report the results of a comprehensive review and meta-analysis of VSL stated preference studies. They recommend that, for analyses that address the OECD as a whole, the VSL range should be $1.5 to $4.5 million with a base estimate of $3 million (2005 US dollars).

A major difference between these estimates is the extent to which they rely on revealed or stated preference studies. Thus the differences in the estimates may reflect differences in the methods used, the criteria applied to select studies for inclusion and the approaches used to combine estimates across studies, rather than solely variation in the values held by different populations.

ADJUSTING FOR INCOME DIFFERENCES

It seems unlikely that VSL would remain constant across populations with substantially different incomes.[12] For example, as discussed earlier, the estimated US population-average VSL is between $9 million and $10 million. A $9 million VSL implies that the average resident is willing to pay $900 for a 1 in 10000 mortality risk change, or 1.6 percent of US gross domestic product (GDP) per capita, which was $56116 in 2015.[13,14] In a low-income country, where GDP per capita may average less than $2000, it seems impossible that the average individual would be willing to spend $900 on the same risk reduction, given the necessity for spending on more basic needs. Overall, individual WTP per unit of risk reduction should decrease as income decreases, resulting in a smaller VSL.

Because relatively few VSL studies are available for lower income countries, analysts typically transfer estimates from higher income settings. These transfers require three types of data: a base VSL, income estimates for both the base VSL and the target populations and an estimate of the change in VSL associated with a change in income, that is, VSL income elasticity. Assuming the elasticity is constant across the income range addressed, the formula is:

$$VSL_{target} = VSL_{base} * (Income_{target}/Income_{base})^{elasticity} \qquad (8.1)$$

One challenge is identifying the appropriate VSL to use as a starting point. As noted above, different approaches yield different base estimates. A second challenge is identifying the appropriate income elasticity, changes in which can alter the results by orders of magnitude. Hammitt and Robinson (2011) report that the then-existing studies found VSL income elasticities ranging from as low as 0.10 to greater than 2.0. In recent reviews, researchers seem to be coalescing around elasticities closer to 1.0 (Robinson 2017). For example, in work conducted for the World Bank, Narain and Sall (2016) use an elasticity of 0.8 for high-income countries and an elasticity of 1.2 to transfer estimates to low- and middle-income countries.

The elasticity may vary depending on the income range considered. However, when extrapolating from high-income countries to much lower income settings, elasticities below 1.0 seem implausible. As income becomes increasingly constrained, the fraction of income individuals are willing to devote to achieving small mortality risk reductions is likely to decrease, due to the difficulties of funding basic needs.

Given these uncertainties, analysts should explore the implications of a range of values when extrapolating VSL across income levels. In some cases, benefits may exceed costs by a large enough amount that the value used may not matter much. In other cases, whether the policy yields positive net benefits may depend on the VSL estimate that is used.

ADJUSTING FOR AGE AND LIFE EXPECTANCY

The base VSL estimates discussed above are generally population-average estimates for adults, while some policies disproportionately affect those who are much younger or much older. Because older individuals have fewer expected life years remaining than the average member of the population, intuition suggests that lower VSL estimates may be applicable. However, both theory (Hammitt 2007) and empirical work suggest that relationship is uncertain. Some argue that the relationship between VSL and age should follow the pattern of consumption over the life cycle, which is typically an inverse-U distribution. Much of the empirical work that considers the trade-off between wages and risks across all workers supports this model (for example, Aldy and Viscusi 2008), although the rate of increase and decrease and the age at which VSL peaks varies across studies.

Stated preference research is needed to address the relationships between age and VSL among individuals older or younger than working age. For older individuals, the evidence is inconsistent. Some studies do not find statistically significant relationships with age, while others find that the VSL decreases among older individuals in varying patterns and amounts. Because children generally lack the independent financial means as well as the cognitive ability needed to respond to WTP questions, related research generally elicits parental WTP. Several studies suggest that WTP for reduced morbidity or mortality risks to children may be noticeably greater than adult WTP to reduce their own risks (perhaps by a factor of two), although the magnitude of the difference varies across studies.

At times, a value per statistical life year (VSLY) estimate is used to adjust for age. In contrast to the VSL, which is the rate at which the individual substitutes money for reductions in mortality risk within the current year or other short time period, the VSLY is the rate at which he or she substitutes money for gains in life expectancy. VSLY is often roughly estimated by dividing VSL by the average (discounted) remaining life expectancy for the population studied. To determine the value per statistical case, the constant VSLY that results is then multiplied by the (discounted) expected years of life extension for individuals affected by the policy. Under this approach, the per-case values are lower for older individuals than for younger individuals, because they have fewer years of expected life remaining.

This approach assumes that VSLY is constant and independent of the number of life years gained, implying that VSL is proportional to the individual's remaining (discounted) life expectancy. However, neither economic theory nor available empirical results support these assumptions, suggesting that the relationship between the VSL and age is very uncertain. Thus, while applying a population-average VSL appears reasonable when a policy affects the general population, it is unclear whether and how the VSL should be adjusted in cases where the very young or the very old are disproportionately affected.

CONCLUSION

When conducting benefit-cost analyses that address mortality risk reductions, analysts can often rely on guidance developed by government agencies to estimate the values. These values typically represent population-average estimates, which may be adjusted for income differences across countries. Adjustments for differences in age or life expectancy are made less frequently, due to gaps and inconsistencies in the available research. Because the VSL concept is often misunderstood, clear communication of the underlying concept and uncertainties in its measurement is essential.

NOTES

1.   Instructors wishing to assign a single, introductory-level reading may find Robinson and Hammitt (2013) useful. Where time permits, adding readings or examples from the cited references may also be helpful.

2. VSL estimates may also be used to derive thresholds for cost-effectiveness analysis, which is often utilized to prioritize spending on health-related policies.
3. For more advanced students, instructors may wish to add a more formal derivation of the underlying economic model. Hammitt (2017) provides a useful overview of this model and its implications.
4. Estimates of willingness to accept compensation (WTA) are also consistent with the benefit-cost analysis framework; however, WTP is generally the appropriate concept for valuing improvements from the status quo.
5. This confusion has led to several proposals to change the terminology, none of which have yet been widely accepted.
6. See Corso et al. (2001) and Cameron and DeShazo (2013) for examples.
7. These studies are often referred to as "hedonic-wage" or "compensating wage differential" studies. See Viscusi (2004) and Kniesner et al. (2010) for examples.
8. Another revealed preference approach considers averting behaviors; that is, defensive measures or consumer products used to protect against perceived health risks, such as the use of bicycle helmets (see, for example, the review by Blomquist (2004)). These studies are applied infrequently in benefit-cost analysis due to concerns about their limitations, including the difficulty of estimating the size of the risk change associated with many behaviors and the need to separately estimate the value of key inputs such as the time spent in the activity.
9. In the United States, Grosse et al. (2009) find that the present value of future lifetime production for a 40 to 44 year old is $1.2 million if both market and nonmarket production are included; $0.8 million if only market production is included (2007 dollars, 3 percent discount rate). These values are much smaller than the US population-average VSL estimates for individuals of about the same age, as discussed later.
10. Because this guidance is periodically updated to reflect new studies and evolving best practice standards, students should check with the relevant agencies for the most recent values.
11. Students should exercise caution in comparing values across sources; the same approach may result in estimates that vary because they are expressed in different year dollars and include different adjustments for changes in real income.
12. The approaches described in this section are typically used to estimate the effects of population-average real income growth over time or of income differences across countries. While they could also be used to estimate the VSL for different income groups within a country, such adjustments are rarely made because they are viewed as inequitable. However, using the same VSL for different income groups ignores the variation in the values that members of each group may place on the risk reductions they receive.
13. While VSL studies often rely on per household or per worker estimates of income, GDP per capita or gross national income (GNI) per capita are often used in transferring VSL across countries because consistently estimated values are available for most countries (Hammitt 2017, Robinson 2017).
14. US per capita GDP estimate in current 2015 dollars from the World Bank as viewed June 2017: http://data.worldbank.org/indicator/NY.GDP.PCAP.CD?name_desc=true, accessed June 1, 2017.

REFERENCES AND RECOMMENDATIONS FOR FURTHER READING

Aldy, J.E. and W.K. Viscusi (2008), "Adjusting the value of a statistical life for age and cohort effects," *Review of Economics and Statistics.* **90**(3): 573–81.
Blomquist, G. (2004), "Self-protection and averting behavior, values of statistical

lives, and benefit cost analysis of environmental policy," *Review of the Economics of the Household.* **2**: 89–110.

Cameron, T.A. and J.R. DeShazo (2013), "Demand for health risk reductions," *Journal of Environmental Economics and Management.* **65**: 87–109.

Corso, P.S., J.K. Hammitt and J.D. Graham (2001), "Valuing mortality-risk reduction: Using visual aids to improve the validity of contingent valuation," *Journal of Risk and Uncertainty.* **23**(2): 165–84.

Grosse, S.D., K.V. Krueger and M. Mvundura (2009), "Economic productivity by age and sex: 2007 estimates for the United States," *Medical Care.* **47**(7): S94–S103.

Hammitt, J.K. (2007), "Valuing changes in mortality risk: Lives saved versus life years saved," *Review of Environmental Economics and Policy.* **1**(2): 228–40.

Hammitt, J.K. (2017), "Extrapolating the value per statistical life between populations: Theoretical implications," *Journal of Benefit-Cost Analysis.* **8**(2): 215–25.

Hammitt, J.K. and L.A. Robinson (2011), "The income elasticity of the value per statistical life: Transferring estimates between high and low income populations," *Journal of Benefit-Cost Analysis.* **2**(1): Art. 1.

Kniesner, T.J., W.K. Viscusi and J.P. Ziliak (2010), "Policy relevant heterogeneity in the value of statistical life: New evidence from panel data quantile regressions," *Journal of Risk and Uncertainty.* **40**: 15–31.

Narain, U. and C. Sall (2016), *Methodology for Valuing the Health Impacts of Air Pollution: Discussion of Challenges and Proposed Solutions.* Washington, D.C.: World Bank Group.

OECD (2012), *Mortality Risk Valuation in Environment, Health and Transport Policies.* Paris: OECD Publishing.

Robinson, L.A. (2017), "Estimating the values of mortality risk reductions in low- and middle-income countries," *Journal of Benefit-Cost Analysis.* **8**(2): 205–14.

Robinson, L.A. and J.K. Hammitt (2013), "Skills of the trade: Valuing health risk reductions in benefit-cost analysis," *Journal of Benefit-Cost Analysis.* **4**(1): 107–30.

Viscusi, W.K. (2004), "The value of life: Estimates with risks by occupation and industry," *Economic Inquiry.* **42**: 29–48.

US Department of Health and Human Services (2016), "Guidelines for regulatory impact analysis." Washington, D.C.: Office of the Assistant Secretary for Planning and Evaluation. https://aspe.hhs.gov/system/files/pdf/242926/HHS_RIAGuidance.pdf, accessed January 17, 2018.

US Department of Transportation (2016), "Guidance on treatment of the economic value of a statistical life (VSL) in U.S. department of transportation analyses – 2016 adjustment," Memorandum to Secretarial Officers and Modal Administrators from M.J. Moran, Acting General Counsel, and Carlos Monje Assistant Secretary for Transportation Policy. https://www.transportation.gov/regulations/economic-values-used-in-analysis, accessed January 17, 2018.

US Environmental Protection Agency (2010, with 2014 update), "Guidelines for preparing economic analyses." Washington, D.C.: National Center for Environmental Economics. https://www.epa.gov/environmental-economics/guidelines-preparing-economic-analyses, accessed January 17, 2018.

9. The arithmetic of efficiency—Or the value of marginal analysis

John Mendeloff

ABSTRACT

This teaching note focuses on two common difficulties for students. The first is the failure to think in terms of marginal effects. Deciding whether something is worthwhile depends upon what other options are available. When confronted with a program that costs more than another but also has greater effects, students often don't realize that they need to examine the marginal cost per marginal effect of the more expensive program relative to the other program. The second, related, difficulty is not realizing that, unless you have a value to place on the effects, you generally can't say whether a project is worthwhile. Instead, students see that buying only one unit may provide a lower cost per unit than buying more units (assuming declining marginal effectiveness). Then they label that the most "cost-effective" option and proceed to recommend that it be adopted. Several variations related to cost-effectiveness are discussed.

MOTIVATION

Two worries motivate this unit. The first is that early students often don't understand that they need to focus on marginal analysis (and they don't know how to do it). The second is confusion about the term "cost-effective." When students see an option that has the lowest cost per unit, they label it the most cost-effective, and from there it is a short step to viewing it as the most efficient. They don't realize that, without putting a value on the effect, you cannot say what option is the most efficient, except in the context of a fixed budget.

Note that this unit does not assume that students have already learned the substance of benefit-cost analysis (BCA). You can understand the arithmetic before you understand why we should care about efficiency or what to count as a benefit or as a cost. On the other hand, this unit could also come after the unit on substance.

This unit starts with the issue of determining the appropriate scale of a project. Thus it skips over the basic question of deciding whether to adopt a single project or the simpler analysis of choosing a set of projects subject to a cost constraint.

Suppose a city is trying to decide how many paramedic units to station in the city. Currently the city has none. The mayor's objective is to prevent heart attack deaths. Each paramedic unit costs $1M per year. The units are subject to declining marginal effectiveness such that one unit prevents a total of six deaths; two units prevent a total of ten; three units, 13; four units, 15; five units, 16 and six units, 16. Declining marginal effectiveness is quite plausible, since the first unit will be placed where it can do the most good; the second unit will allow the two to be placed where they can do the most good and so on. At some point a paramedic and ambulance on every corner won't help much.

For the first part of the analysis, I ask students to assume that the value placed on preventing these heart attack deaths is $600 000. Then, I ask them to work through with me to produce a table with the following for each level of units: the total costs (TC), the total effects (TE), the marginal costs (MC), the marginal effects (ME), the total benefits (TB), the marginal benefits (MB), the net benefits (NB), the average cost per heart attack prevented (AC) and the marginal cost per extra heart attack prevented (MC/ME). I think it helps to work it through together so that they can see where each comes from and how they are related.

In this way, we generate Table 9.1.

Table 9.1   Purchasing ambulance units when you have a value for effects

	(1)	(2)	(3)	(4)	(5)	(6)	(7)	(8)	(9)
Calculation							(5)-(1)	(1)/(2)	(3)/(4)
Units	Total Cost	Total Effect	Marg. Cost	Marg. Effect	Total Ben.	Marg. Ben.	Net Ben.	Av. Cost/ HA Prev.	Marg. Cost/ Extra HA Prev.
	$M		$ M		$ M	$ M	$ M	$ k	$ k
1	1	6	1	6	3.6	3.6	2.6	167	167
2	2	10	1	4	6.0	2.4	4.0	200	250
3	3	13	1	3	7.8	1.8	4.8	230	333
4	4	15	1	2	9.0	1.2	5.0	267	500
5	5	16	1	1	9.6	0.6	4.6	313	1000
6	6	16	1	0	9.6	0	3.6	375	infinite

Suppose an ambulance salesman visits the mayor and suggests that the city buy six ambulances. The total cost is $6M and the total benefits are $9.6M, so it clearly is a big win for the city, net benefits of $3.6M. Or, to look at it another way, the average cost of the deaths prevented with the six units is only $375k while the city values the prevention of each death at $600k.

Of course, the analyst should ask what would happen if the number of ambulance units were changed a little, maybe up to seven or down to five. An honest answer would quickly show that six units couldn't possibly be the best choice because the sixth unit prevented nothing.

Since in this case we do have a value on the effects that we can plug in, we can follow the rule of maximizing net benefits. As we should know, this is the same as expanding the program as long as the extra benefit exceeds the extra cost. Both approaches lead us inexorably to a choice of four ambulance units. Is one unit better than zero? Of course it is; NB increase by $2.6M. Is two better than one? We can compare step by step. We stop at four units because the extra cost of the fifth unit ($1M) exceeds the extra benefit of the fifth unit ($600k), which means that NB will decrease by $400k.

We can point out that the use of the average cost figure would be appropriate only if we had to make a choice between doing nothing and buying six. In that case, six units would indeed be the best choice. That leads to a profound point: whether something is worth doing depends upon what the alternatives are. This is simply a restatement of the need for consideration of opportunity costs. But it helps to focus the mind on determining what those alternatives are.

WHAT ABOUT WHEN WE HAVE NO VALUE OF THE EFFECTS?

Suppose no one has proposed or stipulated what the value is that should be placed on preventing heart attacks. What can the analyst say in this situation?

Most importantly, the analyst *cannot* say what choice is best or most efficient. Why? Because whether it is worth spending more money depends on the benefits we get for the investment. Without a value on the effects, we can't say what the investment is worth.

Table 9.2 presents the same information as Table 9.1, except that it does not include any valuation on the effects. Thus the only calculations concern costs and effects. One mistake people often make is to look at Table 9.2 and reason as follows:

Table 9.2   *The same information on ambulance units, but no value on the effects*

	(1)	(2)	(3)	(4)	(5)	(6)
Calculation					(1)/(2)	(3)/(4)
Units	Total Cost	Total Effect	Marg. Effect	Marg. HA Prev.	Av. Cost	Marg. Cost/ Marginal Effect
	$ M		$ M		$ k	$k
1	1	6	1	6	167	167
2	2	10	1	4	200	250
3	3	13	1	3	230	333
4	4	15	1	2	267	500
5	5	16	1	1	313	1000
6	6	16	1	0	375	infinite

Buying only one unit provides effects at the lowest cost. If we buy more, the effects become more costly. Buying only one unit is the most cost-effective decision, so I would recommend that choice.

This reasoning ignores that deciding not to buy a second unit implies that we do not value preventing four more deaths at a cost of $1M or $250k per death prevented. If we do, we should certainly purchase a second unit. But we don't know if that valuation is appropriate, so we can't say what should be done.

This is a situation where we have neither a value to plug in to calculate net benefits nor a budget constraint. In this case, all the analyst can contribute is to point out the information in the last column, which explains how much you would need to value each effect to justify that level of investment. If you value preventing these deaths less than $167k, you should not buy any ambulance units; if you value them more than $167k but less than $250k, you should buy one unit; if you value them more than $250k but less than $333k, you should buy two and so on.

To confirm that these statements are correct, you can choose a value in the range, insert it in a calculation of net benefits and see that it indeed is the level of investment that maximizes net benefits. For example, if we chose a value of $300 000, the net benefits of one unit would be $1.8M (6 × $300k) minus $1M, or $800k. The net benefits of two units would be $3M (10 × $300k) minus $2M, or $1M. The net benefits of 3 units would be $3.9M (13 × $300k) minus $3M, or $900k. Thus, we can confirm that, as calculated in the preceding paragraph, a valuation of $300k per death prevented should lead to a choice of two units.

Note that the average cost is lowest with only one unit. A proponent of one unit might have argued that with more units the average cost would go up. True, but irrelevant. With declining marginal effectiveness, the average costs will always go up as we expand a program. However, the important point is that the average cost is only relevant when the choice is between that level and doing nothing. It tells you the cost per extra unit of effect compared to doing nothing. If there are other options than doing nothing, then you must look at the MC and MB in comparing the options, not the average cost.

Students may ask "Don't you always have a fixed budget?" In the short run, the answer is often yes. If you run a public agency like emergency medical services and have been given your budget for the year, then your budget is fixed. But suppose you want to see if a new service is warranted and, if so, what level of service is warranted. Then you are no longer talking about a fixed budget. For decision criteria in the case of fixed budget, see Chapter 1. The case when an agency must take an action is discussed further on.

The policymakers will have to decide what to do with the information in Table 9.2. Perhaps they already are spending much higher amounts to prevent other deaths, leading them to use those higher valuations in this case.

OTHER EXAMPLES OF THE IMPORTANCE OF MARGINAL ANALYSIS

Let's take another example. Suppose OSHA is proposing to issue a standard that would limit exposures to a cancer-causing chemical. The current exposure limit is 10 parts per million (ppm) and OSHA is proposing to reduce the limit to 1 ppm, a 90 percent reduction. If we assume that the dose-response curve is linear, the number of cancer deaths will also decline by 90 percent. At the current exposure limit, 20 workers will die from the exposures. So, at 1 ppm, 18 deaths would be prevented. The expected cost of reducing exposures to that level is expected to be $54M. The average cost per death prevented would be $3M ($54M/18). This sum is well below the figure of about $7M currently used by government agencies to value preventing a death. So this regulation appears to be beneficial. It would have benefits of $126M (18 x $7M) and costs of $54M.

But suppose that OSHA could also adopt a standard of 2 ppm instead of 1 ppm and that the costs and effects were as Table 9.3.

In this case, it is relatively cheap to reduce exposures down to 2 ppm, but going from 2 ppm to 1 ppm is much more expensive. These numbers are not far from the actual ones, capturing the fact that the slope of the

Table 9.3   Another example of the need to focus on marginal effects

Exposure limit	# of deaths	Cost	Marginal effect	Marginal cost	MC/ME
20 ppm	20	0	0	0	0
2 ppm	4	$20M	16	$20M	$1.25M
1 ppm	2	$54M	2	$34M	$17M

Table 9.4   Robbery prevention—Raw data

	Cost	Effect	Cost/Effect
Program A	$1M	100	$10k
Program B	$2M	125	$16k

marginal cost curve typically increases, raising the cost per unit of effect as you get closer to zero exposure.

In this second scenario, the implicit value needed to justify an exposure limit of 1 ppm is no longer $3M per death prevented. Now, it is $17M per death prevented, the valuation needed to justify 1 ppm instead of 2 ppm. Of course, the value needed to justify a 2 ppm standard is only $1.25M. This scenario is analogous to introducing options between zero ambulances and six ambulances in the previous example. In this case, inventing a new option—a 2 ppm standard—would allow us to attain a more efficient outcome.

Another example shows a problem that students often get wrong. Suppose that robbery prevention program A would prevent 100 robberies for $1M. Program B would prevent 125 robberies for $2M. The programs are mutually exclusive. Which is preferable? The answer, as before, is that unless we know the value of preventing robberies, we don't know which is more worthwhile or whether either one of them is. If we show the data as Table 9.4, students usually opt for program A because the cost per effect is lower. If they perceive that "doing nothing" is an option, they may note that you must value preventing a robbery at a minimum of $10k to justify even the cheapest program.

It takes time for them to learn that what they need to do is look at the marginal costs and effects (Table 9.5):

And that the answer is (a) do neither if the value is below $10k; (b) chose Program A if the value is above $10k and below $40k and (c) choose Program B only if the value is above $40k. Only in that case are the extra 25 robberies prevented worth more than the extra million dollars in cost.

Table 9.5   Robbery prevention with marginal metrics

	Cost	Effect	Cost/Effect	Marg. Cost (MC)	Marg. Effect (ME)	MC/ME
Program A	$1M	100	$10k	$1M		
Program B	$2M	125	$16k			
B vs A				$1M	25	$40k

THREE CASES

So far, we have identified two cases:

1) You have a value for effects and you can plug it in to calculate what level of investment maximizes net benefits.
2) You do not have a value for effects and you do not have a budget constraint. All you can do is show what values would be needed to justify different levels of investment.

The third case is where you have no valuation, but you do have a budget constraint. This is the true case for cost-effectiveness analysis (CEA). You want to either maximize the effects for the budget you have or minimize the costs of achieving a given level of effects. The crucial difference in this third case is that whether the program is worthwhile is not addressed. The task is simply to choose the approach that gives the greatest bang for the buck.

MORE ON COST-EFFECTIVENESS

Returning to the ambulance case, suppose that our decision-maker is a state government and that it has to decide how to allocate ambulances among several cities. Suppose further that its budget of $6M is now devoted to only one city (City A) and that all of the cities have the same set of marginal costs and effects. We might approach our task by asking whether the last million dollars we are spending would be more valuable if it were reallocated. Since the last million is preventing no deaths, and since it would prevent six deaths if reallocated to any of the other cities, the answer is yes. So reallocate it. Then we could ask the same question about the fifth million we are spending in City A. We are preventing one death in City A. We could prevent four deaths if we reallocated to the city that just

Table 9.6   *Programs to prevent infant mortality—Number of infant deaths prevented*

	Prenatal Care	Nutrition	Neonatal Intensive Care
1st $1M	5	4	6
2nd $1M	5	3	4
3rd $1M	4	3	1
4th $1M	3	3	0
5th $1M	2	3	0
6th $1M	1	2	0
Column Total	20	18	11

got its first million. But we would get six deaths prevented if we gave it to one of the other cities that still has no units. (It's good to show this on the board, moving the dollars around.)

In this manner, we would keep on reallocating as long as the marginal effect in the new city were greater than the marginal effect in the old one. By definition, the point at which we stop gives us the greatest total effect— if it didn't, we would keep on reallocating.

Another example might consider comparisons of different programs to reduce infant mortality in a region. One program might pay visiting nurses to provide prenatal care. A second might emphasize nutrition for pregnant women. A third might provide neonatal intensive care. If you had $6M to spend, what allocation among these programs would be best in terms of preventing the most infant deaths? Table 9.6 presents hypothetical data.

If you could choose only one program, it would be prenatal care because it provides the greatest effect for the $6M investment. But if you could choose combinations, and if we started with all of our money for prenatal care, you would start by asking whether you can get more for the sixth million now being spent on prenatal care. The answer is yes, and you would transfer that money to provide $1M for neonatal intensive care, preventing six deaths instead of only one. Then you would ask about the fifth million being spent on prenatal care. Again, we can gain the most by adding it to the intensive care budget. And we would keep on switching until there are no more opportunities for gains. In this example, you would end up with $3M on prenatal care, $1M on nutrition and $2M on neonatal care. At that point, the marginal effect of the last dollar spent on each program is equal. (Because investments are "lumpy," the numbers won't be exactly equal.) Now, you would be preventing a total of 28 deaths instead of the 20 when all the money went for prenatal care.

Unfortunately, in practice we rarely have evidence that neatly shows the marginal effect of each unit of spending in each program. Moreover, there may be important interactions among programs so that the contribution of an added unit of spending on one depends on the level of spending in the others. Programs could either be substitutes for each other so that the effect of both is less than the sum of their individual effects or complements, in which it would be greater.

Despite these obvious practical difficulties, the principle here is important. A cost-effective allocation is one in which the marginal effectiveness of the last dollar spent in each program is equal. If we suspect diminishing marginal effectiveness within a program, for example, it may well be that shifting some resources to a different program component would increase impact. If all the crime prevention resources are going into one neighborhood, then the total impact might be enhanced by some reallocation. (Note here that we are not raising any of the distributional issues that might arise; we focus here only on total effectiveness.)

MORE CEA—"FLAT OF THE CURVE," "CRITICAL MASS" AND "MUST DOS"

We mentioned earlier the assumption about declining marginal effectiveness. In graphical terms, we could show this with effects on the vertical axis and costs on the horizontal. At first, effects rise quickly with spending but then start to level off so that more spending brings little added impact. The region where the curve starts to flatten is referred to as the "flat of the curve." Sometimes analysts suggest that a program should not be expanded once it reaches this region. It is easy to see the logic of this position, but, again, without knowing something about how these effects are valued, it is not possible to draw a certain conclusion based solely on costs and effects. Well, not true. If the curve stopped rising entirely, then it would be right to conclude that expansion has no value.

Frequently, proponents of a program are faced with evidence that, despite considerable spending, there is no evidence of any impact. Sometimes, they respond that the impact depends upon attaining a "critical mass" of spending that hasn't yet been achieved. In graphical terms, the effectiveness curve is flat but, if we only increased spending somewhat more, effectiveness would suddenly shoot up. Although a possibility, this claim should be viewed with skepticism unless there is a sound theory or evidence to support it.

REFERENCES AND RECOMMENDATIONS FOR FURTHER READING

Boardman, A., D. Greenberg, A. Vining and D. Weimer (2011). *Cost-Benefit Analysis: Concepts and Practice*, Chapter 18. Upper Saddle River, NJ: Prentice-Hall.

Rhoads, S. (1985). *The Economist's View of the World*, Chapter 3. Cambridge: Cambridge University Press.

Silver, N. (2006). "Is Alex Rodriguez overpaid," in J. Keri (ed.), *Baseball Between the Numbers*. New York: Basic Books.

Stokey, E. and R. Zeckhauser (1978). *A Primer for Policy Analysis*, Chapter 9. New York: W.W. Norton.

10. Treatment of employing and disemploying workers

David Greenberg

ABSTRACT

Government projects may cause workers in the private sector to lose their jobs by replacing the functions they perform or, alternatively, to be hired away from the private sector in order to work on the project. Similarly, new regulation may decrease employment in some sectors of the economy and increase employment in others. This chapter attempts to clarify these situations through a simple illustration: a city that is building a subway that will replace an existing privately owned bus system. It first examines what happens when private sector workers (for example, the bus drivers) lose their jobs as a result of a government project. In doing this, it assumes that new jobs are available to these workers, although sometimes not immediately. The chapter then examines hiring persons to work on the project (such as construction workers needed to build the subway) from a labor market in which there is considerable unemployment.

WHY SHOULD I TEACH HOW TO TREAT INCREASES OR DECREASES IN EMPLOYMENT?

Government projects may cause workers in the private sector to lose their jobs by replacing the functions they perform or, alternatively, to be hired away from the private sector in order to work on the project. Similarly, new regulation implemented by the government may decrease employment in some sectors of the economy and increase employment in other sectors. The appropriate treatment of such changes in benefit-cost analysis (BCA) is often confusing to students, especially when unemployment is high.

DESCRIPTION AND OBJECTIVES OF THE CHAPTER

This chapter attempts to clarify these situations through a simple illustration: a city that is building a subway that will replace an existing privately owned bus system. It first examines what happens when private sector workers (for example, the bus drivers) lose their jobs as a result of a government project. In doing this, it assumes that new jobs are available to these workers, although sometimes not immediately. The chapter then examines hiring persons to work on the project (such as construction workers needed to build the subway) from a labor market in which there is considerable unemployment.

THE COST OF LAYING OFF WORKERS IN A COMPETITIVE LABOR MARKET

Assume that in building the subway, the old privately owned bus system would be forced out of business. This would mean that the employees of the bus company would lose their jobs. These lay-offs raise the obvious question of whether they should be counted as part of the social cost of building the subway. This is in fact a major issue in connection with most large public projects. Politically, such projects are often discussed in terms of jobs that will be created and jobs that will be lost.

What we are really interested in for BCA purposes is the net incremental costs of building and operating the new subway system. In other words, we need to compare the status quo of continuing with the existing bus system to the counterfactual of building the new subway system.

How to treat the laid-off bus company employees in a BCA can be framed in terms of opportunity costs. To the extent the resources used by the bus company can be transferred to equally productive uses elsewhere, no social costs are involved. In fact, in such instances, they may be viewed as "offsets" to the gross cost of operating the subway.[1]

For example, if the bus drivers lose their old jobs, but can find an equally productive job elsewhere that pays a similar wage, they do not suffer a loss, and neither does society as a whole. But if they suffer a long period of unemployment or end up in a lower paying, less productive job than previously, they are clearly worse off. Moreover, society no longer receives as much output from them, resulting in a social cost.

From a social point of view, the earnings of workers who are "freed up" through lay-offs but can be used elsewhere as productively should be netted out of the gross costs of operating the subway. Perhaps, this can be seen most clearly if the subway system simply hires the drivers from the old bus company as subway drivers. In this case, there is no social cost, no lost opportunities. The bus drivers are simply transferred from one productive use to another equally productive use. They are not worse off than before and neither is society.

Obviously, it really does not matter if instead of hiring the bus drivers, the subway system hires people who are currently working at productive jobs elsewhere and the bus drivers move elsewhere into other productive jobs. The cost of employing the old bus drivers should still be netted out of the cost of building the subway system.

This netting out only becomes complicated if resources become unemployed. This could happen, for example, if bus drivers do not have the right skills to become subway drivers and it takes some a while before they locate a new job. What we are concerned with here is a net increase in unemployment. If a bus driver becomes unemployed, but an unemployed person becomes a subway driver, there may not be any net increases in unemployment.[2] Economists sometimes refer to this sort of thing as "displacement."

Assuming that there is a net increase in unemployment, the implications for BCA can be illustrated in the form of a hypothetical numeric example:

	Social cost
Gross labor cost of running subway	−$1 000 000
Gross labor cost of running the bus company (cost offset)	+700 000
Net loss of earnings in economy via increased unemployment	−**200 000**
Total social cost of labor if subway built	−$500 000
[Value of leisure gain to those unemployed]	+

The $200 000 loss in earnings resulting from an increase in unemployment (which is shown in bold in the tabulation) is a cost to both the bus drivers and, in the form of reduced production, to society as a whole. The drivers lose earnings. Society loses output.

Any unemployment insurance the unemployed bus drivers may receive can be ignored from the social perspective because it is a transfer of funds from the government (a cost) to the unemployed bus drivers (a benefit to them) and thus nets out to zero from the social perspective.

In principle, those who become unemployed have more leisure time at their disposal. This presumably is of value to them and thus a benefit. If it were not, then they would be willing to work for free. This benefit, however, is difficult to measure and is therefore simply shown with a plus sign. (An approach to treating changes in leisure time that result from changes in employment status is developed in the second part of this chapter.)

To summarize, the main point is that when the government provides a service, those in the private sector who are currently providing the service may suffer losses, at least initially. However, if they can be transferred somewhere else where they are equally productive, there is no net loss to them or to society. In other words, costs in one place are offset by benefits somewhere else.

Of course, if the resources of the alternative provider aren't used as productively or, worse yet, end up sitting idle, real social costs are incurred. Those conducting a benefit-cost analysis must obviously make a fairly detailed investigation of actual conditions and then exercise their best judgment. For example, if local labor market conditions are tight, the laid-off bus drivers may not suffer from much unemployment; but if they are loose, some of them are likely to become unemployed. Even if they do, however, they may merely replace other unemployed persons who become employed (for example, as new subway drivers). In this instance, there are no increases in unemployment and, therefore, no net losses to society. Such losses only occur if net unemployment increases.

THE COST OF HIRING WORKERS FROM A LABOR MARKET WITH HIGH UNEMPLOYMENT[3]

How should the social cost of hiring workers for a government project be measured if the workers were unemployed before they were hired? This is not a trivial issue because almost any government project is going to absorb some unemployed labor. And there are some government programs, such as public works projects, that are specifically aimed at putting unemployed workers to work.

In thinking about hiring the unemployed to work on a government project, we are going to again use the subway example. Unemployment is typically high among construction workers and building the subway may well absorb a number of unemployed construction workers. Now, let us see what happens if there are unemployed workers that construction of the subway absorbs. We are going to examine this issue with Figure 10.1, which is the standard graph that is used to show unemployment in a labor market. This diagram implies that something in the market – perhaps a union or the minimum wage – is holding wages in the market above the market clearing wage. As a result, N_2 people want jobs, but only N_1 people can find them. In other words, there is unemployment.

In building the subway, the demand curve shifts out and some of the unemployed workers get jobs. The newly employed workers are represented by the difference between N_1 and N_3, and those who are still unemployed by the difference between N_3 and N_2.

The budgetary cost of hiring workers for the subway can be calculated

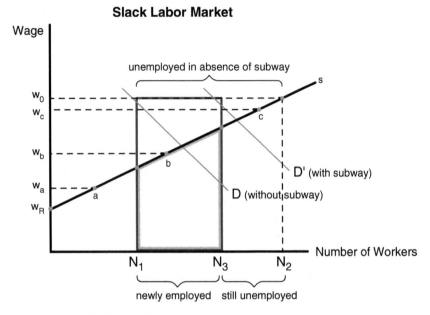

Notes: As described in detail in the text, the measures can be summarized as:
Measure 1: Social cost = Budgetary cost = $W_0 (N_3 - N_1)$
Measure 2: Social cost = 0
Measure 3: Social cost = Trapezoid between N_1 and N_3
Measure 4: Social cost = ½ $(W_0 + W_R) (N_3 - N_1)$
Measure 5: Social cost = ½ $(W_0 + 0) (N_3 - N_1)$ = ½ $W_0 (N_3 - N_1)$, assuming W_R equals zero

Figure 10.1   Measures for employing and disemploying workers

by multiplying the number of workers hired by the wage they are paid. This
is shown in Figure 10.1 as a rectangular area with a width of $N_3 - N_1$ and
a height of W_0.

Measure 1: Social cost = Budgetary cost = $W_0 (N_3 - N_1)$
This is one possible measure of the social cost of hiring the unemployed,
but it is probably not a very good measure. Unlike the situation in which
there is no unemployment and workers transfer from one job to a roughly
equally productive job elsewhere, it is not clear that the budgetary cost is a
very good approximation of social cost when the newly hired workers were
previously unemployed.

The reason has to do with opportunity costs. When an employed worker
leaves his old job to work on a government project, the wages paid pretty
much reflect the opportunity costs involved. But what are the opportunity

costs involved in taking a worker from an unemployed status and putting him in a job? In other words, what does society give up if the worker is no longer unemployed? Some people might say nothing. Therefore, zero is another possible measure of the social cost of hiring the unemployed.

Measure 2: Social cost = 0
This probably is also not a very good measure of social cost. The very fact that most unemployed persons would refuse to work for a zero wage indicates that they view the time they spend unemployed as having some positive value. Moreover, because they are also part of society, a cost to them is a cost to society.

In fact, the supply curve in Figure 10.1 indicates the value that both employed and unemployed workers put on their time. For example, an unemployed worker who is represented at point a on the supply curve in the diagram would value an hour of his time at wage W_a. In other words, W_a is a measure of his opportunity costs—that is what he sees as the lowest wage he would have to receive before he would be willing to accept a job. Unemployed workers at points b and c would also have opportunity costs that are reflected by where they are located along the supply curve. These opportunity cost wage rates provide a measure of what the unemployed feel they give up to go to work on the subway. They are also the social cost of hiring the unemployed to work on a government project.

This suggests that a third possible measure of the social cost of hiring the unemployed to work on a government project is the trapezoidal area below the supply curve and between N_1 and N_3.

Measure 3: Social cost = trapezoid between N_1 and N_3
Thus, Measure 3 implies that the social cost of hiring the unemployed is only part of Measure 1 costs—that is, the budgetary cost shown as the rectangular area in Figure 10.1. The problem with Measure 3 is that all unemployed workers are not confined to the trapezoidal area. For example, unemployed workers at points a and c have opportunity cost wage rates that are, respectively, well below and above any of those represented in the trapezoidal area.

If we could compute the average value of the opportunity cost wage rates for all the unemployed workers hired by the subway, we could then compute the total cost incurred by the unemployed in going to work for the subway.

How might this average opportunity cost wage rate be computed? If the hired unemployed are more or less distributed randomly along the supply curve, and the supply curve is linear as drawn, the average would be approximately midway between the bottom of the supply curve at W_R and W_0.

Measure 4: Social cost = $\frac{1}{2}(W_0 + W_R)(N_3 - N_1)$
[Note: $\frac{1}{2}(W_0 + W_R)$ is a "shadow wage."]
In theory, Measure 4 is probably the best possible measure of the social cost involved in hiring the unemployed to work on a government project. However, it is not a very practical measure in conducting an actual benefit-cost analysis. The problem is that researchers are unlikely to know where W_R, the lowest wage that any unemployed person would be willing to accept, is located.

One possibility is to simply assume that it is located at the origin. In other words, we could assume that W_R equals zero, even though we know it actually is likely to be larger.

Measure 5: Social cost = $\frac{1}{2}(W_0 + 0)(N_3 - N_1) = \frac{1}{2}W_0(N_3 - N_1)$, when assuming W_R equals zero
Measure 5 is obviously simply half the government's budgetary cost. If W_R actually exceeds zero, as seems likely, Measure 5 can be viewed as providing a lower bound estimate of Measure 4. Measure 1, as previously discussed, is clearly an upper bound estimate.

Measures 4 and 5 both use shadow wage rates that are lower than W_0 (the value assumed in Measure 1), but much higher than a zero wage (the value assumed in Measure 2). What this suggests is that the social costs of hiring the unemployed to work on a government project are likely to be considerably lower than the budgetary cost of hiring these persons, but they are also likely to be well above zero.

The five measures that are developed in this section are summarized in Table 10.1, which can be used as a handout:

KEY LEARNING OUTCOMES

If a government project or a government regulation causes private sector workers to lose their jobs, the only important cost that results is if these workers become unemployed for a long period of time or take new jobs in which they are less productive. In these instances, the resulting losses should be counted as costs in a BCA.

In hiring for a government project from a labor market with high unemployment, the information needed to provide an exact estimate of social costs is unlikely to exist. However, two simple, if inaccurate, measures are readily available. The first of these, the government's budgetary cost is likely to be too large an estimate of the true social cost of hiring the unemployed, while the second measure, half the government's budgetary cost, provides too small an estimate. Both estimates are practical, however, in the sense that they can be readily obtained. Therefore, they

Table 10.1   Summary of measures

Models	Text Measure	Empirical Cost Measure	Notes
Budgetary expenditure	Measure 1	$W_0 (N_3 - N_1)$	Assumes an efficient market with no impact on prices (where opportunity cost equals expenditures). This is inconsistent with the assumed existence of a wage floor causing unemployment.
Zero cost	Measure 2	0	Assumes workers have zero opportunity cost (reservation wage). Understates social opportunity cost. Generally considered incorrect.
Area under labor supply curve for L'	Measure 3	Trapezoid between N_1 and N_3	Assumes unemployed are drawn from the segment of the supply curve between N_1 and N_3 in Figure 10.1.
Average reservation wage	Measure 4	$½ (W_0 + W_R)$ $(N_3 - N_1)$	Assumes newly employed are drawn uniformly from the range of reservation wages.
Assume lower bound of reservation wage is zero	Measure 5	$½ (W_0 + 0)$ $(N_3 - N_1) =$ $½ W_0 (N_3 - N_1)$	Assumes lower bound of reservation wage not observed so assumes it is zero. Easiest to compute; note it is 50% of Measure 1.

can be used to obtain upper and lower bound estimates in a sensitivity analysis.

NOTES

1. If it is assumed that the subway requires more workers than the bus company did, and also that the bus and subway workers are hired out of the same labor market, the notion of a cost offset can be seen in a demand and supply curve diagram that shows the market demand curve first shifting to the right to meet the subway's requirement for workers and then shifting part of the way back to the left as workers leave the bus company.
2. See also Chapter 17 on Distributional Accounting where it matters who gains and who loses.
3. This part of the chapter uses a methodology developed by the author that also appears in Boardman et al. (2018).

REFERENCES AND RECOMMENDATIONS FOR FURTHER READING

Boardman, A., D. Greenberg, A. Vining and D. Weimer (2018), *Cost-Benefit Analysis: Concepts and Practice*, 5th edition, Cambridge: Cambridge University Press.
Haveman, R. and S. Farrow (2011), "Labor expenditures and benefit-cost accounting in times of unemployment," *Journal of Benefit-Cost Analysis*, **2** (2), 1–7.
Haveman, R. and D. Weimer (2015), "Public policy induced changes in employment: Valuation issues for benefit-cost analysis," *Journal of Benefit-Cost Analysis*, **6** (1), 112–53.

11. Uncertainty and risk

Nicolas Treich

ABSTRACT

Uncertainty is prevalent in policymaking, and is thus an important dimension of policy evaluation and BCA. This chapter introduces the methods and practices to take uncertainty into account in BCA. The pedagogical approach consists in building on the contrast between two related concepts, such as risk versus uncertainty, static versus sequential analysis or *ex ante* versus *ex post* BCA.

INTRODUCTION

Uncertainty is prevalent in policymaking. Take for instance the famous *Stern Review* (Stern 2007). This review develops a benefit-cost analysis (BCA) of climate policy. It estimates that global warming is equivalent to an immediate and permanent loss of 5 percent of world gross domestic product (GDP), and that this loss can rise to 20 percent of GDP or more. This represents a considerable loss. But this also represents a considerable uncertainty about that loss.

When uncertainty is very large, it is often suggested that BCA cannot, and even should not, be done. Yet, uncertainty is not reduced by not doing BCA. Instead, as illustrated by the *Stern Review*, BCA may be useful to give an order of magnitude of the impact of uncertainty. However, if uncertainty dominates the analysis, it is important that BCA does not give an illusion of precision. Hence it is important to well communicate about how uncertainty has been accounted in the analysis, and to explain carefully how the results of the BCA depend on uncertainty.

RISK VERSUS UNCERTAINTY

In economics, it is common to distinguish risk from uncertainty. Risk is usually associated with known probability while uncertainty is associated with unknown probability. For instance, a situation of risk can be illustrated by the probability that a coin falls on heads. The so-called "objective" probability is 50 percent. A situation of uncertainty can be illustrated by the probability that it will rain next Tuesday in Paris. There is no objective probability here.[1] Economics is usually concerned by the "subjective" beliefs people hold about risk. Even in the case of the coin, people might disagree with the statement that the probability is 50 percent that the coin falls on head. The coin may not be fair, or some people may hold magical beliefs about the coin.

The BCA method relies, as usual, on the willingness to pay (WTP). People's WTPs are expected to capture people's subjective beliefs about the risks. Indeed, a person's willingness to bet on events (such as the throw of the coin or future weather conditions) reveals her subjective beliefs about those events. In other words, the observation of people's WTP provides in principle relevant information to account for risk/uncertainty in the practice of BCA.

PEOPLE'S RISK VERSUS ANALYST'S UNCERTAINTY

It is useful to distinguish two types of uncertainties:

Type 1 uncertainty: The risk faced by economic agents (consumers, firms);
Type 2 uncertainty: The uncertainty faced by the BCA analyst (or the policymaker).

Examples of type 1 uncertainty include the risks that we discuss in the previous section, as the weather risk faced by an agent. It may also include the risks about future health or future income, or the risk that a firm faces over the future price at which it will sell its product. Type 1 uncertainty is part of economic welfare. Following what we said earlier, this uncertainty is reflected in WTPs, typically in consumers' or producers' surpluses. A key ingredient in economic theory to understand how uncertainty affects WTPs is the concept of risk aversion; see the example below.

Example 1 (risk aversion): Suppose that an agent may lose *$10000* with probability *5* percent (think of a yearly risk of a car accident for instance). What is the benefit of eliminating this risk of financial loss? It is tempting to answer *$500*, that is, *5* percent multiplied by the loss *$10000*. But this computation ignores risk aversion. The benefit should be based on the agent's WTP for risk elimination. The agent might express, for instance, a WTP of *$800* (this information may be inferred from the yearly car insurance premium paid by the agent). The difference $300 = $800 - $500 corresponds to the risk premium of the agent, and captures his risk aversion. In other words, a risk averse person is willing to pay more for risk elimination than the expected loss. Note that it is not essential here from the analyst's viewpoint to know the subjective probability held by the agent about the risk of accident. What is important is to know the agent's subjective value associated with the benefit of risk elimination, that is, the agent's WTP. This information can then be used in the BCA of a policy that reduces, or eliminates, risks.

Type 2 uncertainty concerns the uncertainty faced by the analyst when she performs BCA. This uncertainty reflects the analyst's lack of information about some parameters used for the computations of the BCA of a policy. For instance, the analyst may not know which parameter to choose regarding the discount rate, the inflation rate, the damage of global warming due to carbon dioxide concentration or the number of people that will die if there is a flood in a specific area. The analyst thus needs to make an assumption about the value of these uncertain parameters and perform the analysis under this assumption. Then, the analyst may want to consider an alternative assumption about the parameters' value and redo the analysis under that new assumption. This is called sensitivity analysis (See Chapter 7 in Boardman et al. 2006). The analyst can more thoroughly set a probability distribution over parameter values and possibly allow for correlations across these random parameters with a Monte Carlo analysis (see Chapter 19 in this book).[2]

UNCERTAINTY VERSUS INFORMATION

It is useful to distinguish uncertainty from information. Information permits one to reduce uncertainty, and is an important ingredient in policymaking. Acquiring information is a form of risk management. In standard decision theory, the value of information is always positive. It is conceived as a signal about the risky future that the decision maker receives and that allows her to make better decisions. The value of information is computed *ex ante*, that is, before any message is received; see example 2.

Example 2 (value of information): Suppose that a firm must decide to invest in a project or not. Following BCA, it invests if and only if the benefit of the project is higher than its cost. The cost of the project is denoted c. The benefit is denoted X and is uncertain. What is the value of knowing X before investing? We take a numerical example to show how to compute the value of information in this case. Suppose that the cost is $c = 50$ and that the benefit is $X = 200$ or 50 with equal probability. We now compute the value of information by comparing the cases of no and perfect information. Under no information, the firm invests since the expected benefit is equal to *125* (that is, $0.5 \times 200 + 0.5 \times 50$) and this is higher than the cost *100*. Under perfect information, the firm receives a signal providing perfect information about the realization of X. Namely, one signal is "good news" (that is, it indicates that $X = 200$), and the other is "bad news" (that is, $X = 50$). Under good news, the benefit is higher than the cost (that is, $200 > 100$) and the firm invests so that the profit is *100*. Under bad news, the benefit is lower than the cost ($50 < 100$) and the firm does not invest so that the profit is *0*. Since each signal is received *ex ante* with equal probability, the expected profit is equal to *50* under perfect information. Hence, the value of information is equal to *25* (that is, $25 = 50 - 25$) in this case.[3]

STATIC VERSUS SEQUENTIAL BCA

Information is crucial in sequential decision making. What should a policymaker do today, given that she will have better information in the future? Should she wait? Should she be more cautious? Most policies can be delayed, and information arrives over time (for example, with scientific progress) which may help make better decisions in the future. Policymakers thus should account for this prospect of arrival of information before deciding the optimal strategy. This is important for designing policies such as climate change policy or policies regarding emerging risks for which the progress of scientific knowledge is expected to be important. This refers to the debates around the Precautionary Principle (Gollier and Treich 2003). In those situations, it is necessary to adopt a sequential approach to BCA. The key notion here is that of option value (Pearce et al. 2006, Chapter 10). This notion implies that there is an additional value associated with the preservation of more flexibility under the prospect of forthcoming information. In example 3, building the highway is irreversible while preserving the forest is flexible since it maintains more options in the future. The choice of preserving the forest thus provides an additional option value which must be accounted in BCA.

Example 3 (option value): Suppose that the choice is about deciding to build a highway that would necessitate to destroy a forest. Consider for simplicity two periods (that is, the present and the future), and no discount rate. The value of preserving the forest is *10* in the first period and is either *10* or *90* with equal probability in the second period (because for instance the forest contains some plants with low or high medicinal properties to be discovered in the future). The cost of building the highway is *15*, and its benefit is *40* in each period. Under static BCA, the value of preserving the forest is *60* (that is, $60 = 10 + 0.5 \times 10 + 0.5 \times 90$) and the value of building the highway is *65* (that is, $65 = 40 - 15 + 40$). Hence the highway should be built (*65>60*). But under sequential BCA, the value of forthcoming information as well as the flexibility offered by the choice of preserving the forest must be accounted. Consider the strategy which consists in delaying the construction of the highway to the second period. In the first period, the forest is preserved and the benefit is *10*. In the second period, the forest is preserved only if it has a high value. The value of this strategy is equal to *67.5* (that is, $67.5 = 10 + 0.5 \times 90 + 0.5 \times (40-15)$). Therefore, unlike static BCA, sequential BCA recommends that the highway is not built in the first period. This is because of the additional option value.

RISK ANALYSIS VERSUS BCA

Risk analysis plays a central role in the regulatory practices of the health and safety agencies such as US EPA or FDA. The approach is usually based on the "individual risk" concept, namely an incremental risk faced by a specific individual, like the maximally exposed individual or the average individual in some population (Adler 2005). The objective of risk analysis often consists in targeting a specific risk cut-off like the 1-in-1-million lifetime excess cancer risk, the 100-year flood or the 500-year earthquake. In risk analysis, there exist a variety of practices to account for type 2 uncertainty. When a parameter is unknown, it is common to introduce a "safety factor." It is also common to consider the percentiles of the distribution of probability (for example, the 95th percentile) so that a worst-case scenario is considered for the analysis. These practices permit to err on the side of safety.

These common practices in risk analysis are not consistent with BCA. They might perhaps be justified on equity or political grounds, but not on efficiency grounds. The general principle of BCA is to compare the marginal cost and the marginal benefit of regulation. BCA does not focus on individual risk but rather on "population risk." That is, what matters in BCA is the risk of the affected population, not the risk faced by a theoretical or maximally exposed individual. If few or no people live around a polluted area, the marginal benefit of regulating the area is low or nil. Also, risk analysis typically ignores the cost of a regulation. Indeed, the target in risk analysis, like the specific risk cut-off, is thus usually set independently from cost considerations. Yet, as is often the case, the cost of reaching the risk target can be very high and possibly infinite (i.e. impossible to attain).

Thus defining such a regulatory target does not seem sensible on efficiency grounds. Finally, there is no clear foundation in BCA for using an arbitrary "safety factor" or a specific 95th percentile in order to account for type 2 uncertainty. Hence BCA and risk analysis should be seen as different, complementary, approaches in risk regulatory practice and evaluation. They propose different ways to deal with risk and uncertainty in policy evaluation.

EX ANTE VERSUS *EX POST* BCA

BCA takes an *ex ante* approach, namely it evaluates a policy before its implementation. It typically compares two scenarios, the one when policy is implemented to the one when the policy is not implemented. Since no scenario has yet been implemented, the causal impacts of both scenarios are to be assumed in BCA. A way to reduce this uncertainty about the causal impacts of the scenarios is to observe *ex post* the effect of a policy when the policy has already been implemented before. That is, the idea is to evaluate the impact of a policy *ex post*, after its implementation (Greenstone and Gayer 2009).

A major difficulty in *ex post* evaluation is that comparing the situations before and after the policy implementation is not enough to identify the causal impact of the policy. Indeed, other things may have changed, like the economic context. For instance, a reduction in unemployment may be due to a specific labor policy or to a better economic context. One common method to address this difficulty is to use randomized controlled experiments: namely, to assign randomly people to treatment groups. One group receives the treatment (for example, the policy) and the other group does not receive the treatment. This permits to compare people in each group other things equal. Randomized experiments are systematically used in medicine for instance to understand the impact of a drug. In the last decades, randomized experiments have been used massively in development economics, for instance to study the effect of vaccination policies. Such *ex post* experimental studies thus permit us to better understand the causal impacts of a specific policy, and in turn to reduce uncertainty regarding the parameters that may be used in BCA to evaluate *ex ante* similar policies in the future.

NOTES

1. Yet, suppose that an expert (for example, a French meteorologist) responds 50 percent. Still, this sounds different from the chance that a coin falls on head. In practice, there

is a continuum of situations that differ by the degree of confidence people have in the probabilities they hold. These issues have long been discussed in decision theory and philosophy, and often refer to the literature on "ambiguity." We do not pursue further this topic here.

2. Note that it is important that the analyst carefully distinguishes type 1 and type 2 uncertainties, in particular to avoid double counting.

3. As an alternative numerical example, assume that X can take the values *140* or *50* with equal probability, and then check that the value of information is equal to *20* in that case.

REFERENCES AND RECOMMENDATIONS FOR FURTHER READING

Adler, M.D. (2005) "Against 'individual risk': A sympathetic critique of risk assessment," *University of Pennsylvania Law Review*, 153, 1121–250.

Boardman, A.E., D.H. Greenberg, A.R. Vining and D.L Weimer (2006) *Cost-Benefit Analysis: Concepts and Practices*, London: Pearson International Edition.

Gollier, C. and N. Treich (2003) "Decision-making under scientific uncertainty: The economics of the Precautionary Principle," *Journal of Risk and Uncertainty*, 27, 77–103.

Greenstone, M. and T. Gayer (2009) "Quasi-experimental and experimental approaches to environmental economics," *Journal of Environmental Economics and Management*, 57, 21–44.

Farrow, S. (2018) "Simulation: Incorporating uncertainty," in S. Farrow (ed.) *Teaching Benefit-Cost Analysis: Tools of the Trade*, Cheltenham, UK and Northampton, MA, USA: Edward Elgar Publishing, Chapter 19.

Pearce D., G. Atkinson and S. Mourato (2006) *Cost-Benefit Analysis and the Environment, Recent Developments*, Paris: OECD.

Stern, N. (2007) *The Economics of Climate Change: The Stern Review*, Cambridge and New York: Cambridge University Press.

12. On defining and valuing the benefits of health policy interventions: How and why CEA in health morphed into CU(B)A and "back-door" BCA

David Salkever

ABSTRACT

For the past five decades, the literature on economic evaluations of health programs or policies has consisted largely of cost-effectiveness analysis (CEA) rather than benefit-cost analysis (BCA). One factor contributing to this orientation was the view that we could not obtain valid estimates of consumers' monetary valuations (that is, willingness-to-pay (WTP) figures) for the benefits provided by these programs or policies. As interest in CEA methods in health expanded, and the limits of simple effectiveness measures in CEA became clearer, further refinements in effectiveness measurement have: (1) brought us closer and closer to actually conducting BCAs for heath programs and (2) generated important new insights into defining and valuing program benefits in WTP terms. This chapter traces these developments in the convergence of the CEA and BCA literatures in health. A simple example is presented to highlight the major challenges to obtaining valid WTP valuations for benefits of health programs, and to compare major strategies used for generating monetary WTP benefit valuation figures.

THE CORE PRINCIPLES OF BCA: A THUMBNAIL SKETCH

BCA, in simplest terms, involves application of accepted principles of neoclassical welfare economics that provide a systematic process for choosing between two alternative states of the world. Typically, the choices are between a "status quo" state that would obtain in the absence of any changes in public policy, and an "alternative" state in which a specified new "policy" is implemented. The relevant differences between these two states constitute the "effects" of the new "policy" (relative to the status quo).

According to BCA theory, *all* the various effects of a new policy should be valued in monetary terms by the willingness to pay (WTP) of any and all individual citizens whose well-being is in fact altered by implementation of the new policy. Each of the separately measurable "effects" of the policy are valued in monetary WTP terms; for some individuals, WTP figures for particular effects will be negative and therefore regarded by them as "costs," while WTP figures for other effects will be positive and will be regarded by them as "benefits." The sum of all WTP figures for any individuals represents their "net benefit" for the policy (relative to the status quo). The unweighted sum of these net benefit figures across all individuals represents the *overall* net benefit of the policy (relative to the status quo).

Finally, the rationale for choosing between states of the world based on the unweighted sum of net benefit figures across all individuals is that a positive (or negative) unweighted sum implies the new policy is (or is not) a potential Pareto improvement relative to the status quo. This rationale assumes any compensation of "losers" by "winners" is feasible and costless.

CRITICISMS OF BCA CORE PRINCIPLES

In the general BCA literature, a number of criticisms have been raised about strict adherence to BCA principles. Some criticisms are based on incorrect understanding of the rationale for BCA; for example, it is often asserted that BCA uses the unweighted sum of WTP figures across individuals as the measure of net benefits because it assumes that $1 of WTP for a poor person is viewed by the evaluator or policymaker as *equal in subjective value* to $1 of WTP for a rich person. In fact, of course, BCA does *not* assume $1 WTP for a rich person is equivalent in subjective value to $1 WTP for a poor person. Instead, BCA separates efficiency decisions (for example, whether to adopt or not adopt a new policy) from distributional choices once the policy has been adopted. Thus, the reason for using the unweighted sum of WTP to measure net benefit in BCA derives from: (1) the assumption that costless transfers are possible, and (2) the overriding efficiency objective of identifying potential Pareto improvements.[1]

Other, more valid criticisms, have focused on the obvious unreality of the assumption that compensation is costless or nearly costless. This criticism, however, can be addressed in at least some instances by developing estimates of compensation costs and using these estimates in evaluating new policy proposals. (The alternative of using "distributional weights" is often proposed but not universally accepted.)

Some other criticisms of strict adherence to core BCA principles may have validity but have been questioned as focusing on problems that could but rarely do arise. An example, is the reversibility problem of positive total WTP for both adopting a policy and for abandoning the same policy once it is adopted. Arguments that such reversals rarely occur in practice can be found in Zerbe and Bellas (2006) and Willig (1976).

Finally, there are serious criticisms about our ability to measure WTP figures that accurately reflect the preferences of well-informed individuals, who accurately perceive precisely how their well-being is in fact altered by implementation of the new policy.

CRITICISMS OF BCA OF HEALTH POLICY INTERVENTIONS AND THE CASE FOR RELYING ON CEA FOR EVALUATING HEALTH POLICIES

As Kenkel (1997) detailed in an early overview of the CEA vs. BCA controversy in health, critics of BCA in health offered criticisms ranging from "ethical" objections to the very act of "placing a monetary value on health," to the presumption that BCA "favors" interventions that help the wealthy over interventions that help the poor, to practical concerns about the validity of WTP estimates as accurate representations of individual's preferences.

The first two of these objections were problematic in that they emanated from an incorrect understanding of BCA and the nature of the "benefits" offered by health policy interventions. Concern about the propriety of "placing a monetary valuation on health" is misplaced since health policies do not offer certain improvements in health; instead, they offer changes in risks of future health levels. BCA of health policies place $ values on these changes in risks rather than $ values on "health per se" (however "health" is defined).

The presumption about BCA "favoring" interventions that help the wealthy presumably derived from the mistaken impression that BCA had distributional preferences "baked in" (for example, $1 of WTP was of equal "subjective" worth for all people). In fact, BCA is precisely designed to separate distributional judgments from the task of identifying potential Pareto improvements.

The most salient and challenging criticism of BCAs of health policies, however, is the argument that WTP values used in such BCAs do not accurately reflect the true preferences that would be revealed by individuals who are fully informed about the impact of these policies on their well-being. While this is, of course, a general concern in BCA across all sectors, the problem for evaluators of health policies is especially difficult because of the complexity of the beneficial effects of these policies.

As noted, these effects are essentially changes in risks of being in various health states. The WTP figures for these effects will likely be inaccurate for two different reasons: (1) problems that individuals have in understanding and dealing with small changes in probabilities, and (2) problems individuals have in fully understanding the ways in which being in a particular health state, that they have never yet experienced, impacts their well-being.

According to the critics of BCA in health, CEA offers a solution to all three of these criticisms. The CEA solution offered is simply to not place *any* monetary value on health policy effects that involve reducing risks of ill health (which are the main benefits of the health policy intervention). Instead these effects are only measured in "physical" (non-monetary) units such as lives saved, years of life extended, cases of a particular disease (for example, influenza) prevented and so on. No input from consumers on the monetary valuations of these effects is required for CEA; all that is needed is to compute the relevant monetary measures of cost for implementing the policy, calibrate "effectiveness" in non-monetary terms, and compute a cost-effectiveness ratio (CER) for any new health policy relative to the status quo.

Of course, the critics of BCA in health also recognized the major limitations of CEA relative to BCA. For example, CEA generally does not provide a clear choice between a new policy and the status quo. Similarly, they recognized that even in choosing between two alternative new policies, comparisons of CERs can indicate a clear choice of one policy over the other only in rare circumstances. Notwithstanding these limitations, the critics of BCA in health have argued that the much less powerful tool of CEA is still preferable because it does not require potentially inaccurate estimates of WTP.

THE INTRODUCTION AND EVOLUTION OF CEA FOR HEALTH POLICIES

The origins of applying CEA to health policies were succinctly described by Klarman (1982):

> The major impetus to applying ... [CEA] ... came with President Johnson's [importation] of the planning, programming, and budgeting system ... from the Department of Defense ... to civilian branches of the ... government in 1965 ... [The DoD] analysis differed from standard [BCA] in at least two

respects: 1) emphasis was on ascertaining the effects [outcomes] of alternative programs; and 2) given the presence of budget constraints and similar kinds of outcomes of competing programs, the analysis [focused on] measurement of program [monetary] cost and [estimating] program benefits in terms of physical units of outcome . . . (N)o attempt was made to take the next step of putting an economic value on the effects of alternative programs.

This simple version of CEA works well in many (but not all) decision problems for choosing among non-mutually exclusive alternative programs that produce the same single kind of output (for example, reduced risk of contracting influenza, reduced risk of motor vehicle traffic deaths prevented) and that only involve costs from the same constrained budget. Complications arise, however, when there are multidimensional outputs (for example, reduced risk of mortality and reduced risk of morbidity), when output units differ in kind across policy alternatives, and/or when mutually exclusive choices require choosing higher vs. lower levels of both costs and output. In these cases, the simple CEA paradigm no longer provides clear bottom-line conclusions about policy choices and additional value judgments (whether intuitive or derived from a WTP assessment) are required.

Two major concerns motivated CEA analysts to find improved ways to characterize output that would mitigate the severe limitations of the simplest CEA analyses that only used homogeneous unidimensional output measures. First, with multidimensional output measures, one cannot define a CER without somehow constructing a single effectiveness measure as the denominator, which implies the use of some weighting scheme to convert the multidimensional effectiveness measures. The first efforts to include weighting were somewhat arbitrary. One well-known example is the Klarman et al. (1968) CEA of chronic kidney disease which compared expected life-years for dialysis with expected life-years for transplantation but adjusted for quality of life differences by assuming the quality of a year on dialysis only equated with a quarter of a year with a transplanted kidney. A similar example by Stason and Weinstein (1977) calculated effectiveness "in terms of increased years of life expectancy from blood-pressure control, adjusted for changes in the quality of life due to the prevention of morbid events, on the one hand, and to medication side effects, on the other."

These both illustrated the general idea that when interventions alter the probability of survival but also alter the probability among survivors of having varying degrees of morbidity, downward or upward adjustments, for more vs. less severe levels of morbidity, provide a weighting scheme to yield a single effectiveness measure even if outcomes are heterogeneous (or multidimensional). Following the terminology of Klarman et al. (1968),

Stason and Weinstein (1977), and Weinstein and Stason (1977), the label of "Quality Adjusted Life Years" (QALYs) has been applied to these effectiveness measures.

Second, the economists doing health care CEA's realized that the only source for these QALY weights that was ultimately non-paternalistic was the preferences of the individuals whose risks for various morbidity levels were being impacted by the policies being evaluated. The idea here was to make the process for deriving weights at least roughly consistent with the BCA stricture that WTPs for health benefits should be based on the expressed preferences of the individuals experiencing these benefits (assuming they are also fully informed of the nature of these benefits). This second concern led to numerous efforts to apply preference assessment methods for deriving the weight for each relevant health state (for example, morbidity level). These methods (for example, using standard gamble (sg) and time trade-off (tto) questions, or visual analog scale (vas) designations) seek to measure the "health utility" of a particular health state relative to extreme health states (for example, perfect health, death).

It is also important to note that this process involves two separate analytic steps: (1) defining each specific health state, and (2) applying an assessment method (for example, standard gamble, time trade-off, visual analog scale) to derive health-state specific utility value (HSSU) for one unit of time (for example, one year) in that specific health state. Various strategies have been used for constructing a "scenario" that defines each specific health state. One common approach is to use the separate dimensions used in a health utility scale for this purpose. For example, using the EuroQOL EQ-5D dimensions (mobility, self-care, usual activities, pain/discomfort, anxiety/depression), a specific health state could be described by specific levels of function vs. disfunction (1=best to 3=worst) for each of the dimensions.

By applying these assessment methods in CEA for each health state, we can obtain the resulting unidimensional measure of effectiveness that is simply the increase in expected "health utility" produced by a new health policy relative to the status quo, or that same increase compared across multiple health policy alternatives. (When multiple time periods are considered and discount rates are used to weight present vs. future "health utility" gains, the corresponding effectiveness measures is simply the discounted expected health utility gain.)

This mode of analysis, which is now termed cost-utility analysis (CUA), offers several advantages over the original simple CEA approach that ignored heterogeneity in outcomes. First, it is in some sense consumer-preference based and does not involve paternalistically imposed weights from "experts" or policymakers.[2] Second, it provides a measure of effectiveness which abstracts from any specific outcomes produced by specific types of interventions (for example, cases of influenza prevented); this means it can be used to compare cost-utility ratios (CURs) across many differing types of health policy interventions.

A SIMPLE EXAMPLE OF USING HEALTH-STATE SPECIFIC UTILITY WEIGHTS TO CALCULATE GAINS IN EXPECTED HEALTH UTILITY

We can illustrate the application of HSSU weights to compute a single effectiveness measure with a simplified example based in part on Drummond et al. (2015, Chap. 9). In this example, we consider two alternative interventions: (1) a policy of treating HIV-positive persons with a single drug therapy ("monotherapy"), and (2) a policy of treating HIV-positive persons with a multiple drug "cocktail" ("combotherapy"). We assume there are just five alternative health states defined by HIV-positive status and CD4 cell count in the blood: (1) healthy and not HIV-positive, (2) HIV-positive but fairly healthy (CD4 count >200 and < 500 cells per mm^3), (3) HIV-positive and less healthy (CD4 count <200 cells per mm^3), (4) full-blown AIDS, and (5) dead. (Note that we also assume persons not HIV-positive at the start of the policy may become HIV-positive in later years of the policy; thus, health benefits are reckoned for these persons as well rather than for person who happen to be HIV-positive at the start of the policy. The general point is that the expected health benefits represented by the change in health-state probabilities extend beyond current patients to a presumably much larger group of potential patient beneficiaries of the policy.)

Assume the health-state transition probabilities for one year to the next for monotherapy and combotherapy policies are given by the two panels in Table 12.1.

Note that the transition probabilities for moving from "healthy" to any other state are the same for both therapies (since they have no primary prevention effect), but the combination therapy reduces the rate of transition from 200<CD4<500 to CD4<200, from 200<CD4<500 to full-blown AIDS, and from 200<CD4<500 to dead.

Since Table 12.1 only gives the initial one-year transition probabilities, we can extend the description of the benefits of combination therapy to longer periods by repeating the transition process for a series of additional years. Assuming a ten-year lifespan, the corresponding ten-year sequences of health-state probabilities are given by Appendix Tables A12.1 and A12.2

Table 12.1   Year-to-year transition probabilities

MONOTHERAPY					
Health State:	Healthy	200<CD4<500	CD4<200	AIDS	Dead
Healthy	0.8	0.194	0	0	0.006
200<CD4<500		0.721	0.202	0.067	0.01
CD4<200			0.581	0.407	0.012
AIDS				0.75	0.25
Dead					1
COMBOTHERAPY					
Health State:	Healthy	200<CD4<500	CD4<200	AIDS	Dead
Healthy	0.8	0.194	0	0	0.006
200<CD4<500		0.86	0.103	0.03	0.007
CD4<200			0.581	0.407	0.012
AIDS				0.75	0.25
Dead					1

respectively. The ten-year sequence of changes in these probabilities due to adopting combotherapy is shown in Appendix Table A12.3. These changes represent the health benefits of combotherapy (relative to monotherapy), and a monetary WTP figure for these changes is needed for a BCA of adopting combotherapy.

Suppose we assume the following HSSU QALY weights: 1 for state (1), 0.8 for state (2), 0.6 for state (3), 0.4 for state (4) and 0 for state (5). The results of applying these weights to the change in health-state probabilities implied by switching from monotherapy to combotherapy are shown in Table 12.2.

The expected QALY gain per person for combotherapy relative to monotherapy is 0.6188 QALYs undiscounted; assuming a 3 percent annual discount rate, the corresponding present value of the expected QALY gain is 0.5428. Assuming there are N potential beneficiaries with a non-zero probability of ever receiving combotherapy (over the time horizon of the policy), and that the QALY weights, discount rate and health-state probabilities are the same across these N persons, the expected QALY gain from the program is simply N times the per person expected QALY-gain figure.

Table 12.2 QALY values of changes in yearly health-state probabilities

			MONO VS. COMBO THERAPIES					
Health State	Healthy	200<CD4<500	CD4<200	AIDS	Dead	Yearly Total	PV of Yearly Total QALYs w. Discount Factor =1/1.03	Discount Factor
HSSU Weight (QALY)	1	0.8	0.6	0.4	0			0.9709
QALY Change								
Year 1	0	0	0	0	0	0	0	1
Year 2	0	0.0216	−0.0115	−0.0029	0.0000	0.0072	0.0070	0.9709
Year 3	0	0.0514	−0.0226	−0.0072	0.0000	0.0216	0.0216	0.9426
Year 4	0	0.0816	−0.0291	−0.0157	0.0000	0.0368	0.0357	0.9151
Year 5	0	0.1083	−0.0310	−0.0235	0.0000	0.0538	0.0507	0.8885
Year 6	0	0.1294	−0.0290	−0.0293	0.0000	0.0711	0.0651	0.8626
Year 7	0	0.1445	−0.0246	−0.0323	0.0000	0.0876	0.0778	0.8375
Year 8	0	0.1539	−0.0189	−0.0327	0.0000	0.1023	0.0882	0.8131
Year 9	0	0.1582	−0.0129	−0.0308	0.0000	0.1145	0.0959	0.7894
Year 10	0	0.1583	−0.0072	−0.0272	0.0000	0.1239	0.1008	0.7664
10-year Total	0	1.0071	−0.1869	−0.2015	0.0000	0.6188	0.5428	

FROM CEAS TO CUAS TO "LEAGUE TABLES" AND "ACCEPTABILITY" THRESHOLDS

Using preference-based effectiveness measures (expected QALY gains), CUA moved beyond the restrictions of the original CEA applications that relied on unidimensional "physical" outcome measures (for example, numbers of influenza cases prevented) that could only compare interventions producing the same types of outcome units and were often funded out of the same constrained public agency budgets. Instead, CUAs could compute CURs with monetary cost measures in the numerator and effectiveness measures of gains in expected "health utilities" in the denominator and could treat these CURs as commensurable across virtually any types of health programs. This implied that choices between qualitatively very different health programs could be compared to one another via "league tables" which simply ranked many different and diverse programs on the basis of their CURs (with lower CURs indicating more "efficient" programs).

Table 12.3 shows an example of a league table. Each row in the table shows a comparison of two different policies – a "new" policy and a "comparator" (which could be a status quo of doing nothing). The second and third columns of the table show the difference in costs between the two policies as well as the difference in "effectiveness" measured in QALYs per person.

The original idea of the league table was that all the comparisons in the tables demonstrated alternative ways to spend funds from a "health sector budget" on the "new" policy. Looking at a single row in the table, you will typically see a "new" policy that involves additional costs but produces additional effectiveness; incremental costs are positive, incremental effectiveness is positive, and the incremental cost-effectiveness ratio (ICER) is also positive. The problem for the policymaker is to decide whether the incremental effectiveness is large enough to warrant spending the incremental costs. Looking at this problem for only a single row (that is, policy choice), the policymaker can only make an intuitive judgment since she(he) does not have a valuation of incremental effectiveness in monetary terms that would be provided by a BCA.

The idea of presenting a league table with multiple rows was devised as a way to facilitate the policymaker's choices on individual programs. All policy choices in the tables are ranked in ascending order of the ICER; the various policy choices involve a wide range of dissimilar interventions, but this is not problematic since effectiveness is measured in commensurable units (QALYs per person) across all choices. The policy choices typically range widely in their ICER values, and they also typically include at least

Teaching benefit-cost analysis

Table 12.3   Selected examples from a league table

Intervention	Change in Cost (2010 $s)	Change in QALY	Cost-Effectiveness Ratio (2010 $s)
Coumadin (warfarin) compared to aspirin for 70-year-olds with atrial fibrillation	3,000	0.81	3,704
Diabetes education and self-management compared to standard care for patients newly diagnosed with type 2 diabetes	200	0.04	5,000
Daily dialysis compared to dialysis every other day for 60-year-old critically ill men with kidney injury	13,000	2.14	6,075
ICD (implantable cardioverter defibrillator) compared to current standard of care to prevent sudden cardiac death for patients who are at risk for sudden death due to left ventricular systolic dysfunction	113,000	3	37,667
HIV counseling, testing and referral compared to current standard of care in high-risk populations (HIV annual incidence 1.2% and prevalence of undiagnosed HIV 0.3%)	1,000	0.03	33,333
Spine surgery compared to non-operative treatment for adult patients with confirmed spinal stenosis and spinal nerve-based (radicular) leg pain	15,000	0.17	88,235
Annual CT screening compared to no screening for 60-year-old heavy smokers who are eligible for lung reduction surgery	6,000	0.04	150,000
Screening for osteoporosis with a bone densitometry and osteoporosis treatment compared to no densitometry or treatment for men age 65 and older with no prior fracture	4,000	0.03	133,333

Source: http://healtheconomics.tuftsmedicalcenter.org/cear4/Resources/LeagueTable.aspx, accessed December 7, 2017.

some choices on which policy decisions have already been made. Thus, policymakers facing the need to make one specific decision can see from the table whether other previous policy choices that involved higher or lower ICERs were or were not in fact adopted.

For example, if the choice in question has a lower ICER than other choices that were previously adopted, the decision makers could view this as supporting the adoption in the current choice since this would not implicitly place a higher value (in terms of dollars per QALY gained) than other interventions that had previously been chosen. By similar reasoning, the retrospective use of the league table could be employed to identify particular previous policy choices that implied a much higher dollars-per-QALY value than other interventions that were not adopted. In the broadest case, one could view *all* recent health policy choices as subject to re-evaluation, and thus use a comprehensive league table to identify the set of non-mutually exclusive policy choices that would maximize overall effectiveness (in terms of QALYs) given the health sector "budget" constraint.[3]

Finally, many commentators have suggested that there is a rough consensus (at least within a particular country) as to the highest ICER value that would be "acceptable" for any policy choice. This ICER "threshold" then becomes the recommended marginal monetary valuation for an incremental gain in effectiveness, and the implication is that the "net monetary benefit" is positive for any intervention with an ICER below this threshold value. In short, the use of CUA coupled with an "acceptable" threshold has allowed us to obtain conclusions about net benefits in dollar terms of policy choices and thereby circumvented the purported limitations and impracticalities of the "textbook" BCA that required measurement of WTP in monetary terms for all relevant effects. As CEA of health policies morphed into CUA of health policies and was paired with "consensus" dollars-per-QALY "threshold" values, the ultimate result was a revival of BCA in health, albeit in the form of cost-utility-benefit-analysis (CU(B)A).

PROGRESS IN MEASURING THE WTP FOR THE BENEFITS OF HEALTH POLICIES?

As noted earlier, the original impetus for use of CEA rather than BCA in health resulted not only from invalid presumptions about BCA "placing a dollar value on health" and biasing policy choices toward the wealthy, but also from valid concerns about the difficulty of obtaining accurate and valid WTP figures for benefits of health policies. The subsequent development, in CUA, of a preference-based approach to effectiveness measurement required a clearer and more useful strategy for defining the nature of the benefits of health policies. Specifically, it led to explicit representation of these benefits as a set of changes in the probabilities of being in any potentially relevant health states over the potential beneficiary's lifespan.

Thus, in our simplified example based on Table 12.2, we described the health benefits of combination therapy for HIV-AIDS relative to monotherapy as the differences between two "lifetime" sequences for probabilities for being in each of five distinct health states over ten different years (see Table A12.3, which is based on the differences between Tables A12.1 and A12.2). Note that this approach of describing health benefits as changes in the lifetime sequences of health-state probabilities can be used for any health policy intervention; "real-world" examples are more complex.

With the development of CU(B)A, we now have at least two different paradigms for deriving a monetary valuation of these health benefits:

1. The "pure" BCA paradigm bases valuation on: (a) informing potential beneficiary consumers of the specific nature of each relevant health state, (b) informing them of the year-by-year changes in the probabilities of being in each of these relevant health states, and (c) eliciting a monetary WTP figure from each consumer for the entire set of these changes in probabilities, and (d) adding up these WTP figures (appropriately discounted) across the population of potential beneficiaries.
2. The typical CU(B)A bases valuation on: (a) obtaining the HSSU QALY weight for the "average" consumer for each relevant health state, (b) computing the change in discounted expected QALYs based on these HSSU weights, (c) applying the "average" consumer's monetary value per QALY to this change in discounted expected QALYs, and (d) multiplying the result (appropriately discounted) by the number of potential beneficiaries.

We expect that the results obtained from these two methods will not necessarily be approximately equal. Several major differences between them should be noted. CU(B)A in its simplest form – focusing on a single "average" potential beneficiary – does not account for heterogeneity among potential beneficiaries in the following:

1. Their HSSU preference weights for any specific health states,
2. their monetary valuations per QALY,[4]
3. their risk preferences,[5] or
4. the influence of the sequence in which specific health states occur on their HSSU weights.[6]

To some extent, heterogeneity among potential beneficiaries could be accounted for in CU(B)A by doing separate analyses for sub-groups of beneficiaries. This would, however, not eliminate the assumptions about risk-neutrality or sequence independence of preferences (items (3) and (4) above). Such assumptions are required in order for the CB(U)A approach to allow the application of a single set of HSSU weights.[7]

The "pure" BCA paradigm does not require these simplifications and assumptions, but the practicalities are daunting. One could attempt to elicit a single WTP figure directly from a representative sample of potential beneficiaries for valuing all of the relevant changes in health-state probabilities. This could be done using any one of a variety of WTP question formats. It would involve presenting, to a representative sample of individual respondents: (1) detailed descriptions (sometimes called "scenarios") of all relevant health state; and (2) the full set of changes in probabilities of being in each relevant state over the respondents' lifetimes.

Is it reasonable to expect that the respondents could understand the scenarios and the changes in probabilities well enough to provide responses to WTP questions that accurately reflected their true preferences? Several considerations suggest that the answer to this question is no. These include the fact that many respondents will never have actually experienced the scenarios corresponding to the relevant health states. It may also be presumed that respondents will have difficulty in processing the meanings of small changes in probabilities and assigning monetary values to these changes that reflect their true preferences.

These practical problems with the "pure" BCA paradigm provide the principal argument for CU(B)A, namely that it provides a simplified strategy for eliciting individuals' preferences for various health states and for coming up with a "shadow price" of QALYs (that is, a "threshold" dollar value for a QALY). On the other hand, the CU(B)A approach involves the series of strong assumptions and simplifications noted earlier.

Finally, note that coupling of the CU(B)A approach with the use of league tables and "consensus" threshold values does not entirely avoid the CU(B)A simplifications and assumptions. In addition, it raises several other major questions. Should we be looking at past decisions on health policy interventions as at all determinative for current health policy decisions? Should we base policy choice decisions on a single "consensus" threshold value in all cases? Is there any consensus at this point about the correct threshold value? Should we instead recognize the possibility that the threshold value depends on the specifics of the policy choice and therefore could vary across differing kinds of decisions? In response to the numerous unanswered questions about the use and level of CEA thresholds, the report of the Second Panel on Cost-Effectiveness in Health and Medicine has labeled further inquiry into these questions as a "key area for future research" (Neumann et al., 2017, Chap. 2).

UNANSWERED QUESTIONS AND THOUGHTS ON NEXT STEPS

As a result of the development of CEA into CUA into CU(B)A described earlier, we are now left with two similar yet different paradigms for devising monetary valuations of health program benefits. In both paradigms, the program benefits are described in terms of year-by-year changes in the probabilities of being in specific health states. One paradigm, CU(B)A, involves simplifying assumptions that may not be valid. The other paradigm, "pure" BCA, presents serious practical challenges in the WTP elicitation process that also raise validity questions. Thus, comparison of results from applying each paradigm to the same policy may be of interest, but is not a test of accuracy per se.

At this point, research toward improving accuracy of results has therefore focused on testing the validity of assumptions in the CU(B)A. Several recent studies by Bobinac and colleagues illustrate some interesting new directions in estimating WTP figures for QALYs. In particular, they published two recent studies (Bobinac et al., 2010; Bobinac et al., 2014) that allow comparisons of WTP-per-QALY values obtained from elicitation methods that specifically include risk vs. results obtained with conventional elicitation methods that involve valuation of an outcome that is certain. In particular, they compared WTP-per-QALY estimates from elicitation questions that explicitly included uncertainty with their own previous results with similar questions about prospects that were certain, a substantial increase in implied WTP-per-QALY was observed. This result: (1) reinforces our conjecture that risk preferences are in fact important in assessing WTP of health policies, while (2) raising concerns about deficiencies in the CU(B)A reliance on HSSU weights based on elicitation questions that assume risk-neutrality.

Bobinac et al. (2010) also find substantial variation among survey respondents in their expressed WTP-per-QALY values based on income differences; this implies that the use of a single "correct" monetary QALY value in the standard CU(B)A approach is at variance with consumer preferences and reinforces the need to look explicitly at distributional equity issues in CU(B)A analyses. They also report empirical results (Bobinac et al., 2012) that do not support an assumption that individuals' WTP-per-QALY figures are invariant to the size of the QALY gains provided by an intervention; this is at variance with the standard CU(B)A procedure of using a single WTP-per-QALY figure to compute "monetary net benefit" of an intervention.

In conclusion, further methodological development is needed both: (1) to devise modifications to the current CU(B)A procedures that are more consistent with this recent empirical evidence, and (2) to better cope with the practical difficulties of implementing BCA valuations that at least approximate the results from applying the BCA paradigm.

NOTES

1. This criticism of using an unweighted sum of WTP figures to measure net benefit is also often based on the argument that the marginal utility of income declines with the level of income so the utility value of one dollar of WTP for the poor is greater than it is for the rich. (See, for example, Bellinger (2016) Chaps. 3 and 6.) From the neoclassical welfare economics perspective, this argument is flawed since it requires interpersonal comparisons of utility (for example, that one "util" is the same for a poor person as for a rich person) that are not empirically verifiable.
2. Also note, however, that CUA does typically treat units of effectiveness in "utility" terms as equivalent across all persons; such interpersonal utility comparisons are not required in BCA.
3. The notion of the relevant budget constraint, however, becomes problematic in CUA. Funding for treatments in the league table comes from sources besides a single public agency's budget (for example, patient-payments, private insurance and so on) and span multiple years (over which agency budgets change). Similar complications arise when the "health sector" cost of treatment is defined to include impacts on all other health services received by the patients undergoing treatment (including costs for "related" and "unrelated" health problems). Inclusion of other "societal" costs in the CUR denominator of "societal" CUAs (for example, patients' time and travel costs, impacts on patients' earnings and non-health resource consumption) led to Meltzer's (1997) fundamental contribution on defining the relevant "societal" resource constraint in constructing the incremental CUR denominator for health interventions. More recent studies have applied Meltzer's societal-cost conceptualization to specific treatment/policy interventions (Huang et al., 2007; Johannesson et al., 1997; Meltzer et al., 2000, and Salkever, 2013). This approach is also recommended by the Second Panel on Cost-Effectiveness in Health and Medicine (Neumann et al., 2017, Chap. 3).
4. Alternatively, this valuation is often a "threshold" value from external sources, that may be quite different from the monetary valuations per QALY of the "average" consumer.
5. In the usual sg approach, respondents are assumed to be risk-neutral. The tto and vas elicitation methods assume that uncertainty is irrelevant, since they entail eliciting responses to choices between certain health states. Risk preferences are, however, of potential importance for assessing interventions with different risk profiles (for example, comparing high-risk surgical interventions with high expected levels of effectiveness vs. lower-risk non-surgical interventions with lower expected levels of effectiveness).
6. CU(B)A assumes that the relevant utility weight for any specific health state is the same regardless of the health states which preceded it in time and/or followed it in time.
7. Also note that the sg, tto and vas elicitation methods assume the resulting utility weights are invariant to the time durations used in the elicitation questions. A disconcerting feature of this assumption is that it implies a discount rate of zero.

REFERENCES AND RECOMMENDATIONS FOR FURTHER READING

Bellinger, W.K. (2016), *The Economics Analysis of Public Policy* (2nd edition). New York: Routledge.

Bobinac, A., N.J.A. van Exel, F.F.H. Rutten and W.B.F. Brouwer (2010), "Willingness to pay for a QALY: The individual perspective," *Value Health*, **13**, 1046–55.

Bobinac A., N.J.A. van Exel, F.F.H. Rutten and W.B.F. Brouwer (2012), "Get more pay more? An elaborate test of construct validity of willingness to pay per QALY estimates obtained through contingent valuation," *Journal of Health Economics*, **31**, 158–68.

Bobinac, A., N.J.A. van Exel, F.F.H. Rutten and W.B.F. Brouwer (2014), "The value of a QALY: Individual willingness to pay for health gains under risk," *PharmacoEconomics*, **32**, 75–86.

Drummond, M.F., M.J. Sculpher, K. Claxton, G.L. Stoddart and G.W. Torrance (2015), *Methods for the Economic Evaluation of Health Programs* (4th edition). Oxford: Oxford University Press.

Huang, E.S., Q. Zhang, S.E.S. Brown, M.L. Drum, D.O. Meltzer and M.H. Chin (2007), "The cost-effectiveness of improving diabetes care in U.S. federally qualified community health centers," *Health Services Research*, **42**, 2174–93.

Johannesson, M., D.O. Meltzer and R.M. O'Conor (1997), "Incorporating future costs in medical cost-effectiveness analysis: Implications for the cost-effectiveness of the treatment of hypertension," *Medical Decision Making*, **17**, 382–9.

Kenkel, D. (1997), "On valuing morbidity, cost-effectiveness analysis, and being rude," *Journal of Health Economics*, **16**, 749–57.

Klarman, H.E. (1982), "The road to cost-effectiveness analysis," *The Milbank Memorial Fund Quarterly: Health and Society*, **60**(4), 585–603.

Klarman, H.E., J.O.S. Francis and G.D. Rosenthal (1968), "Cost effectiveness analysis applied to the treatment of chronic renal disease," *Medical Care*, **6**(1), 48–54.

Meltzer, D.O. (1997), "Accounting for future costs in medical cost-effectiveness analysis," *Journal of Health Economics*, **16**(1), 33–64.

Meltzer, D.O., B. Egleston, D. Stoffel and E. Dasbach (2000), "Effect of future costs on cost-effectiveness of medical interventions among young adults: The example of intensive therapy for type 1 diabetes mellitus," *Medical Care*, **38**(6), 679–85.

Neumann, P.J., G.D. Sanders, L.B. Russell, J.E. Siegeland and T.G. Ganiats (eds) (2017), *Cost-Effectiveness in Health and Medicine* (2nd edition). Oxford: Oxford University Press.

Salkever, D. (2013), "Social costs of expanding access to evidence-based supported employment: Concepts and interpretive review of evidence," *Psychiatric Services*, **64**(2), 111–19.

Stason, W.B. and M.C. Weinstein (1977), "Allocation of resources to manage hypertension," *New England Journal of Medicine*, **296**(13), 732–9.

Weinstein, M.C and W.B. Stason (1977), "Foundations of cost-effectiveness analysis for health and medical practices," *New England Journal of Medicine*, **296**(13), 716–72.

Willig, R. (1976), "Consumer surplus without apology," *American Economic Review*, **66**(4), 589–97.

Zerbe, R.O. and A.S. Bellas (2006), *A Primer for Benefit-Cost Analysis*. Cheltenham, UK and Northampton, MA, USA: Edward Elgar Publishing.

APPENDIX

Table A12.1   Ten-year sequence of yearly health-state probabilities: Monotheraphy

Health State	Healthy	200<CD4<500	CD4<200	AIDS	Dead
Year 1	0.800	0.194	0.000	0.000	0.006
Year 2	0.640	0.295	0.039	0.013	0.013
Year 3	0.512	0.337	0.082	0.036	0.023
Year 4	0.410	0.342	0.116	0.083	0.040
Year 5	0.328	0.326	0.136	0.132	0.068
Year 6	0.262	0.299	0.145	0.177	0.108
Year 7	0.210	0.266	0.145	0.212	0.158
Year 8	0.168	0.233	0.138	0.235	0.217
Year 9	0.134	0.200	0.127	0.248	0.280
Year 10	0.107	0.170	0.114	0.251	0.347

Table A12.2   Sequence of yearly health-state probabilities: Combotherapy

Health State	Healthy	200<CD4<500	CD4<200	AIDS	Dead
Year 1	0.800	0.194	0.000	0.000	0.006
Year 2	0.640	0.322	0.020	0.006	0.012
Year 3	0.512	0.401	0.045	0.018	0.020
Year 4	0.410	0.444	0.067	0.044	0.031
Year 5	0.328	0.462	0.085	0.073	0.048
Year 6	0.262	0.461	0.097	0.103	0.073
Year 7	0.210	0.447	0.104	0.131	0.104
Year 8	0.168	0.425	0.106	0.154	0.143
Year 9	0.134	0.398	0.106	0.171	0.187
Year 10	0.107	0.368	0.102	0.183	0.234

Table A12.3   Changes in yearly health-state probabilities: Combotherapy vs. status quo (Monotherapy)

Health State	Healthy	200<CD4<500	CD4<200	AIDS	Dead
Year 1	0.000	0.000	0.000	0.000	0.000
Year 2	0.000	0.027	−0.019	−0.007	−0.001
Year 3	0.000	0.064	−0.038	−0.018	−0.003
Year 4	0.000	0.102	−0.049	−0.039	−0.009
Year 5	0.000	0.135	−0.052	−0.059	−0.020
Year 6	0.000	0.162	−0.048	−0.073	−0.035
Year 7	0.000	0.181	−0.041	−0.081	−0.054
Year 8	0.000	0.192	−0.032	−0.082	−0.074
Year 9	0.000	0.198	−0.022	−0.077	−0.094
Year 10	0.000	0.198	−0.012	−0.068	−0.113

13. Harmful addiction

David Weimer

ABSTRACT

Addiction harms individuals and the rest of society. It poses a challenge to conventional benefit-cost analysis (BCA) because it involves sovereign consumers apparently making mistakes. Although the neoclassical approach to addiction, the rational addiction model, does not adequately explain harmful addiction, it introduces the useful notion that the utility of current consumption can depend on the stock of prior consumption. Behavioral economics offers a number of explanations for addiction: non-exponential time discounting, presentism, cue-dependent consumption choices, and costly self-control in the face of temptation. The latter provides some normative leverage: addictive consumption involves a loss of individual welfare when the individual would be willing to pay to avoid facing the tempting choice. Practical BCA can assess the welfare loss from addictive consumption if a marginal valuation schedule for non-addicted consumption can be distinguished from the market demand schedule. Unfortunately, it is currently unclear how to identify the non-addicted demand schedule from revealed preference data. Further, the task is complicated because consumption of most goods commonly classified as addictive involves both addictive and non-addictive consumption.

The consumption of substances or engagement in activities that involve self-harm poses a challenge to the application of BCA to assess the relative efficiencies of public policies. The valuation of policy impacts through revealed preferences assumes individuals make choices that maximize their utility. Addiction, as the term is commonly used, brings into question this normative interpretation of consumer sovereignty. How should BCA interpret self-harm that results from addiction?

Although we do not have a definitive answer, this question is worth exploring for several reasons:

1. Addiction causes much harm to individuals and the rest of society. For example, smoking contributes to disease; some recreational drugs, such as opiates, involve mortality risks for users and impose costs on others; compulsive gambling often immiserates gamblers and their families.
2. Although there is a model of rational addiction, there are also several behavioral models that explain harmful addiction—exploring addiction provides an introduction to these models.
3. Assessing policy interventions directed at reducing harmful addiction provides an illustration of the importance of taking account of heterogeneous preferences and behaviors in BCA.

WHAT IS ADDICTION?

Perceptions of addiction, which have ranged from moral weakness to brain disease, affect the extent to which it is treated primarily as either a criminal justice or a medical problem. Neuroscience research has found that consumption of substances commonly thought of as addictive change the structure and functioning of the brain. This has prompted calls for addiction to be considered a brain disease (Leshner 1997; Volkow and Li 2004). The definition adopted by the American Society of Addiction Medicine in 2011 heeded these calls: "Addiction is a primary, chronic disease of brain reward, motivation, memory and related circuitry. Dysfunction in these circuits leads to characteristic biological, psychological, social and spiritual manifestations. This is reflected in an individual pathologically pursuing reward and/or (sic) relief by substance use and other behaviors" (ASAM 2016, 1; Smith 2012). It includes not only chemical, or substance, addictions, such as to alcohol, illicit drugs, and tobacco, but also compulsive, or behavioral, addictions, such as to gambling, sex, or internet use. The observation of "addiction hopping," through which individuals switch to a new expression of addiction when an old one is blocked, suggests that a more general disease of addiction may underlie any particular manifestation (Richter and Foster 2014); so too do similarities in neurological processes associated with addiction (Goodman 2008).

Accepting this definition would help clarify addictive consumption for purposes of BCA by allowing analysts to treat it as they would self-harmful behaviors resulting from mental illness; that is, not as a manifestation of "true" preferences. However, the definition of addiction as a brain disease is not universally accepted. Critics point to growing evidence of substantial neuroplasticity throughout life, arguing that any repeated behavior can change brain structure and function (Hall et al.

2015). Changes in neural function must be sufficient to cause impairment for it to be considered a disease, which is not always the case (Levy 2013, 3389): "addiction is not a brain disease (though it is often a disease, and it may always involve brain dysfunction)." Neuroplasticity also suggests that, unlike some other chronic diseases, it may be possible to reverse addiction through either abstinence or the repetition of behaviors less harmful than the addiction.

NEOCLASSICAL APPROACH: RATIONAL ADDICTION

The rational addiction model seeks to explain addiction as the result of individuals maximizing their utilities over time (Becker and Murphy 1988). The key modeling insight is to make utility depend not just on the current consumption of a good, but on some "stock" of the good that depends on past consumption. In its simplest form, such intertemporally dependent preferences can be written such that an individual's period-specific utility at some time τ is:

$$U_\tau = u(x_\tau, s_\tau, S_\tau) \qquad (13.1)$$

where x_τ is a vector of non-addictive goods consumed, s_τ is the quantity of the addictive good consumed and S_τ is the accumulated stock of the addictive good. The function u is assumed stable and therefore not subscripted for time.

The accumulated stock of the addictive good S_τ is a function of the quantities of the addictive good consumed in prior periods. An example of a particular function for S_τ is:

$$S_\tau = S_{\tau-1} + s_\tau - dS_{\tau-1} \qquad (13.2)$$

where d is the rate at which the stock depreciates. S_τ could be modified to allow the person to make expenditures on "anti-market" goods (Winston 1980), such as nicotine gum by cigarette smokers, to reduce its effective size.

The rational addiction model assumes that the consumer maximizes global utility, which is the discounted sum of utilities over the consumer's time horizon. The actual optimization is complicated and can have several solutions. However, absent a mistake by the consumer, the decision to consume the addictive good is optimal from the perspective of the individual. Without external effects, such as driving while impaired by alcoholics, or information asymmetries, such as lack of knowledge about the risks of consuming new "designer drugs," public policies to reduce addiction could not increase efficiency.

Many harmful addictions begin during adolescence—few people begin smoking cigarettes in adulthood. One might think of adolescents as ignoring the consequences of their decisions on their future selves. Thus, they may make consumption decisions that impose a large S_τ on their adult selves, who then follow the rational addiction model. In such situations, the adolescent imposes an "internality" on his or her future self (Herrnstein et al. 1993). From this perspective, policies that restrict adolescent behavior could increase efficiency.

Why might adolescents impose internalities on their future selves? A variety of explanations can be offered: a very high discount rate, earlier peaks in thrill and novelty seeking than full development of self-control, and peer pressure. The more interesting question is: Why would adults, such as those who have gone "cold turkey," resume harmful consumption? Psychologists and behavioral economists have addressed this question (Bickel and Marsch 2001; Redish et al. 2008; Bickel et al. 2014).

BEHAVIORAL EXPLANATIONS

Three behavioral explanations have received the most attention: non-exponential discounting, cues, and presentism (Weimer 2017).

1. Only exponential discounting, using the familiar present value formula in the discrete case, is time consistent. That is, only if a person discounts the future exponentially will he or she want to stick with a plan made today about future consumption. For example, most people would prefer to receive two apples a year and a day from now to one apple a year from now. However, the same person might very well prefer to have the one apple today rather than the two apples tomorrow.

    Alternatives to exponential discounting include hyperbolic and quasi-hyperbolic discounting. For example, quasi-hyperbolic discounting of an outcome occurring at time T takes the following form:

$$QH_T = \beta[1/(1 + d)^T] \tag{13.3}$$

    where $T \geq 1$ is the number of periods beyond the present, $0 < \beta < 1$ captures the degree of immediate impatience (a smaller β shows greater impatience), and d is the discount rate. Note that if $\beta = 1$, then the formula reduces to that for exponential discounting.

Higher levels of consumption of addictive goods occur if non-exponential discounting is substituted for exponential discounting in the rational addiction model (Gruber and Köszegi 2001). If one assumes that individual welfare requires exponential discounting, then this modification of the rational addiction model could provide internal benefits from public policies aimed at reducing the consumption of harmfully addictive goods.

2. Cues are environmental circumstances that trigger increased demand for the addictive good (Laibson 2001; Bernheim and Rangel 2004). For example, being with someone who is smoking may create an urge for a former smoker to smoke; so too might stressful circumstances or consumption of complementary goods such as alcohol. The cues can be thought of as shifting the decision process from one that fully takes account of the future consequences of immediate consumption to one the focuses on immediate gratification.

3. Presentism recognizes that people face temptations for immediate consumption that they wish to avoid and that resisting the temptation is psychologically costly (O'Donoghue and Rabin 2015). Like hyperbolic or quasi-hyperbolic, it produces time inconsistency. Indeed, because the evidence for individuals behaving as if they are employing these non-exponential discounting procedures is strongest in studies that observe behavior over relatively short time frames (Frederick et al. 2002), presentism combined with otherwise exponential discounting may provide a better description of time-inconsistent behavior. Further, cues can be thought of as affecting the costs of self-control in the face of temptations. Connecting back to the neoclassical model, one can think of S_τ as the primary mechanism driving the costs of self-control against temptations for harmfully addictive consumption.

NORMATIVE INTERPRETATION

In standard consumer theory, an individual is always better off with more consumption options. Given a choice over two sets of alternatives in which one set is a proper subset of the other, the consumer will always choose the fuller set over the proper subset because it provides more consumption options. However, an individual aware of his or her own presentism may very well choose the proper subset if it removes the temptation (Schelling 1984). Stepping back from an actual choice, such as whether or not to have an alcoholic drink in a particular social situation, to the selection of the set of alternatives from which a choice will be made, such as avoiding the social situation, provides a way of gaining information about the costs of self-control from revealed preferences (Gul and Pesendorfer 2004, 2005, 2007). To the extent that public policies restrict sets of alternatives to those that would be selected voluntarily by individuals, they can be thought of as promoting efficiency.

For example, bans on indoor smoking restrict the set of alternatives available to smokers. Nonetheless, such bans now enjoy support not just from non-smokers but also from some current smokers, especially those who plan to try to quit (Hersch 2005).

It is difficult to think of situations in which willingness to pay (WTP) for a reduced set of alternatives can be inferred from observed behaviors. Until clever researchers find ways to make such revealed preference inferences, analysts may turn to stated preference methods to assess WTP for reductions in available alternatives.

TAKING ACCOUNT OF HETEROGENEITY IN CONSUMPTION OF POTENTIALLY ADDICTIVE GOODS

Practical BCA often imputes values from demand (marginal valuation) schedules in markets. If all consumption in the market were harmfully addictive consumption, then it would be at least plausible to ignore losses in conventional consumer surplus in predicting the costs and benefits of an intervention that reduces consumption. This is the approach often advocated by public health economists with respect to goods like cigarettes (Song et al. 2014; Chaloupka et al. 2015). Yet, even though nicotine is one of the most addictive substances known to science, some youth who experiment with smoking do not become regular smokers and some adults can limit their consumption to smoking at special occasions.

Consider alcohol. Although current alcoholics fall prey to the temptation of harmful addictive consumption, most alcohol consumers can easily limit their consumption to levels that do not cause them individual harm and may even provide positive health benefits. The market demand for alcohol includes both the addictive and non-addictive demand. Ignoring all losses in consumer surplus in the market from an intervention like a higher excise tax would fail to take account of the losses suffered by non-alcoholics. (Of course, there may be externalities from consumption by either those addicted or those not addicted, such as accident risks that would have to be taken into account in a BCA.)

The analysis of a market that mixes addictive and non-addictive demand was proposed in the context of gambling by the Productivity Commission (1999) in Australia. The analysis assumes that for most people gambling

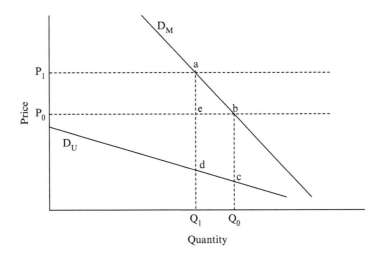

Source: Adapted from the Productivity Commission (1999), Appendix C, 11–13.

Figure 13.1 Combining both addictive and non-addictive demand

is a recreation where one pays the expected loss as a price, but for some people gambling is a compulsion (addiction) that often immiserates them and their families. Other researchers have applied this model, which follows, to cigarettes (Laux 2000; Weimer et al. 2009; Ashley et al. 2015).

In Figure 13.1, the market demand schedule, which could be estimated from market data over time or across jurisdictions, is labeled D_M. If price were increased by a tax from P_0 to P_1 and the good were treated in the usual way, then the loss in consumer surplus would be the area of trapezoid P_1abP_0. The area of the rectangle inscribed by P_1aeP_0 would be the increased government revenue that would offset some consumer surplus loss resulting in a net (deadweight) loss equal to the area of triangle abe.

Rather than treating the market demand schedule as the relevant marginal valuation schedule for the good, assume that, if no one were addicted to the good, the demand schedule, and the marginal valuation schedule, would be D_U. In this case, rather than the reduction in consumption from Q_0 to Q_1 creating a deadweight loss of abe, it would create a gain equal to the area of trapezoid bcde, the difference between prior expenditure on these units (rectangle Q_0beQ_1) and the prior valuation (trapezoid Q_0cdQ_1). Thus, the consumer surplus loss would be the area of rectangle P_1aeP_0 minus the area of trapezoid bcde. Again, with offsetting government revenue, instead of a social loss equal to the area of triangle abe, there would be a social gain equal to the area of trapezoid bcde.

The challenge in moving from this conceptual framework to application in BCA is finding ways to position the unaddicted demand schedule, D_U. An approach employed by Weimer et al. (2009) specified a simple utility function for cigarette demand that related the position of D_U to the position of the market demand schedule in terms of the WTP of addicted smokers for being unaddicted. The researchers then employed a contingent valuation survey to estimate this WTP and the implied position of D_U.

SUMMARY

Harmful addiction poses a challenge to conventional BCA because it involves sovereign consumers apparently making mistakes. Public policy interventions to reduce harmful consumption, or its consequences, can often be justified in terms of external effects. However, a full analysis should also take account of the internal effects on those who consume the addictive good. Unfortunately, market demand schedules for addictive goods do not convey enough information to estimate internal effects. A challenge for applied economists is finding a way to estimate these internal effects when both addictive and unaddictive demand are present.

REFERENCES AND RECOMMENDATIONS FOR FURTHER READING

American Society of Addiction Medicine (ASAM) (2016) Definition of Addiction. Accessed January 3, 2018 at http://www.asam.org/quality-practice/definition-of-addiction.
Ashley, E.M., C. Nardinelli and R.A. Lavaty (2015) "Estimating the benefits of public health policies that reduce harmful consumption." *Health Economics* **24**(5), 617–24.
Australia, Productivity Commission (1999) *Australia's Gambling Industries*. Inquiry Report No. 10, 26 November.
Becker, G.S. and K.M. Murphy (1988) "A theory of rational addiction." *Journal of Political Economy* **96**(4), 675–700.
Bernheim, B.D. and A. Rangel (2004) "Addiction and cue-triggered decision processes." *American Economic Review* **94**(5), 1558–90.
Bickel, W.K., M.W. Johnson, M.N. Koffarnus, J. MacKillop and J.G. Murphy (2014) "The behavioral economics of substance use disorders: Reinforcement pathologies and their repair." *Annual Review of Clinical Psychology* 641–77.
Bickel, W.K. and L.A. Marsch (2001) "Toward a behavioral economic understanding of drug dependence: Delay discounting processes." *Addiction* **96**(1), 73–86.
Chaloupka, F.J., J. Gruber and K.E. Warner (2015) "Accounting for 'lost pleasure' in cost-benefit analysis of government regulation: The case of food and drug

administration's proposed cigarette labeling regulation." *Annals of Internal Medicine* **161**(1), 64–5.

Frederick, S., G. Loewenstein and T. O'Donoghue (2002) "Time discounting and time preference: A critical review." *Journal of Economic Literature* **40**(2), 351–401.

Goodman, A. (2008) "Neurobiology of addiction: An integrative review." *Biochemical Pharmacology* **75**(1), 266–322.

Gruber, J. and B. Köszegi (2001) "Is addiction 'rational'? Theory and evidence." *Quarterly Journal of Economics* **116**(4), 1261–303.

Gul, F. and W. Pesendorfer (2004) "Self-control, revealed preference and consumption choice." *Review of Economic Dynamics* **7**(2), 243–64.

Gul, F. and W. Pesendorfer (2005) "The revealed preference theory of changing tastes." *Review of Economic Studies* **72**(2), 429–48.

Gul, F. and W. Pesendorfer (2007) "Harmful addiction." *Review of Economic Studies* **74**(1), 147–72.

Hall, W., A. Carter and C. Forlini (2015) "The brain disease model of addiction: Is it supported by the evidence and has it delivered on its promises?" *Lancet Psychiatry* **2**(1), 105–10.

Herrnstein, R.J., G.F. Loewenstein, D. Prelec and W. Vaughan (1993) "Utility maximization and melioration: Internalities in individual choice." *Journal of Behavioral Decision Making* **6**(3), 149–85.

Hersch, J. (2005) "Smoking restrictions as a self-control mechanism." *Journal of Risk and Uncertainty* **31**(1), 5–21.

Laibson, D. (2001) "A cue-theory of consumption." *Quarterly Journal of Economics* **116**(1), 81–119.

Laux, F.L. (2000) "Addiction as a market failure: Using rational addiction results to justify tobacco regulation." *Journal of Health Economics* **19**(4), 421–37.

Leshner, A.I. (1997) "Addiction is a brain disease, and it matters." *Science* **278**(5335), 45–7.

Levy, N. (2013) "Addiction is not a brain disease (and it matters)." *Frontiers in Psychiatry* **4**(24.10), 3389–95.

O'Donoghue, T. and M. Rabin (2015) "Present bias: Lessons learned and to be learned." *American Economic Review* **105**(5), 273–9.

Redish, A.D., S. Jensen and A. Johnson (2008) "A unified framework for addiction: Vulnerabilities in the decision process." *Behavioral and Brain Sciences* **31**(4), 415–37.

Richter, L. and S.E. Foster (2014) "Effectively addressing addiction requires changing the language of addiction." *Journal of Public Health Policy* **35**(1), 60–64.

Schelling, T.C. (1984) "Self-command in practice, in policy, and in a theory of rational choice." *American Economic Review* **74**(2), 1–11.

Smith, D.E. (2012) "The process addictions and the new ASAM definition of addiction." *Journal of Psychoactive Drugs* **44**(1), 1–4.

Song, A.V., P. Brown and S.A. Glantz (2014) "When health policy and empirical evidence collide: The case of cigarette package warning labels and economic consumer surplus." *American Journal of Public Health* **104**(2), e42–e51.

Vining, A.R. and D.L. Weimer (2010) "An assessment of important issues concerning the application of benefit-cost analysis to social policy." *Journal of Benefit-Cost Analysis* **1**(1), 1–38.

Volkow, N.D. and T.-K. Li (2004) "Drug addiction: The neurobiology of behaviour gone awry." *Nature Reviews Neuroscience* **5**(12), 963–70.

Weimer, D.L. (2017) *Behavioral Economics for Cost-Benefit Analysis: Benefit Validity when Sovereign Consumers Seem to Make Mistakes.* New York, NY: Cambridge University Press.

Weimer, D.L., A.R. Vining and R.K. Thomas (2009) "Cost-benefit analysis involving addictive goods: Contingent valuation to estimate willingness-to-pay for smoking cessation." *Health Economics* **18**(2), 181–202.

Winston, G.C. (1980) "Addiction and backsliding: A theory of compulsive consumption." *Journal of Economic Behavior & Organization* **1**(4), 295–324.

14. Supplementing benefit-cost analysis: Models for transportation and land use decisions

Emile Quinet

ABSTRACT

This chapter is devoted to models for transport, trade and land use decisions. They complement traditional benefit-cost analyses (BCA) insofar as they allow describing the distribution of effects and coping with market imperfections such as externalities and market powers. They can be classified according to several types: dynamic or static, taking into account or not the land market, and also ranked according to their degree of complexity. Their use for BCA is presented, along with some recommendations on how they can help to assess projects and schemes.

INTRODUCTION

The great advantage of usual BCA procedures is that they require very little information: they are based on a partial analysis, limited to the market where the change happens. The required information pertains just to the market of interest, where the change to be assessed takes place. It requires only the quantities consumed in the initial configuration and the demand function. This information enables the provision of the quantities consumed: in the case of transport, traffic flows and the traffic model. A basic result (for example, Lesourne 1964) is that this information is sufficient to ascertain the change in welfare for the whole collectivity: this result states that welfare produced by the initial change is exactly equal to the sum of the consumer's surplus and the producer's surplus of the partial market from which comes the initial change.

However, this procedure has two important drawbacks. First, it does not provide the final effects of the measure to be assessed. Through the Walras general equilibrium properties, the change provided to consumers of the market under consideration is diffused across the whole economy. By the economic mechanisms of substitution and complementarity, it is transformed in changes in the quantities produced and traded and in the prices of all other goods. The partial analysis gives no clue about the final distribution of the effects, a matter of concern for decision makers. Also, in order to get to know the final beneficiaries, it is necessary to follow the transmission mechanisms of the initial change.

Second, the basic aforementioned result is valid only under strict assumptions which are not realistic: (1) the changes under consideration are marginal; (2) there is no externality and no market power (first best assumptions, see also Chapter 5);[1] (3) income distribution is optimal and (4) market prices reflect the collective value of the good. The deviations from these assumptions are common in economic life: it often happens that the price of some good does not reflect its collective value, as it is the case in presence of subsidies or specific taxes; there are many externalities, either negative – such as environmental externalities – or positive – for instance in the case of agglomeration effects; and many markets are not competitive, with some firms benefiting from market power.

Those two limits (distribution effects and restrictive assumptions) are especially binding in situations where space is at stake, namely in the case of transport, regional issues and international trade. In those cases, the spatial distribution of effects and market imperfection are especially important: in terms of distribution, which one of the two regions linked by a new means of transport will benefit more from this change? In terms of unfilled assumptions, the roots of geographical economics are increasing return to scale and agglomeration, externalities.

Limiting ourselves to these cases where space is at stake, we will explore a way to overcome these drawbacks, through the use of general equilibrium models. General equilibrium models aim at describing the whole economy and allow detailing the effects of the change under consideration. They do so either in a framework of first best assumptions, or in a more general framework taking into account both market imperfections and distributive effects (for example, see Mayeres and Proost (1997) for more developments). In the special case of transport and trade where we limit ourselves in this chapter, these general equilibrium models imply a spatial dimension.

GENERAL STRUCTURE

In situations where space is involved, the study area is split into geographical zones. The spatial distribution of activities (residential, industrial, commercial, health, education, administration, green spaces and so on) between zones is described with a different level of detail according to the model. This spatial distribution generates displacement flows on transport networks that connect these different places. These flows depend on the supply of transport in terms of capacity, cost and quality of service. This is the *ex ante* situation.

The change under consideration in transport or trade costs, for instance due to a new motorway, induces changes in economic activity: customers will go to different shops; workers will apply to firms which are more distant than before; some households will move. The aim of the model is to assess the changes that will be brought about by the new motorway in terms of both economic activities and transport costs and flows. The issue is that there is in general a reverse causality between transport and economic activity: changes in transport costs induce changes in locations and level of activities in each zone. On the other hand, those changes in traffic flows induce changes in transport costs (due for instance to congestion effects), which themselves bring about results in new changes in location of economic activities and so on.

In terms of software, these models are generally composed of two modules which are typically run iteratively:

- An economic module evaluating the structures of production and consumption in every zone. The links between the sectors are represented by the coefficients of input-output matrices or other modeling approaches. The demand for each commodity is satisfied through domestic production and imports from other zones, the volume of which depends on a comparison of prices with other regions and on the costs of transport. Locations of firms and households depend on the accessibility to firms, amenities and shops.
- A transport module which relates transport flows to the costs of transport. This module is a normal common transport model similar to those currently used in transport economics.
- On balance, the transport costs and traffic flows output of this transport module should be equal to the transport costs and traffic flows of the previous step of the iterative process.

Figure 14.1 is drawn from Simmonds and Feldman (2005) and shows the general structure of those models, using the example of the Delta model (DELTA stands for Development, Employment, status and commuting, Location and property market, Transition and growth, and Area quality).

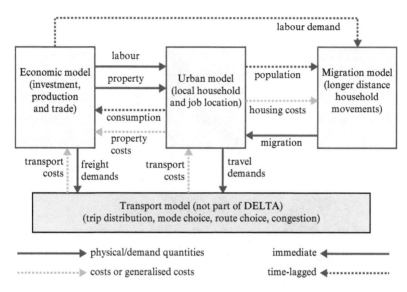

Source: Simmonds and Feldman (2005).

Figure 14.1   Overall structure of a DELTA base model

OUTPUTS

This sort of model generates aggregate results such as gross domestic product (GDP), employment, export and import and population for each zone. It also provides large numbers of more detailed results, depending on the degree of complexity of the model in terms of size and number of zones, of number of production sectors, of variety of households and so on. As an illustration, let us show a particular output of the implementation of the SGEurope model (Bröcker et al. 2004). Figure 14.2 shows the forecasted impacts of the Trans-European Networks (TEN) and Transportation Infrastructure Needs Assessment (TINA) infrastructure programs of the European Union. As it clearly appears, there are winners and losers; positive effects on some regions, negative on others. The polarization of activity resulting from this new infrastructure can also be seen: activity tends to grow in those regions most directly affected at the expense of those both far away or in the "shadow" created by the infrastructure.

Transport intervenes in this model in various ways:

● The choice of mode and route and the amount of induced traffic depend on the characteristics of transport supply.

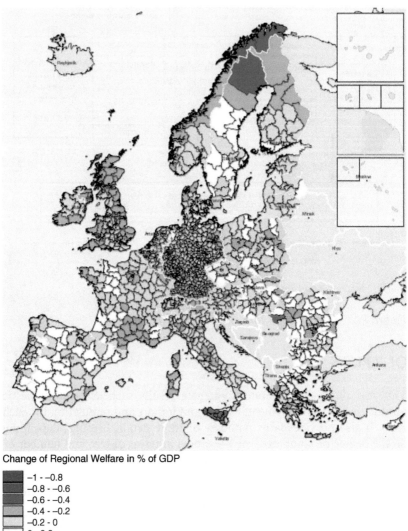

Change of Regional Welfare in % of GDP

- −1 - −0.8
- −0.8 - −0.6
- −0.6 - −0.4
- −0.4 - −0.2
- −0.2 - 0
- 0 - 0.2
- 0.2 - 0.4
- 0.4 - 0.6
- 0.6 - 0.8
- 0.8 - 1
- 1 - ...

Source: Bröcker et al. (2004).

*Figure 14.2   Consequences of the TINA and TEN European projects in
terms of GDP per head*

- Interregional trade depends on the allocation of the trade of one region with each other region, this depending on the nature of the good transported, the price of the good in each region, and as an element in this, the cost of transportation for that good.
- The evolution of transport costs affects the change in the coefficients of the input-output matrix and the share of transport in the added-value of each good.
- The migration of population between regions is determined by incomes per head and unemployment levels in each zone and costs of transport between zones.
- Investment by region and by sector depends on changes in (expectations of) production levels in each region, which can be altered by proposed changes in transport and accessibility.

CLASSIFICATIONS

There is no exhaustive and unanimously accepted classification of these models, but many surveys have been made; among them let us mention those of Wegener (2011), Bröcker and Mercenier (2011), while the use of models is developed in Vickerman (2007). Building on Quinet and Raj (2017), let us here present some distinctions relevant for our purpose which is to see to what extent these models can improve on current BCA.

Static and Dynamic Models

A first distinction lies between static and dynamic models. Static models do not take into consideration time; they assume that an equilibrium is reached, telling neither how nor when, and they describe this equilibrium. They are well suited to comparative statics, and especially BCA, where two situations are assessed: a situation of equilibrium without the infrastructure (the situation "without") and with it (the situation "with").

As an example of this type, let us quote Anas's Regional Economy Land Use and Transportation (RELU-TRAN) model (Anas and Liu 2007). This model has been used for the assessment of the Grand Paris Express, a ring mass transit system around Paris, about 10 kilometers from the center of the city. Based on Anas and Chang (2017) this model and Table 14.1 allow one to assess the welfare effects of this new infrastructure and break down the impact between consumers, landowners, the state (revenues from taxes) and importers.

As an example of the dynamic models, let us mention UrbanSim (Waddell 2002). In such models, all variables are time dependent; a time lag

Table 14.1   Welfare consequences of the implementation of the Grand Paris Express

Impact	Euros per Consumer Present value 2005–2030
Consumer CV	2685
Real Estate Values	2209
Tax Revenue	
Sales	110
Income	764
Importer CV	6881
Total Welfare	12 649

is introduced between the two modules: to make things simple, the outputs of the transport model of period t, which are the costs of transport, are introduced in the economic module of year t + 1 as inputs. In such a framework, there is no equilibrium; all markets are out of equilibrium, except in infinite times. So no welfare calculation is possible. However, the model allows predicting the evolutions of the variables of interest.

Land Use Issues

An important dimension for many transportation infrastructure investments relates to how precisely the models take into account the land use market. In many models, which deserve the name of Land Use Transport Integration (LUTI) models, the land market is explicitly introduced, the price of land is fixed either through a bidding process, or according to heuristics using accessibility as a driver of rents and displacements of goods and people. As a consequence, the zones are small (the size of zones may be 10 000 square meters at most, often less) as the land rent is quite variable depending on the location. Accordingly, the description of the transport system must be very accurate and the economic module is data demanding (population, sectorial activities, imports and exports for each zone). This type of model is appropriate at the scale of an agglomeration.

Other models do not include the land market; they deal with larger zones and are well designed for interregional or international issues. Consequently, the transport system can be described in a simpler way. Those models deal with transport as a simple activity, with a unique cost that generally depends upon distance many of them imply no migration of household and labor.[2] They can be named Spatial General Equilibrium models (SGEM). These SGEM models are traditionally used in intercity studies, trade and in interregional issues.

Perfect or Imperfect Competition

It is not always easy for the external observer to check whether a model is based on perfect competition assumptions or not, although it seems that most of them are based on perfect competition. And the same model can easily cope with both assumptions. For instance, the initial version of RELU-TRAN does not imply departure from first best assumption, but the further versions introduce possible agglomeration externalities (the productivity of each firm is proportional to the proximity of other firms, measured by an accessibility index).

Other models integrate increasing returns from the start. In the SGEM category, CGEurope (Bröcker 2002) assumes monopolistic competition. In the RAEM (Tavasszy et al. 2011), each sector consists of identical firms each producing a unique specification of a particular commodity, according to the monopolistic competition paradigm. Households and domestic sectors consume transport services in their consumption and production activities. Martínez and Araya (2000) introduce agglomeration externalities in the land use MUSSA model (Martínez and Donoso 2004) through the presence in the utility function of the agent of a parameter representative of the advantages of the location, which depends on the accessibility of the place and its characteristics (for example, neighborhood).

Several spatial models are built according to the framework of the New Economic Geography paradigms, and then imply departures from the first best assumptions: monopolistic competition, agglomeration externalities and a taste for diversity. The models of Puga (1999), Forslid et al. (2002) and Bosker et al. (2010) are based on monopolistic competition. Ahlfeldt et al. (2015) uses agglomeration externalities both for households and for firms to explain the pattern of land use in Berlin and its evolution.

Issues of Size and Complexity

Other dimensions of classification are the size and complexity of the models. Though rarely addressed, these issues are of major importance to the practitioners as they command both the details of the results and the amount of data to be gathered. From such a point of view, there is a continuum of models, but several types can be identified.

At the higher level of complexity, we find the LUTI models. Reproducing the land market and housing market, they are more directed towards urban areas; they imply very detailed zoning, with a lot of data, both on households and on firms; the transport sector is modeled with detail; usually the traffic modeling is achieved through a classical four steps model, which interacts with an activity model. Hence, their geographic spread is—for the time being—a limitation.[3] Moreover, there may be problems of convergence of the calculations—for example, in the presence of increasing returns. The numerous parameters of these models are estimated through econometric methods for some of them, through calibrations and expert guesses for many other ones. Due to the size of the models it is not easy to tell what the important parameters are. Already mentioned examples of such models are RELU-TRAN and UrbanSim. They often deserve the criticism of being black boxes.

The SGEM models have a lower degree of complexity. As opposed to LUTI models, they do not try to precisely model land markets or housing markets. Usually their description of the transport sector is simpler and limited to the distribution and generation steps, possibly including the modal choice, but neither route choice nor congestion. Their parameters are also calibrated both through econometric methods and through simulation. They can integrate complex economic mechanisms outside of transport. For example, many include increasing returns and externalities. They are calibrated both through sound econometric studies and through expert guesses.

A third category differs from the two previous ones in that the parameters are not calibrated by simulation or guess but by sound econometric methods. We will name them "structural models." Usually they concentrate on a special form of causality or a special form of mechanism; they are not able to answer all of the questions of decision makers. They have many less parameters than the previous models that sought to reproduce as accurately as possible a global reality. It is then possible to assess those using econometric methods that estimate the significance of their parameters. They are especially fit for estimating specific parameters such as elasticities. Examples of such models are those of Puga (1999) and Bosker et al. (2010). The simplest ones of them just imply basic mechanisms, for instance, the models designed by Anderson and Van Wincoop (2004) for the gravity equation or Redding and Venables (2004) for the wage equation. The description of transport is very crude, often just a cost between each origin and each destination, without taking into account any congestion effect. The geographical zoning is quite variable, depending on the availability of data and on the phenomenon at stake. These models are more frequent in the trade and geographical economics traditions than in the transport tradition, dominated by large LUTI and SGEM models.

CONCLUSION

There is a wide array of models able to supplement the usual welfare calculation and to correct its well-known drawbacks such as lack of indication of the distribution of effects and, limiting assumptions of absence of externalities and market powers. They are based on a general equilibrium framework, and can have various specificities: some are able to model the land market, they are usually very data demanding and entail a high degree of complexity; they are especially appropriate for urban issues. Others are more simple and do not take into account the land market; they are more prone to deal with regional and international issues. Many of these models cannot be calibrated by econometric methods; they imply estimation of many parameters through expert guesses or transfer values. Other models, often named structural models, imply fewer parameters. They have not the aim of explaining all variables but concentrate on some variables; their parameters are estimated through sound and rigorous econometric methods.

How to use them, and which type should be chosen? There is no general model able to answer all questions; the choice between the various possibilities depends on the specificities of the situation, the time and budget available. Depending on their level of disaggregation, LUTI or SGEM models are useful for a breakdown of the consequences of an isolated project, but they are justified only for large projects and when the cost and time of implementation is affordable. They are more justified for sets of projects, master plans or programs. However, due to the number of parameters they take into account, their results are subject to errors, possible manipulations and black box effects. Structural models do not suffer from the black box effect and can thus provide insights on stylized facts in a more robust way.

NOTES

1. This is a necessary condition for the partial analysis on a single impacted market to represent the surplus that will benefit the whole economy, and will transmit with no distortion to the rest of the economy. This useful property (Lesourne 1964, and Jara-Diaz 1986) enables the calculation of the economic surplus from the initially impacted market, without having knowledge of how the surplus will share out, and without having to follow the complex path of the transformations in which the impact will result.
2. In CGEurope, for example, there are several modes, whose costs are constant (and not dependent on the traffic), and the choice between them is represented by a Logit model; so the outcome boils down to a unique mode whose cost is the logsum of the costs of the elementary modes.
3. This might change with the rise of Big Data and the development of computers' capacity.

REFERENCES AND RECOMMENDATIONS FOR FURTHER READING

Ahlfeldt, G.M., S.J. Redding, D.M. Sturm, D.M. and N. Wolf (2015), "The economics of density: Evidence from the Berlin Wall," *Econometrica*, **83**, 2127–89.

Anas, A and H. Chang (2017), "How and how much do public transport megaprojects induce urban agglomeration? The case of the Grand Paris project," Communication to the ITEA conference, Barcelona, June.

Anas, A. and Y. Liu (2007), "A regional economy, land use, and transportation model (RELU-TRAN)," *Journal of Regional Science*, **47**(3), 415–55.

Anderson, J.E., and E. Van Wincoop (2004), "Trade costs" (No. w10480). National Bureau of Economic Research.

Bosker, M., S. Brakman, H. Garretsenand and M. Schramm (2010), "Adding geography to the new economic geography: Bridging the gap between theory and empiric," *Journal of Economic Geography*, **10**(6), 1–31

Bröcker, J. (2002), "Spatial effects of European transport policy: A CGE approach," in G. Hewings, M. Sonis and D. Boyce (eds) *Trade, Networks and Hierarchies*, Berlin: Springer-Link.

Bröcker, J., R. Meyer, N. Schneekloth, K. Spiekermann and M. Wegener (2004), "Modeling the socio-economic and spatial impacts of EU transport policy," IASON Deliverable 6, Funded by the 5th Framework RTD Programme. Kiel/Dortmund: Christian-Albrechts-Universität Kiel/Institut für Raumplanung, Universität Dortmund.

Bröcker, J. and J. Mercenier (2011), "General equilibrium models for transportation economics," in A. de Palma, R. Lindsey, E. Quinet and R. Vickerman (eds) *A Handbook of Transport Economics*, Cheltenham, UK and Northampton, MA, USA: Edward Elgar Publishing.

Forslid, R., J.I. Haaland and K.H.M. Knarvik (2002), "A U-shaped Europe?: A simulation study of industrial location," *Journal of International Economics*, **57**(2), 273–97.

Jara-Diaz, S.R. (1986), "On the relation between users benefits and the economic effects of transportation activities," *Journal of Regional Science*, **26**(2), 379–91.

Lesourne, J. (1964), *Le Calcul Economique*, Paris: Dunod.

Martínez, F. and C. Araya (2000), "Transport and land-use benefits under location externalities," *Environment and Planning A*, **32**, 1611–24.

Martínez, F. and P. Donoso (2004), "MUSSA: A behavioural land use equilibrium model with location externalities, planning regulations and pricing policies." Working paper available at http://www.cec.uchile.cl/~dicidet/fmartinez/Mussa. PDF, accessed January 2, 2017. University of Chile.

Mayeres, I. and S. Proost (1997), "Optimal tax and public investment rules for congestion type of externalities," *The Scandinavian Journal of Economics*, **99**(2), 261–79.

Puga, D. (1999), "The rise and fall of regional inequalities," *European Economic Review*, **43**(2), 303–34.

Quinet, E. and A. Raj (2017), "Assessing the impact of connectivity," Working Paper P147759, The World Bank.

Redding, S. and A.J. Venables (2004), "Economic geography and international inequality," *Journal of International Economics*, **62**(1), 53–82.

Simmonds, D.C. (1999), "The design of the DELTA land-use modelling package," *Environment and Planning B: Planning and Design*, **26**(5), 665–84.

Simmonds, D. and O. Feldman (2005), "Land-use modelling with DELTA: Update and experience." Proceedings of the Ninth International Conference on Computers in Urban Planning and Urban Management (CUPUM). Available at http://www.dav idsimmonds.com/files/resourcesmodule/@random4767836fd9d18/1200086520_cu pum_paper_354.pdf, accessed January 2, 2017.

Tavasszy, L.A., M.J. Thissen and J. Oosterhaven (2011), "Challenges in the application of spatial computable general equilibrium models for transport appraisal," *Research in Transportation Economics*, **31**(1), 12–18.

Vickerman, R. (2007), "Cost—benefit analysis and large-scale infrastructure projects: State of the art and challenges," *Environment and Planning B: Planning and Design*, **34**(4), 598–610.

Waddell, P. (2002), "UrbanSim: Modeling urban development for land use, transportation and environmental planning," *Journal of the American Planning Association*, **68**(3), 297–314.

Wegener, M. (2011), "Transport in spatial models of economic development," in A. de Palma, R. Lindsey, E. Quinet and R. Vickerman (eds) *A Handbook of Transport Economics*, Cheltenham, UK and Northampton, MA, USA: Edward Elgar Publishing.

15. Evaluating knowledge projects and R&D infrastructures with an example

Massimo Florio and Chiara Pancotti

ABSTRACT

What is the benefit for society of capital-intensive investment in research and development (R&D) infrastructure? This chapter concisely presents a model for applying benefit-cost analysis (BCA) to such projects and shows its application through a quantitative case study. The content of this chapter relies on the experience gathered by the team of the University of Milan and the Centre for Industrial Studies (CSIL) in a research project on how to apply *ex ante* BCA for major R&D infrastructures as well as years of teaching activities for an international audience of young professionals and early career researchers. The objective is to illustrate both theoretical and empirical approaches to address the evaluation of R&D infrastructural projects which are an essential driver of scientific progress and economic growth.

INTRODUCTION

What is the benefit for society of investment in research and development infrastructures (RDI)? The ultimate goal of such projects is to provide new knowledge, but how can we measure their welfare effects to different social groups? This chapter is based on research activities performed by a team from the University of Milan (Italy) and the Centre for Industrial Studies (CSIL) on how to apply *ex ante* BCA for major R&D infrastructures as well as years of teaching experience in the University of Milan for an international audience of young professionals and early career research-ers (PhD students and post-docs) with a variety of backgrounds (public administration, economics, science). The R&D infrastructures we are discussing here include facilities such as genomics platforms, astronomic observatories, nanoelectronics laboratories, oceanographic vessels and particle accelerator facilities, and not facilities for data collection and storage, like databases, archives, libraries and computer grids. An extended although hypothetical example of a new research institute is included in this chapter.

The evaluation of RDI is usually given by stakeholders in such projects in the form of qualitative case studies or of lists of widely different indicators, such as jobs created, publications or number of firms involved. In practice, the appraisal and selection of RDI traditionally rest on science's own internal quality control mechanisms. Usually, these involve a peer review process that assesses the project merit in scientific terms, sometimes complemented by a 'business case' (Pancotti et al., 2014). Notwithstanding such an approach is usually informative, it is not suitable for systematically comparing both intertemporal costs and benefits on a unique accounting basis, thereby assessing the net welfare change attributable to a project.

Is BCA able to provide an answer to the same question? In principle, the answer may be affirmative, as BCA systematically compares both intertemporal costs and benefits on a unique accounting basis, thereby assessing the net welfare change attributable to a project. However, two issues have traditionally slowed down the use of BCA in the R&D sector, namely:

- *The uncertainty associated with the outcomes of R&D activity.* In fact, the nature of knowledge creation is such that *ex ante* the results of a discovery can be estimated only in probabilistic terms and only to some extent (De Roeck, 2016). Also, the effects of a discovery may appear in the very distant future, long after the discovery itself or even the decommissioning of the infrastructure.
- *The intangible nature associated to the outcomes of R&D activity.* The main intangible output produced by basic research projects is pure knowledge, whose value is, by its own nature, unmeasurable, before economic applications have been identified. However, even when knowledge does not find some use sooner or later, this does not mean that it does not have an intrinsic value in itself. People may have social preferences for knowledge per se (Catalano et al., 2016).

A BCA MODEL FOR R&D PROJECTS

R&D facilities share some features of any infrastructure. As such, the general BCA fundamentals should be exploited and adapted as best as possible. In this perspective, the framework model for applying BCA to R&D facilities uses: (1) shadow prices to capture social benefits beyond the market or financial value; (2) a counterfactual scenario to ensure that all costs and benefits are estimated in incremental terms relative to a 'without project' world (that is, if the project is not built, what would happen?); (3) discounting to convert any future value in their present value equivalent. At the same time, a BCA framework to assess R&D facilities contains some novelties addressing specific challenges posed by the typical outputs of R&D projects – for example, their intangible nature[1] and their uncertainty.[2] These major novelties include:

1. The stochastic nature of the BCA model. This means that whenever possible all the critical variables affecting a project are associated to probability distributions instead of deterministic values. A Monte Carlo simulation (see Chapter 19) is then used to approximate the probability distribution functions of the performance indicators – usually the Economic Net Present Value (ENPV) – and their main parameters. Through this process, the measurable uncertainty associated to a project is embedded into the model, while what is intrinsically non-measurable is deliberately left aside. What does it mean? Simply, it means taking into account the effects (that is, discoveries and innovations) that can be estimated when the funding decision is made. What cannot be estimated *ex ante* (that is, unpredictable effects such as a new set of services and possible uses of the infrastructure that arise during its life cycle) we assume to have a non-negative effect and it is omitted from the quantitative analysis. Actually, forecasting the probability of occurrence and magnitude of such unpredictable effects is usually impossible.
2. The identification of the core types of beneficiaries in terms of the standard economic agents – firms, consumers, employees, taxpayers – and the presentation of the possible benefits associated with R&D projects in this perspective. R&D infrastructure projects have in fact the mostly unique peculiarity that some producers of services are also their beneficiaries. This is the case of scientists: they produce knowledge, but are also users of such knowledge. This coincidence may generate confusion over the agents and determinants of supply and demand, thereby leading to what we identify as errors in the valuation of benefits, such as including the scientists' employment and salary among the project benefits (see Chapter 10 on employment).
3. The breakdown of benefits into two broad classes. On one hand, there are 'use benefits', accruing to different categories of direct and indirect users of the infrastructure services, such as scientists, students starting their career within the facility, firms benefitting from technological spillovers, consumers benefitting from innovative services and products and general public visitors of the facility or those enjoying outreach activi-

ties. On the other hand, there are 'non-use benefits', denoting the social value for the discovery potential of the R&D infrastructure regardless of its actual or future use. In other words, the BCA model takes the form of a simple yet comprehensive equation (Florio and Sirtori, 2016):

$$\mathbb{E}(ENPV_{RDI}) = \mathbb{E}(EPV_{B_u}) + \mathbb{E}(EPV_{B_n}) - \mathbb{E}(EPV_{C_u}) \qquad (15.1)$$

In this frame, the BCA consists of forecasting, in incremental terms, the expected ($\mathbb{E}$) economic (E) net present value (NPV) of the R&D infrastructure projects ($\mathbb{E}(ENPV_{RDI})$). This is defined as the sum of the expected present value of economic benefits associated with any actual or predictable practical use of the infrastructure services ($\mathbb{E}(ENPV_{B_u})$) and the additional expected value of discovery (new knowledge) for which a possible use is not yet identified ($\mathbb{E}(ENPV_{B_n})$) but for which a social value can be empirically estimated (non-use value), minus the expected present value of the costs ($\mathbb{E}(EPV_{C_u})$).

TYPICAL BENEFITS

An overview of typical benefits which can be attached to different groups of beneficiaries of an R&D infrastructure project is provided in the following figure (15.1) together with the suggested estimation methods. In the rest of the chapter we will focus on some of the effects listed in Figure 15.1 which are considered the most widespread among R&D projects, but case by case adaptation will be needed in practice. Further detail may be found in CSIL (2016).

THE CASE STUDY

To teach practitioners how to apply the aforementioned framework it may be helpful to recur to a quantitative case study approach. Consider a project that concerns the construction and operation of a National Institute for promoting applied research and commercialisation of a new disruptive technology (labelled β). The Institute will include a large research lab and two 'cleanrooms', where experiments can be carried out without contamination.

Project Objectives

The objectives of the hypothetical National Institute are:

- To increase the number of people researching the new technology related topics and, in turn, the production of scientific articles and patents.

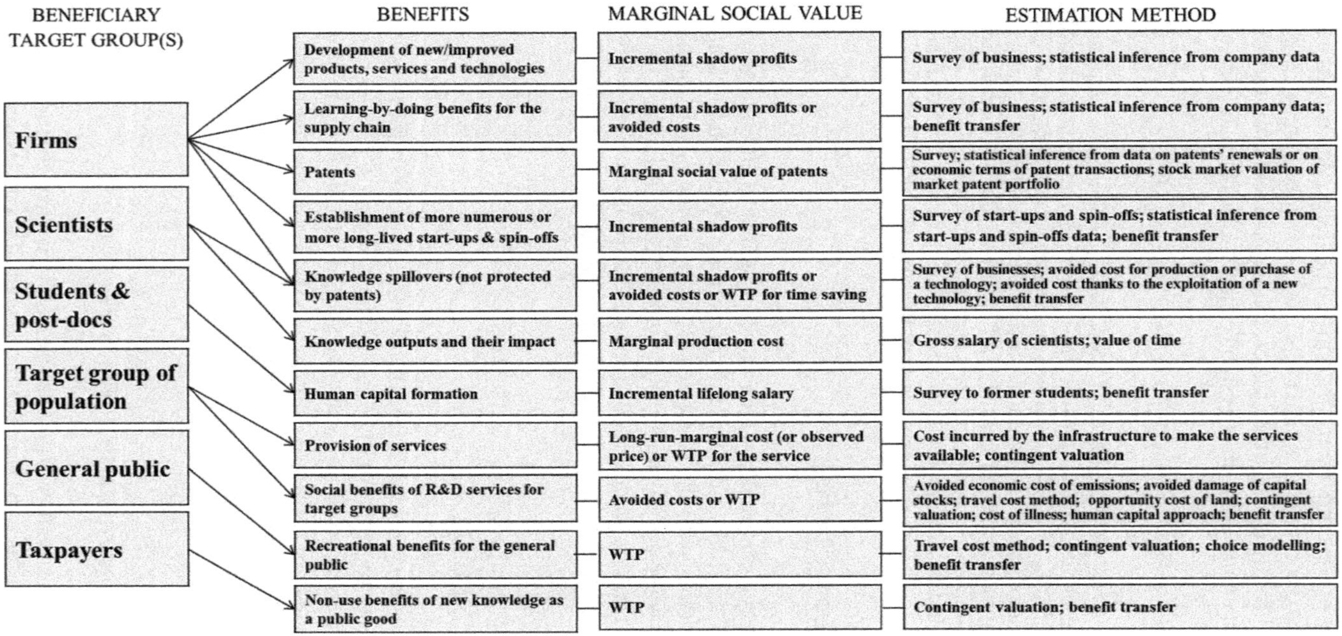

BENEFICIARY TARGET GROUP(S)	BENEFITS	MARGINAL SOCIAL VALUE	ESTIMATION METHOD
Firms	Development of new/improved products, services and technologies	Incremental shadow profits	Survey of business; statistical inference from company data
	Learning-by-doing benefits for the supply chain	Incremental shadow profits or avoided costs	Survey of business, statistical inference from company data; benefit transfer
	Patents	Marginal social value of patents	Survey; statistical inference from data on patents' renewals or on economic terms of patent transactions; stock market valuation of market patent portfolio
Scientists	Establishment of more numerous or more long-lived start-ups & spin-offs	Incremental shadow profits	Survey of start-ups and spin-offs; statistical inference from start-ups and spin-offs data; benefit transfer
	Knowledge spillovers (not protected by patents)	Incremental shadow profits or avoided costs or WTP for time saving	Survey of businesses; avoided cost for production or purchase of a technology; avoided cost thanks to the exploitation of a new technology; benefit transfer
	Knowledge outputs and their impact	Marginal production cost	Gross salary of scientists; value of time
Students & post-docs	Human capital formation	Incremental lifelong salary	Survey to former students; benefit transfer
Target group of population	Provision of services	Long-run-marginal cost (or observed price) or WTP for the service	Cost incurred by the infrastructure to make the services available; contingent valuation
General public	Social benefits of R&D services for target groups	Avoided costs or WTP	Avoided economic cost of emissions; avoided damage of capital stocks; travel cost method; opportunity cost of land; contingent valuation; cost of illness; human capital approach; benefit transfer
	Recreational benefits for the general public	WTP	Travel cost method; contingent valuation; choice modelling; benefit transfer
Taxpayers	Non-use benefits of new knowledge as a public good	WTP	Contingent valuation; benefit transfer

Source: Adapted from CSIL (2016).

Figure 15.1 Classification of potential beneficiaries and typical benefits associated with R&D infrastructure projects

- To offer a dynamic research environment to a number of PhD students.
- To increase collaboration between universities and industry partners and, in turn, the commercialisation of the new technology.
- To create some spin-offs.

Project Time Horizon

Let us assume that the time horizon of the project is 15 years including three years of construction and 12 years for the operating phase, which will allow sufficient time for research, testing and developing of new technology related products. After such horizon, the project is assumed to have no value given the pace of innovation in the field.

Project Costs

The investment cost is EUR 45 million. Initial funding is exclusively in the form of two grants to an agency in charge of the RDI: EUR 25 million from the national (state or regional) government and EUR 20 million from a supranational organisation (or a federal government). The Institute will operate as a 'hub and spoke' model, working with other research institutions involved in the same technology and individual research projects are planned to be funded by a number of organisations. The operating costs (salaries, space costs, collaborative industrial research, conferences and seminars, sponsored activities and so on) amount to EUR 9 million from the first year of operation until the end of the time horizon. See Table 15.1 summing up the costs of the project considered at their accounting prices, for example, financial flows have been corrected with suitable conversion factors.

Employment Effect

The implementation of the project will allow for the creation of about 100 jobs (including 80 scientific jobs) for the entire operational phase. Moreover, nearly 500 external scientists will be able to use the new infrastructure each year, and in three years of the completion of the investment it will be also used by PhD students.

Project Revenues

The revenues of the project (that is, cash inflows directly paid by project users) are:

Table 15.1 Illustrative table for the calculation of the economic performance (EUR, million)

Year	1	2	3	4	5	6	7	8	9	10	11	12	13	14	15
Design	3.00														
Construction	5.50	17.00	5.50												
Equipment		4.50	5.50												
Residual value									2.50						−2.80
Total investment costs	8.50	21.50	11.00	0.00	0.00	0.00	0.00	0.00	2.50	0.00	0.00	0.00	0.00	0.00	−2.80
Administrative personnel				0.40	0.40	0.40	0.40	0.40	0.40	0.40	0.40	0.40	0.40	0.40	0.40
Scientific personnel				3.36	3.36	3.36	3.36	3.36	3.36	3.36	3.36	3.36	3.36	3.36	3.36
Maintenance				0.39	0.39	0.39	0.39	0.39	0.39	0.39	0.39	0.39	0.39	0.39	0.39
Conference & seminars				0.15	0.15	0.15	0.15	0.15	0.15	0.15	0.15	0.15	0.15	0.15	0.15
Energy				0.75	0.75	0.75	0.75	0.75	0.75	0.75	0.75	0.75	0.75	0.75	0.75
Consumable materials				0.65	0.65	0.65	0.65	0.65	0.65	0.65	0.65	0.65	0.65	0.65	0.65
Services				0.35	0.35	0.35	0.35	0.35	0.35	0.35	0.35	0.35	0.35	0.35	0.35
Total operating costs	0.00	0.00	0.00	6.05	6.05	6.05	6.05	6.05	6.05	6.05	6.05	6.05	6.05	6.05	6.05
Commercialisation of new/improved products	0.00	0.00	0.00	0.00	0.00	12.00	12.00	12.00	12.00	12.00	12.00	12.00	12.00	12.00	12.00
Social value of patents	0.00	0.00	0.00	0.00	0.00	1.50	1.50	1.50	1.50	1.50	1.50	1.50	1.50	1.50	1.50
Production of knowledge in the form of publications	0.00	0.00	0.00	3.36	3.36	3.36	3.36	3.36	3.36	3.36	3.36	3.36	3.36	3.36	3.36
Human capital formation	0.00	0.00	0.00	0.00	0.00	0.06	0.10	0.14	0.18	0.22	0.27	0.32	0.37	0.42	14.18
Establishment of spin-offs	0.00	0.00	0.00	0.00	0.00	0.00	0.00	0.00	0.50	0.50	0.85	0.85	1.20	1.20	12.92
Total social benefits	0.00	0.00	0.00	3.36	3.36	16.92	16.96	17.00	17.54	17.58	17.98	18.03	18.43	18.48	43.96

Licensed revenues gained from patent commercialisation	Entry fees charged to external researchers and enterprises	PhD fees	Revenues from industrial research contract	Total operating revenues	Net cash flow
0.00 (*)	0.00	0.00	0.00	0.00	−8.50
0.00 (*)	0.00	0.00	0.00	0.00	−21.50
0.00 (*)	0.00	0.00	0.00	0.75	−11.00
0.00 (*)	0.40	0.03	0.35	0.75	−1.94
0.00 (*)	0.40	0.03	0.35	0.78	−1.94
0.00 (*)	0.40	0.03	0.35	0.78	11.65
0.00 (*)	0.40	0.03	0.35	0.78	11.69
0.00 (*)	0.40	0.03	0.35	0.78	11.73
0.00 (*)	0.40	0.03	0.35	0.78	9.77
0.00 (*)	0.40	0.03	0.35	0.78	12.31
0.00 (*)	0.40	0.03	0.35	0.78	12.71
0.00 (*)	0.40	0.03	0.35	0.78	12.76
0.00 (*)	0.40	0.03	0.35	0.78	13.16
0.00 (*)	0.40	0.03	0.35	0.78	13.21
0.00 (*)	0.40	0.03	0.35	0.78	41.49

Note: (*) Licensed revenues gained from patents commercialisation are not included for avoiding double counting with the benefit 'social value of patents' which reflects both the private return and the knowledge spillovers brought about by patents.

- Licensed revenues gained from patent commercialisation.
- Entry fees to the laboratory and to use research equipment charged to external researchers and enterprises.
- PhD fees.
- Revenues from industrial research contract and pre-commercial procurement contracts.

Grants awarded by national organisations and public agencies are not included among operating revenues but among financing sources since they are simply transfers from state budget rather than payment against a service directly rendered by the project promoter (European Commission, 2014 and CSIL, 2016). See Table 15.1 summing up the revenues of the project considered at their accounting prices, that is, financial flows have been corrected with suitable conversion factors.

Project Benefits

The project is associated with the following main benefits:

- Development and commercialisation of new/improved products.
- Social value of patents.
- Production of knowledge outputs in the form of publications.
- Social value of human capital formation.
- Spin-off creation.

The estimation of these benefits is discussed in what follows. In particular, for each benefit a brief introduction to the theoretical background underpinning the empirical estimation is first presented and then the illustrative calculations are provided.

Development and Commercialisation of New/Improved Products

When a project entails the development of innovative products the social value of these goods is expressed using the *incremental shadow profits* expected from their sale. In particular: 'incremental' means that profits expected from the sale of new/improved products generated by the project must be compared with the profits in the without-the-project scenario; and, 'shadow' means that market distortions should be duly considered; for instance, the shadow profit is higher than the gross financial profit if the infrastructure is located in an area of high unemployment and hires local unskilled personnel.

Given that i is the number of innovations (for example, new products) over time t, $\mathbb{E}(\Pi_{it})$ represents the expected incremental profits directly imputable to these innovations and s_t represents the discount factor. Then, the expected present value of developing new/improved products, services and technologies (Z) is expressed as (CSIL, 2016):

$$\mathbb{E}(Z) = \sum_{i=1}^{I} \sum_{t=0}^{T} s_t \cdot \mathbb{E}(\Pi_{it}). \tag{15.2}$$

In the case under consideration, it is expected (hypothetically, on expert judgement) that annually six enterprises will benefit from the use of testing and prototyping shared laboratories of the National Institute. These activities will eventually lead to the development of new marketable products. Data necessary for calculating the annual incremental shadow profit of each company directly imputable to the commercialisation of new developed products are:

- The yearly average amount of revenues per company is zero for the first two years and then real EUR 4 million.
- The yearly salaries for unskilled workers amount to EUR 0.4 million, while those for skilled workers amount to EUR 0.5 million.
- The conversion factor for unskilled labour is estimated at 0.8 due to unemployment in the region, while that for skilled labour is estimated equal to 1.
- The yearly average production cost (excluding labor) is EUR 1.2 million.
- The conversion factor for production costs is assumed equal to 1.

The baseline annual incremental shadow profit per each company since year three is then:

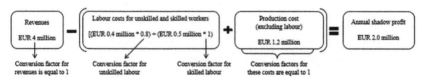

Figure 15.2   Baseline annual incremental shadow profit for each company

Social Value of Patents

When a patent is registered, it produces a private return to the inventor and potential knowledge spillover to society. Patent citations reveal 'prior art' that an inventor has learned and make them potential measures of the knowledge spillovers from past inventions to the current invention. Both the private returns and the knowledge spillovers brought about by patents granted by an R&D infrastructure represent a benefit that should be considered. Hence, the *marginal social value of the patent generated by an R&D infrastructure* should be forecasted.[3] Given *i* as the number of patents over time t, $MSV_{(pvit,exit)}$ as the patent marginal social value, and s_t as the discount factor, the expected present value of this benefit is expressed as (CSIL, 2016):

$$\mathbb{E}(P) = \sum_{i=1}^{I} \sum_{t=0}^{T} s_t \cdot \mathbb{E}(MSV_{(pvit,exit)}), \qquad (15.3)$$

where the marginal social value (*MSV*) includes both the private value (pv_{it}) and the externality (ex_{it}), that is, the knowledge spillover brought about by patents granted by an R&D infrastructure.

Let us assume that the National Institute is envisaged to produce on average two patents per year from the third year of operation onwards. This might be based on the past track record of similar infrastructures. According to data retrieved from a meta-analysis carried out by the academics of the two universities based in the same country as the National Institute, the median market value of patents in the field as the β technology is EUR 300,000. Moreover, according to statistics on patent citations retrieved from databases maintained by similar facilities, the median number of backward and forward citations in the field is respectively ten and 15. Assuming that the externalities are linear in the number of citations, the new patent benefits from ten previous discoveries, and will benefit 15 future ones. Hence, the yearly social value of patents would be EUR 1.5 million, as follows:

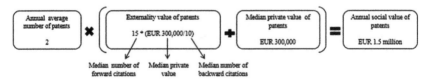

Figure 15.3   Yearly social value of patents

Production of Knowledge in the Form of Publications

For scientists and researchers one of the main benefits to working at an R&D infrastructure is the opportunity to access and process new experimental data, to contribute to the creation of new knowledge, and – ultimately – to produce scientific output that may take the form of articles in scientific journals. The social benefit related to the production of scientific publications can be valued using their *marginal production cost*, that is, the time spent by scientists to conduct research and produce knowledge outputs valued at appropriate shadow wages. However, not all scientific output has the same value for the relevant scientific community. For this reason, weighing the influence of a paper by multiplying the value of the scientific publications *by a multiplier of impact* is advisable to capture the additional value attributable to citations that the outputs receive. It is important to stress that the value of the publication is not the same as the knowledge embodied in it, which can be much higher or much lower. One can think of an article as the output of a publishing business, whatever its content (which can be very 'good' or very 'bad' in a broader perspective).

Given $\mathbb{E}(Y_t)$ as the expected social cost of producing knowledge outputs (shadow cost of production) at time t, s_t as the discount factor and $\mathbb{E}(m)$ as the expected multiplier of impact, the expected present value of this benefit is expressed as (CSIL, 2016):

$$\mathbb{E}(O) = \sum_{t=0}^{T} (s_t \cdot \mathbb{E}(Y_t) \cdot \mathbb{E}(m)). \tag{15.4}$$

As already mentioned, on average 80 scientists will be annually employed in the National Institute. Given the field and the track record of existing similar infrastructures in other countries:

- the expected average yearly productivity of scientists within the infrastructure is three articles;
- the average time devoted to research is 80 per cent (the remaining time is devoted to administrative and other tasks);
- the average gross yearly salary of scientists using the infrastructure is EUR 42,000;
- the median number of citations of scientists expected to work in the infrastructure is ten;
- the average number of references in the scientific field is 40 per paper;
- the time needed to evaluate someone else's paper and decide to cite it is one hour.

As a result, the total discounted social value of publications is:

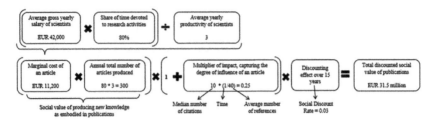

Figure 15.4　Total discounted social value of publications

Social Value of Human Capital Formation

For PhD students, postdoctoral researchers and visiting young scientists who enjoy the possibility of spending time working within a major R&D infrastructure, the main expected benefit is a 'premium' on their future salaries. This premium stems from the acquisition of human capital, that is, new capacity and skills, and can be proxied by the incremental lifelong salary earned by students and young scientists over their entire careers compared with the without-the-project scenario. See Camporesi et al., 2017 for an empirical example.

The expected present value of human capital accumulation benefits, $\mathbb{E}(H)$, can be defined as the sum of the expected increasing earnings, $\mathbb{E}(E_{it})$, gained by PhD students and young scientists indexed by i, from the moment (at time φ) they leave the R&D infrastructure and they enter different labor markets (CSIL, 2016). In formula:

$$\mathbb{E}(H) = \sum_{i=1}^{I} \sum_{t=\varphi}^{T} s_t \cdot \mathbb{E}(E_{it}). \tag{15.5}$$

As already mentioned, in three years from the completion of the investment the National Institute is expected to host PhD students. In particular, every year 20 students will be hosted for a training period of two years. After their training period, students are expected to immediately enter the labour markets. In particular, they are supposed to enter three possible professional sectors with the following probabilities:

- 30 per cent for academia;
- 30 per cent for other research centres in the same technology field;
- 40 per cent in industries working within the same technology field.

The salary curve associated with the three possible future professional careers of 40 years are presented in Figure 15.5.

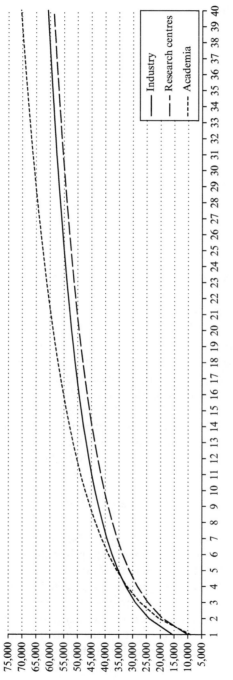

Figure 15.5   Salary curve for three possible professional careers

Based on statistical information, a salary premium of 3 per cent over the total future salary is expected for PhD students having spent a training period at the National Institute as compared to their peers who have not enjoyed the same experience. Accordingly, the expected total discounted human capital benefit, estimated as the present value of the total annual gross incremental salary gained by all students trained during the project time horizon over their entire work career, is EUR 11 million. The following formula applies:

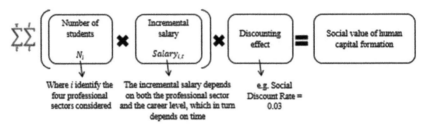

Figure 15.6   Expected total discounted human capital benefit

Establishment of Spin-offs

When an R&D infrastructure is expected to contribute to the establishment of start-ups and spin-offs, the economic value of this benefit is valued as the *expected shadow profit* gained by the created business during its overall expected lifetime compared with the without-the-project scenario.

Given that i is the number of spin-offs established over time t, $\mathbb{E}(\Pi_{it})$ represents the expected incremental profits directly imputable to the project and s_t represents the discount factor. Then, the expected present value of establishing a spin-off (F) is expressed as (CSIL, 2016):

$$\mathbb{E}(F) = \sum_{i=1}^{I} \sum_{t=0}^{T} s_t \cdot \mathbb{E}(\Pi_{it}). \tag{15.6}$$

According to the initial feasibility study, the National Institute is expected to support the creation of five new enterprises during the entire time horizon. In particular, the first spin-off is expected in the sixth year of the time horizon and then a new enterprise is expected every two years. The following assumptions hold: (1) the average survival rate of each spin-off is 70 per cent after five years, 40 per cent after ten years, 10 per cent after 15 years and 0 per cent after 20 years in both the with- and without-the-project scenarios; (2) the average shadow profit of the new enterprises for the first three years will be zero; it then increases to EUR 0.5 million per year.

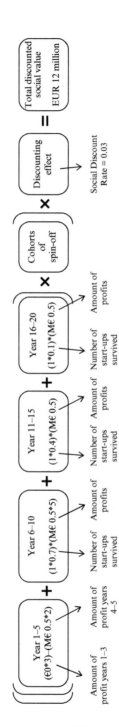

Figure 15.7   *Total discounted social benefit of spin-offs established*

195

In a deterministic or baseline model, the total discounted social benefit (Figure 15.7) is the sum of the shadow profits gained by all the enterprises created thanks to the project during the firm's overall expected lifetime provided that the survival rate is as given in the above assumptions.

Bottom Line: The Socioeconomic Performance of the Project

Once the economic inflows and outflows associated with the infrastructure have been identified and their baseline values (that is, most likely values) have been valued in monetary terms, the investment's economic perform- ance can be calculated using the standard indicators, that is, the ENPV,[4] the economic internal rate of return (ERR)[5] and the benefit/cost ratio.[6] In the case under examination the estimated performance indicators are:

- ENPV = EUR 68 million (estimated at a social discount rate = 3 per cent, currently adopted by the European Commission, 2014);
- ERR = 15 per cent;
- B/C ratio = 1.7.

However, given the *ex ante* uncertainty of forecasting future effects the last step of the analysis must comprise a fully-fledged quantitative risk assessment, meaning that costs and benefits become part of a probabilistic model. In other words, it requires assigning each critical variable a specific probability distribution instead of considering a set of 'most likely' values. For instance, in the case under examination, among others, the following critical variables can be considered:

- The number and the value of patents. As an example, the yearly number of new patents can have a discrete probability distribution taking the value of 1, 2 or 3, while the value of a patent can have a normal distribution with mean of EUR 300,000 and standard devia- tion of EUR 100,000.
- The ratio between cited and citing patents. As an example, a trian- gular distribution (minimum value = 0.5; modal value = 1.5 and maximum value = 2.5) can be assumed.
- The annual incremental shadow profit of firms developing new products. For instance, a rectangular distribution can be hypoth- esised taking any value between EUR 1.5 million and EUR 2.5 million per year with a mode of EUR 2 million.

Using a Monte Carlo simulation technique (Florio, 2014; and Chapter 10 of this book) these probabilities distributions can be combined to calculate the probability distribution functions of the ENPV and the ERR and their cumulative distribution functions.

CONCLUDING REMARKS

The illustrative case study, while based on the simple model presented above, relies on a number of assumptions, which should be critically considered by the practitioner. For example, only expert assessment and comparisons with the past experience can suggest how realistic are the forecasts on the number of patents, PhD students attracted, number of publications and their impact, number and value of the spin-offs and so on. The approach rests on treating the uncertainty with a Monte Carlo approach that requires that experts provide the (often subjective) probability distributions attached to different possible outcomes.

One way to think to the implementation of the above mentioned risk analysis is to structure a questionnaire based on such assumptions, to select a group of respondents and to check their agreement on the probabilities attached to the different possible outcomes. This may lead to the elicitation of areas of (strong) disagreement. At that stage, the evaluator can recur to a more sophisticated forecasting method, a well known precursor of which is the Delphi approach (developed around the 1950s in the RAND Project (see, for example, Helmer, 1963 and 1967 and Sackman, 1974)), where typically the survey is in two or more rounds: the first one to discover disagreement and the second and subsequent ones to try to reach consensus (or to form a more precise elicitation of a majority/minority opinion). More recent advances in information and communication technology suggest to design the Delphi exercise as a web conference (see, for example, National Research Council, 2010) which in some cases may involve more than 100 experts.

The combination of benefit-cost analysis and science and technological forecasting in the Delphi tradition and its recent online advances can then be implemented as a systematic revision of the probability distributions for the computation of the project performance. In such a way, the Monte Carlo exercise would be based on the informed weighing of alternative scenarios by the evaluator. In a teaching room, this can be simulated by asking the participants to reconsider their case study assumptions after having surveyed online a small group of virtual experts (with preset divergent answers to some questions).

NOTES

1. For instance, the output of basic research typically is in the form of new ideas or pure knowledge, which are something intangible and have no immediate monetary value.
2. Actually, R&D activities involve the generation of new knowledge, and the probability of success depends on many factors, not all of which are under the direct control of the R&D project's promoter.
3. Caution must be used in order to avoid double counting with the previous benefit (that is, change in the expected profit from the sale of innovative products).
4. It is defined as the difference between the discounted total benefits and the discounted total costs.
5. It is the specific social discount rate that produces an ENPV equal to zero.
6. It is the ratio between the discounted total benefits and the discounted total costs.

REFERENCES AND RECOMMENDATIONS FOR FURTHER READING

Camporesi, T. (2001), 'High-energy physics as a career springboard', *European Journal of Physics* **22**, 139–48.
Camporesi, T., G. Catalano, M. Florio and F. Giffoni (2017), 'Experiential learning in high energy physics: a survey of students at the LHC', *European Journal of Physics* **38**(2).
Carrazza, S., a. Ferrara and S. Salini (2016), 'Research infrastructures in the LHC era: a scientometric approach', *Technological Forecasting and Social Change* **112**, 121–33.
Catalano, G., M. Florio and F. Giffoni (2016), 'Willingness to pay for basic research: a contingent valuation experiment on the large hadron collider', paper produced in the frame of the research project 'Cost/Benefit Analysis in the Research, Development and Innovation Sector' sponsored by the EIB University Research Sponsorship programme (EIBURS). Available at: https://arxiv.org/abs/1603.03580, accessed 5 January 2018.
CSIL (2016), 'Exploring cost-benefit analysis of research, development and innovation infrastructures: an evaluation framework', paper presented at the EIBURS-UNIMI Workshop hosted by DG Research – European Commission Brussels, November 13, 2015. Available at: https://ideas.repec.org/p/mst/wpaper/201601.html, accessed 5 January 2018.
De Roeck, A. (2016), 'The probability of discovery', *Technological Forecasting and Social Change* **112**, 13–19.
Del Bo, C.F. (2016), 'The rate of return to investment in R&D: The case of research infrastructures', *Technological Forecasting and Social Change* **112**, 26–37.
European Commission (2014), *Guide to Cost-benefit Analysis of Investment Projects. Economic Appraisal Tool for Cohesion Policy 2014-2020*, Directorate-General for Regional and Urban Policy, Luxembourg: Publications Office of the European Union.
Florio, M. (2014), *Applied Welfare Economics: Cost-Benefit Analysis of Projects and Policies*. London: Routledge.
Florio, M. and Sirtori, E. (2016), 'Social benefits and costs of large scale research infrastructures', *Technological Forecasting and Social Change* **112**, 65–78.

Florio, M., S. Forte and E. Sirtori (2016), 'Forecasting the socio-economic impact of the large Hadron Collider: a cost-benefit analysis to 2025 and beyond', *Technological Forecasting and Social Change* **112**, 38–53.

Helmer, O. (1963), 'The systematic use of expert judgment in operations research', the RAND Corporation, Santa Monica, California, US. Available at: http://www.rand.org/pubs/papers/P2795.html, accessed 5 January 2018.

Helmer, O. (1967), 'Analysis of the future: the Delphi method', the RAND Corporation, Santa Monica, California, US. Available at: http://www.rand.org/content/dam/rand/pubs/papers/2008/P3558.pdf, accessed 5 January 2018.

Marsilio, M., G. Battistoni, M. Genco, C. Pancotti, S. Rossi and S. Vignetti (2016), 'Cost-benefit analysis of applied research infrastructure. Evidence from health care', *Technological Forecasting and Social Change* **112**, 79–91.

National Research Council (2010), *Persistent Forecasting of Disruptive Technologies— Report 2*, Washington, DC: The National Academies Press. Available at: https://www.nap.edu/read/12834/chapter/1, accessed 5 January 2018.

Pancotti, C., J. Pellegrin and S. Vignetti (2014), 'Appraisal of research infrastructures: approaches, methods and practical implications', DEMM Working Paper n. 2014–13.

Sackman, H. (1974), 'Delphi assessment: Expert opinion, forecasting, and group process', a report prepared for US Air Force Project Rand, the RAND Corporation, Santa Monica, California, US.

16. Cost estimation in education: The ingredients method

Clive Belfield, A. Brooks Bowden and Henry M. Levin

ABSTRACT

In this chapter, we describe the ingredients method as a simple but formal way to estimate costs for the purposes of benefit-cost analysis. The ingredients method distinguishes between input quantities and prices; the product of quantities and prices yields an estimate of the total social cost of an intervention, program or policy. We begin by clarifying what is meant by "cost" and why budgetary information is unlikely to be adequate for cost analysis. We then describe the ingredients method – how to identify inputs and price out these inputs so that they reflect opportunity cost. Next, we explain why the ingredients method is preferred in terms of transparency, informational content, and ease of sensitivity testing. We conclude with an exercise that illustrates how the ingredients method is applied and why it is preferred to alternative costing methods.

INTRODUCTION

We recognize that cost analysis is rarely the most exciting part of benefit-cost analysis; and even in regulatory impact assessments it is sometimes given short shrift. In this module we describe the ingredients method as a simple yet – importantly – a formal way to estimate costs. In conjunction, as well as referring to the potential pitfalls if cost analysis is performed cursorily, we emphasize that performing cost analysis with the ingredients method is fundamental to a full understanding of a social intervention and its theory of action.

In this description of the ingredients method we use examples of education interventions, although the method applies generally across social programs.

CLARIFYING COST TERMS

We start with terminology: the term "cost" is often used loosely in every-day language (and may be confused with expenditure or economic burden such as the "cost of high school failure"). We define cost as "cost per unit of delivery" (to distinguish it from the textbook definition of "cost per unit of output"). Next, we clarify what "per" refers to in a given educational context: it might be cost per student, cost per completer or cost per school, for example. This definition leads us to consider costs as "all the resources needed to *implement* a social intervention, regardless of who funds or bears the cost of that intervention". We emphasize implementation in contrast to all the economic consequences that happen after implementation. Once we have this idea of implementation in mind we can itemize all the possible resources a school, college or other educational agency might utilize.

Analysts might think that budgetary documents are sufficient to under-stand costs. They almost certainly are not; and it is useful to discuss why they are not. Budgets rarely include information on all the resources used to provide a social program. They typically omit contributed resources such as volunteers, donated equipment and services and other "unpaid" inputs. Often resources are paid for from multiple sources of funding so several budget statements would be needed. Regardless of the number of budgets, standard budget practices may distort the true costs of an ingredient (especially for public sector programs or those where some capital investments are amortized over a single year). Often, the costs of any particular intervention are embedded in a budget or expenditure state-ment covering a much larger unit of operation. Finally, most budgetary documents are plans for how resources will be allocated rather than how they actually were allocated; there is usually a difference and that difference may be relevant for modeling benefits (for example, if more counselors are hired instead of teachers, behavioral outcomes might improve relative to academic outcomes). Thus, analysts should not rely on budgetary or expenditure documents to ascertain the costs of interventions.

Instead, analysts should collect data on costs directly. Our preferred approach is to apply the ingredients method (for other methods, see Boardman et al., 2011).

WHAT IS THE INGREDIENTS METHOD?

The ingredients method conceptualizes costs as a detailed recipe of all resources used in implementing a social intervention to achieve an outcome. It involves a set of steps to yield cost estimates. First, the analyst must identify and describe the inputs used to implement the intervention. Second, these inputs should be priced out. Third, the analyst must calculate total cost and analyze costs in such a way that the cost results relate to the theory of change for the relevant intervention. These cost estimates are reported in a template spreadsheet. With this cost information, the ingredients method results can be paired with impacts to complete a benefit-cost analysis. (A full explication of the ingredients method and its long history is in Levin et al., 2017, Chapters 2–6).

IDENTIFYING INPUTS

The analyst should start by identifying and specifying all inputs or ingredients used to implement the social intervention. For consistency, ingredients can be grouped into several categories: (1) personnel; (2) training; (3) materials; (4) facilities and (5) other inputs. Often, personnel (for example, teachers, counsellors, instructional support staff and volunteers) are the biggest group of ingredients, reflecting the labor-intensive technology of education and social services. Training inputs may also be important: in order to implement a new education or social program, current personnel must change their practices or systems of operation; they must be trained in how to make such changes. One challenge is to identify the other inputs; these might include transportation or prizes.

The ingredients should be specified in sufficient detail so that their value can subsequently be ascertained. Thus, in addition to quantities, information will be needed on the qualifications of staff, characteristics of physical facilities, types of equipment and other inputs. The degree of specificity and accuracy in listing ingredients should depend upon their overall contribution to the total cost of the intervention.

After identifying ingredients, the next step is to address how they are financed across agencies (for example, school staff and district-level personnel). This part of the analysis lends itself to future replication or consideration of the feasibility of a program as an alternative. It can be critical to the success of the program to define which costs were borne by the school, local volunteers, parents and others. This portion of the analysis would also address any financial transfers that may occur through fees or subsidies.

Initially, this task can be simulated as a desk exercise but it will of course need to be verified and corrected using actual data from sites implementing the intervention. Given the variation in potential benefits from social programs, we emphasize the collection of ingredients data across many sites where an intervention is being implemented. The sites should be sampled using a sampling frame equivalent to a sampling frame needed to estimate benefits.

As an illustration, the ingredients utilized to implement the HighScope Perry Preschool Program were as follows (Nores et al., 2006). *Instructional staff:* Four teachers were employed in each year of the program; these teachers were of median experience and qualifications and were eligible for benefits and pension claims. *Administrative and support staff:* Program staff managed the special education program, including a special services director. *Facilities:* The local public school district provided the facilities, including regular classroom space. *Materials and equipment:* Equipment was purchased especially for the program to transform a school space into a preschool space; learning materials were supplied and children were provided with food services. *Other inputs:* A screening process was used to determine child eligibility for the program. The public school district provided resources, including maintenance, utilities and general administrative and non-teaching staff. Client inputs were judged negligible: no fees were charged to parents; all supplies were given to parents; families lived within walking distance of the school, so transportation services were unnecessary; parental involvement was minimal and voluntary.

PRICING OUT INPUTS

The next step is to price each of the ingredients individually. Prices can be derived separately from the input usage by drawing on databases of existing prices. There are many sources for input prices (for example, the US Bureau of Labor Statistics earnings data), market rates for facilities space and market purchase prices (such as for materials). Analysts should search these databases for prices that most accurately reflect the opportunity cost of using each input. Often, opportunity cost is best captured by market prices, but this need not always be the case (for example, if some facilities are highly regulated).

There are several advantages in applying extant prices. Using independent prices reduces the likelihood of researcher bias in the choice of prices. By drawing on lists of prices, the analyst can more readily examine how prices might vary (especially hourly wages versus salaries) and apply sensitivity tests using different prices. Also, existing databases may be useful either for hard-to-specify prices (for example, rental rates for school spaces) or for assumptions (such as the expected life of a capital asset such as a college building). Finally, relying on extant prices allows for greater comparability across interventions.

Table 16.1   Sample worksheet for total costs across stakeholders

Ingredients	Input Quantities	Input Prices	Total Cost	Net Cost per Stakeholder (Program Sponsor, Government Agency, Private Organizations, Students/Parents)
Personnel				Reported in separate
Training				column per stakeholder
Facilities				Net of user fees / cash
Materials and equipment				subsidies
Other inputs				Net cost per stakeholder
Required client inputs				should sum to Total
				Ingredients Cost
Total Ingredients Cost				

Source: Adapted Levin et al. (2017, Table 6.2).

INGREDIENTS SPREADSHEET

Inputs and their respective prices can be put together in a simple spreadsheet. See Table 16.1 for a template.

The rows of the spreadsheet are the inputs needed to deliver the program. The columns refer to who is funding each ingredient. The bottom panel of the spreadsheet shows the total ingredients cost. If there are any user fees or subsidies across agencies, these can be included to derive the net cost for the program. Given the number of participants served by the program, the average cost of the program can straightforwardly be calculated.

ADVANTAGES OF THE INGREDIENTS METHOD

Cost estimation is not easy to do: there are many errors and slips analysts can make; and sometimes it is hard to explain what is included in a cost estimate (see Harrington et al., 2000). The ingredients method, in part because of its simplicity, mitigates some of these challenges.

There are three main advantages of the ingredients method: the estimated costs are transparently derived; the results are informative; and the estimated costs can easily be subjected to sensitivity testing. These advantages become clear when the initial spreadsheet (Table 16.1) is reported.

The ingredients method is transparent. It shows what inputs are used and how intensively they are used; it also presents information on how each input is priced. This transparency is a big advantage. It clarifies what is often ignored in reporting of costs – whether cost estimates are "site-specific" or "expected". Site-specific costs are those calculated precisely for the intervention as it is delivered in a specific context based on local prices (for example, at high schools in Chicago where the program is implemented). By contrast, expected costs are those calculated using national or adjusted prices and so are applicable for all high schools across the US, for example. For expected costs, the inputs are unchanged but the prices for inputs are adapted. This distinction is important for educational and social programs because there are likely to be many sites and therefore many local variations in input availability and input prices. (This is in contrast to the cost for, say, a hydroelectric dam which will only be implemented once and on a specific river).

The ingredients method yields results that are informative. Readers can look at an ingredients spreadsheet and see very easily how an intervention is structured and implemented. For example, by itemizing inputs, the reader can see if an intervention is labor or capital intensive, if there are expensive materials used (such as for computerized learning) and if there is heavy reliance on donated resources. Next, the reader can see which of those inputs represents a high price per unit. Fundamentally, describing the inputs and their prices is equivalent to describing the intervention itself and articulating its theory of action. For example, if an intervention relies extensively on highly paid teachers, but no additional counselling personnel, we might expect benefits in terms of improved achievement but not in terms of student behavior. In addition to this descriptive function, results from the ingredients method may help guide further analysis of issues such as economies of scale, input substitutability and implementation fidelity.

Finally, the ingredients method offers a simple way to perform sensitivity testing. First, how accurately were the inputs estimated? It may be that the analyst is uncertain about the usage of some inputs, such as administrative time or facilities. Second, how accurately were the prices of inputs estimated? It may be that prices for inputs vary across sites or implementation quality. Straightforwardly in the spreadsheet format, the analyst can model what would happen if input quantities are changed and if input prices are changed. If the distribution of inputs and or prices can be determined, a distribution of cost estimates can also be calculated. Robustness checks on cost estimates are therefore formalized, either through variation of key parameters or Monte Carlo simulation.

CONCLUSION

Logically, analysts should pay just as much attention to accurate estimation of cost as to accurate estimation of benefits. Yet cost estimation is typically thought of as straightforward or easy. This is a mistake and can lead to substantial errors. The ingredients method is a simple but formal approach that divides the task into three steps. It helps the analyst systematically focus on what inputs are used, what each input costs and how they combine to become total cost. Importantly, it motivates the analyst – and readers of the analysis – to better understand the intervention as it is delivered and thence predict its benefits.

Student Exercise: There is some evidence that afterschool programs for youth can help to increase academic performance, improve behavior and enhance attachment to school (Ciocanel et al., 2017). Let us assume that the social benefits of afterschool programs are valued at $21 000. This amount is per youth who participates for three consecutive years and is expressed as a present value at the time of initial enrollment in afterschool.

You decide to open an afterschool agency that will serve 6000 youth across ten sites/centers. At each site, the maximum group size is 25, and children are in afterschool for two hours and 180 days per year. At each site, the staffing will require a principal, a part-time administrative assistant and a group leader; posted full-time salaries per annum for these positions are $60 000, $30 000 and $50 000 respectively. Full-time teachers are paid $40 000. Each facility will be 2000 square feet; rent is assumed to be the same as for commercial space. Each child receives food services paid directly by the state government of $5 per day and is provided with transport that the centers can claim reimbursement for from the federal government of $10 per day. Materials costs are estimated at $100 per child per year. Finally, parents are expected to volunteer 20 hours each year.

Create an ingredients worksheet with columns for costs to the afterschool company, government agencies and other groups. Calculate the total cost of afterschool provision and the cost per child per year. What sensitivity tests would you perform on your estimates? How would you relate these costs to the expected benefits of the afterschool program? Is this afterschool program a good investment from the social perspective?

Key Learning Outcomes

- Cost estimation requires just as much attention as impact or benefits estimation and can be as challenging to do.

- Cost estimation should be based on a formal method, such as the ingredients method.
- It is important to specify separately the inputs used and the opportunity cost of each input.
- The ingredients method has advantages with respect to transparency, informativeness and sensitivity testing.

REFERENCES AND RECOMMENDATIONS FOR FURTHER READING

Boardman, A.E., D.H. Greenberg, A.R. Vining and D.L. Weimer (2011), *Cost-Benefit Analysis: Concepts and Practice, Fourth Edition*, Upper Saddle River, New Jersey, USA: Pearson Education, Inc.

Bowden, A.B. and C.R. Belfield (2015), "Evaluating TRIO: A benefit-cost analysis and cost-effectiveness analysis of talent search," *Journal of Benefit-Cost Analysis*, **6**(3), 572–602.

Ciocanel, O., K. Power, A. Eriksen and K. Gillings (2017), "Effectiveness of positive youth development interventions: A meta-analysis of randomized controlled trials," *Journal of Youth and Adolescence*, **46**(3), 483–504.

Harrington, W., R.D. Morgenstern and P. Nelson (2000), "On the accuracy of regulatory cost estimates," *Journal of Policy Analysis and Management*, **19**(7), 297–322.

Levin, H.M., P.J. McEwan, C.R. Belfield, A. Brooks Bowden and R. Shand (2017), *Economic Evaluation of Education: Cost-Effectiveness and Benefit-Cost Analysis, Third edition*, New York, NY, USA: Russell Sage.

Nores, M., C.R. Belfield, W.S. Barnett and L. Schweinhart (2006), "Updating the economic impacts of the High/Scope Perry Preschool Program," *Educational Evaluation and Policy Analysis*, **27**(3), 245–61.

17. Distributional accounting in benefit-cost analysis

Kerry Krutilla

ABSTRACT

This chapter demonstrates how to integrate distributional effects within public evaluation and benefit-cost analysis, using the Kaldor-Hicks Tableau format for distributional accounting. This format adds policy-relevant insight to the traditional efficiency evaluation.

INTRODUCTION

Benefit-cost analysis (BCA) is conducted from the "societal perspective," and so distributional effects have to be addressed either implicitly or explicitly. This chapter describes the nuances that characterize this evaluation context, and then introduces the "Kaldor-Hicks Tableau" (KHT) format to represent distributional effects. Kaldor-Hicks Tableaus provide a conceptually consistent and transparent picture of distributional impacts at a chosen level of stakeholder representation. This format embodies the usual efficiency evaluation, and as such, can be used to integrate efficiency and distributional considerations within the benefit-cost analysis.

Key concepts in this chapter include the idea of stakeholder standing, geographic accounting perspectives, economic efficiency, the Pareto criterion, the Kaldor-Hicks standard and the Kaldor-Hicks Tableau.

THE PUBLIC EVALUATION CONTEXT

In a world where resources are scarce and demands for produced goods and services are essentially unlimited, diverting resources (such as labor, capital, materials and energy) to increase some public good like health services reduces the resources available to do other things.

Benefit-cost analysis compares the value of resources in a public good against their value in a best alternative use (their "opportunity cost"). Policymakers can use this comparison to judge whether public projects, programs or policies should be undertaken (*ex ante* analysis), or to assess public programs retrospectively to determine whether they should be continued, expanded or abandoned (*ex post* analysis).

Comparing benefits to costs is an intuitively logical way to inform decision-making, as noted by Benjamin Franklin in this famous remark:

> [M]y way is to divide half a sheet of paper by a line into two columns; writing over the one Pro, and over the other Con.
> Then, during three or four days consideration, I put down under the different heads short hints of the different motives, that at different times occur to me, for or against the measure.
> When I have thus got them all together in one view, I endeavor to estimate their respective weights . . .
> And, though the weight of reasons cannot be taken with the precision of algebraic quantities, yet when each is thus considered, separately and comparatively, and the whole lies before me, I think I can judge better, and am less liable to make a rash step, and in fact I have found great advantage from this kind of equation, in what may be called moral or prudential algebra.[1]

Modern benefit-cost analysis can be distinguished from Franklin's prudential algebra along two dimensions: the breadth of the stakeholder representation and the degree of "monetization" (See Figure 17.1). To define terms, a "stakeholder" is someone who has a "stake" in the outcome of the public decision and whose well-being matters, that is, a person who has "standing." "Monetization" refers to the use of money metric measures, like market prices, to provide the "weight of reasons" described by Ben Franklin.

Because benefit-cost analysis is used to help policymakers make public decisions, the "stakeholder perspective" in BCA must be "societal." That is, the decision's impact on anyone with standing must be recorded. As such, BCA addresses the opposite end of the stakeholder continuum from Ben Franklin's prudential algebra, which describes rational individual decision-making. That said, the "societal perspective" itself is usually circumscribed. First, the "accounting domain" – the geographic space within which "the society" is defined – is generally some subset of the world. For example, the Office of Management and Budget (OMB) instructs US federal agencies preparing "Regulatory Impact Analyses" or RIAs (see Chapter 6) to only count benefits and costs falling within the United States. However, a several-country accounting perspective is appropriate for an international lending institution such as the World Bank or European Bank for Reconstruction and Development when evaluating a highway project spanning several countries. Some authors argue that, from

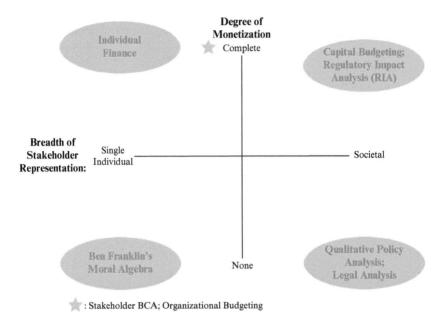

: Stakeholder BCA; Organizational Budgeting

Figure 17.1   Evaluation contexts

a philosophic perspective, the accounting domain should be global (Howe, 1987). This is not a consensus view in the BCA field, however.

A current debate in the United States about the "social cost of carbon" (SCC) illustrates some of the different perspectives in the BCA field on geographic accounting stances. The SCC provides a monetary measure of the present value of reducing one ton of carbon emissions; it was used in RIAs during the Obama administration to measure the global climate benefits of federal regulations that reduce energy consumption. The accounting perspective underlying the SCC is global, and some authors argue that the accounting domain for climate damages should instead follow OMB's standard recommendation to use the national accounting perspective. The logical consequence would be to reduce the estimates of global warming damages to the share falling on the United States.[2] Other scholars believe that the global accounting stance underlying the SCC is appropriate. In this view, the effects on global climate in other countries will have negative repercussions for the United States, and should be reflected in public decision-making.[3]

More common than expanding the accounting stance beyond a national boundary is restricting it to some sub-region within a country. For example, a state or regional government that is deciding whether to fund a local road network might not consider the welfare of out-of-state travelers. The mayor and city council considering the pros and cons of a municipal recycling program might not consider the welfare of those living outside the city.

In fact, the appropriate scope for the accounting domain is an inherently contextual and philosophic issue. Moreover, an analyst can demarcate different accounting stances in the same benefit-cost analysis, giving a distributional or stakeholder accounting representation from the largest accounting domain considered. For example, a national highway system can be evaluated from a national accounting perspective, but the benefits, costs and financial effects falling on different states and regions can also be identified. It will be argued further on that this kind of depiction adds value to the benefit-cost analysis.

Another kind of restriction on the "societal" notion was alluded to earlier: the decision about which residents in the accounting domain have "standing." Citizens without criminal records will always have "standing." One question is whether the welfare of those with criminal records, or non-citizen residents, should also be counted. Again, this is a philosophical question. See Chapter 4 in this volume for further discussion.

Turning from the societal perspective in whatever way it is defined, it is also possible to conduct evaluations from the perspective of a subset of society's stakeholders. These kinds of evaluations occur at intermediate points on "the breadth of stakeholder representation" axis in Figure 17.1, and are common in the health policy literature. For example, a hospital might consider whether future cost savings in avoided treatments from using a new kind of diagnostic equipment will cover the costs of the equipment. The health evaluation literature describes this accounting stance as the "health care provider perspective." Such evaluations contribute to rational decision-making from the perspective of the evaluator. But because they leave out effects that fall on individuals who would be defined as "stakeholders" in the societal perspective, most economists would not consider this kind of evaluation as a benefit-cost analysis proper. For example, not only will the diagnostic equipment reduce costs to health care providers, it will also reduce patient commuting trips to the hospital, improve patients' sense of well-being and increase the time patients spend in productive work. Of these benefits, it is relatively easy to monetize the value of additional work, for example, as predicted additional work hours multiplied by an assumed wage rate. Suppose an evaluator finds that the sum of the value of additional work and health care cost savings are larger than the costs of the diagnostic equipment, but that the health care cost savings alone do not justify the investment. In short, using the "health care provider perspective," the hospital would not purchase the equipment, while from a societal perspective, it should. This kind of discrepancy is what benefit-cost analysis is designed to identify. Based on the benefit-cost analysis, it might make sense in this case for a national health service to subsidize the purchase of the diagnostic equipment.

The presentation so far has focused on the horizontal axis of Figure 17.1. Let us now consider axis 2 – the degree to which benefits and costs are monetized. As a start, it is useful to identify what the terms "benefit" and "cost" mean, and how they relate to the economic efficiency concept.

In standard BCA, benefits are defined as the most a stakeholder is willing to pay (WTP) for some good or service, while costs are defined as "opportunity costs" and measured by the minimum compensation payment that a resource supplier will accept to give up the resource that they own (WTA). These concepts provide an intuitive basis for defining economic efficiency: if a resource supplier needs less compensation to supply a resource than a new resource owner is willing to pay for it, then the value of the resource goes up when it moves from the first to the second owner. Getting more value from the same resource, or WTP –WTA > 0, defines economic efficiency. Benefit-cost analysis measures the sum of the WTPs of the stakeholders who gain from a project, and compares this aggregated sum of the WTAs of the losers, to judge whether the value of a new resource allocation is higher than the old one.

Many resources have market prices, a starting point for monetizing the cost side, but many public goods do not; that is, the benefit side starts out unmonetized. The degree to which market prices, when they exist, can be used to measure WTA or WTP is well worked out in the theoretical BCA literature and is beyond the scope of this chapter. Similarly, the theory and empirical literature on imputing WTP measures to unpriced public goods (like air quality improvements or airport noise reductions) is well developed.[4] What is relevant here is that benefit-cost analysis is based on the monetization of benefits and costs, rendering them comparable.

The upper right point in Figure 17.1 gives two examples that exemplify standard evaluation contexts for benefit-cost analysis; that is, the evaluation of public decisions from a societal perspective in which benefits and costs are mostly monetized. (The "mostly" qualification will be discussed in a moment). "Capital budgeting" refers to the choice among public investment options when funds are too limited to finance all the options that would pass a benefit-cost test. Many states in the United States have "capital budgets" for big-ticket investment items. The country of Chile has a system of national investment evaluation in which all proposed projects above a threshold have to be considered. Regulatory Impact Analyses, the benefit-cost analysis of federal regulatory proposals, is another evaluation context. In the US, RIA is required for all "economically significant" regulations proposed by cabinet agencies. This part of Figure 17.1 is the focus of standard textbooks in benefit-cost analysis.

The "mostly complete" qualification is made because monetizing all the benefits and costs is usually not possible for evaluations conducted from the societal perspective, in view of the distribution of impacts over numerous and diverse stakeholders. RIAs of federal environmental regulations rarely monetize all of the environmental effects of the regulations, for example. More complete monetization is often easier for capital projects, if they do not have significant environmental effects. Take for example the expansion of a utility grid in a less developed country. In this case, market prices exist for the electricity produced, and also for the resources used as inputs. These market prices provide the starting point for a virtually complete monetization of the benefits and costs.

In general, however, there are diminishing returns to monetization for evaluations conducted from the societal perspective; beyond a certain point, the value of the additional information may not be worth the cost of producing it. Returning to the evaluation of the diagnostic equipment in the hospital example discussed earlier, for example, suppose that the value of the medical cost savings were larger than the cost of the equipment, so that the decision to purchase the equipment could be justified without considering other benefits. In this case, an analysis from the societal perspective could be based on the health care cost savings alone, with the qualification offered that the benefits left out of the analysis would only reinforce the conclusion. In which case, the only difference between the "health care provider perspective" and the "societal perspective" would be a qualification offered about the analysis itself.

On the other hand, if the hospital faced a capital budget that restricted the choice between the diagnostic equipment and some other investment option, the left-out benefits could be crucial to the comparison. Partial monetization is inherently problematic in the capital budgeting context, or more generally, when more than one alternative is compared. These choice contexts require a careful assessment of the implications of differing degrees of monetization.

The other parts of Figure 17.1 represent varying degrees of stakeholder representation and monetization. For evaluations conducted from an individual or organizational stakeholder perspective, complete monetization is often possible for some class of decisions, for example, financial investments or organizational budgeting. In many cases, however, decisions from a less-than-the-societal stakeholder perspective must also be made without the monetization of trade-offs. Some classes of policy analyses, for example, legal analysis or decisions about foreign policy, are made from the societal perspective, but also do not rely on monetary assessments of the trade-offs (lower right-hand corner of Figure 17.1).

Given the nuances in defining the societal perspective, the boundary between the upper right-hand corner and the interior regions in Figure 17.1 is not always sharp.[5] Nonetheless, many evaluation contexts are limited in their stakeholder perspective and degree of monetization *ipso facto*; for example, decisions made within organizations to promote organizational goals. Evaluations in such contexts do not qualify as benefit-cost analyses proper even if, like Ben Franklin's "prudential algebra," they embody a thoughtful evaluation of trade-offs.

DISTRIBUTIONAL EFFECTS IN BENEFIT-COST ANALYSIS

Public decisions always impact numerous residents with standing in a defined, geographic accounting domain. These effects must be aggregated and compared. The remainder of this note explains the standard approach in benefit-cost analysis for aggregating stakeholder effects, and suggests a framework for better representing stakeholders in the evaluation.

It is the nature of pure public goods that everyone consumes at the same level. And because people have different preferences, a public decision to provide more of a public good like clean air or national defense will be favored by those who want more and opposed by those who want less. The suite of public goods offered in a national election campaign is the limiting extreme of this reality: everyone must "consume" the winner's policy package.

In contrast, consumers have the flexibility to tailor their private consumption choices over private goods to satisfy their individual preferences. The person who likes more wine and less orange juice is not forced to consume excess orange juice and too little wine. Consumers can optimize their consumption mix of wine and orange juice when they shop at the grocery store (see Chapter 13 for a qualified perspective related to addiction).

Kaldor-Hicks Tableaus can be used to illustrate the distributional distinction between private and public choices. KHTs present a complete and conceptually consistent picture of the benefits, costs and transfers that stakeholders experience at a chosen level of stakeholder representation. This representation provides transparency about the distributional effects of decision-making.

KHT1 represents a voluntary market exchange when a consumer is willing to pay 100 dollars for a good that has an opportunity cost of 25 dollars to supply (see Table 17.1). The price paid for the good, the

Table 17.1   Private market exchange for consumer good, KHT1

	Buyer	Seller	Net
Benefit (maximum WTP)	B(100)		B(100)
Transfer (price paid)	−T(75)	T(75)	0
Cost (minimum compensation)		−C(−25)	−C(−25)
Net	B − T	T − C	B−C
	(100 − 75=25)	(75 − 25 = 50)	(100 − 25) = 75

transfer payment, is 75 dollars. The net effects (or distributional effects) on stakeholders are shown in the bottom row, which sum the rows above. The net effect on the buyer ("consumer surplus" or "buyer surplus") is B − T = 25 dollars. The seller receives the net ("seller surplus") of T − C = 50 dollars. Given that the distributional effects in this case are non-negative, the exchange will take place.

The sum of the distributional effects along the bottom row gives benefits less costs (B − C) in the lower right-hand cell (the price "T" paid for the good, as a "transfer payment," drops out in the summation). This summation is the equivalent of comparing the value of the good to the buyer (B = 100) less the opportunity cost of supplying it (C = 25), ignoring the transfer payment. This comparison is shown on the right-hand column of the KHT, which sums the columns to the left.

Assume that the buyers and sellers are perfectly informed about the quality of the good and all the effects associated with a market transaction are borne by buyers and sellers, as shown in KHT1. In this case, the distributional effects of voluntary exchange will always be non-negative, as shown in KHT1. As a rule, participants do not undertake voluntary exchanges that worsen their own situation (see Chapter 13 for behavioral anomalies like addictions that are an exception to this rule). The context where resource reallocations impose no net losses on any stakeholder is known as "Pareto improving." Pareto improving resource reallocations provide the highest bar for economic efficiency. Private market transactions always meet this test (in the standard case absent third party effects and asymmetric information), given the flexibility of the participants in market exchanges to voluntarily make choices in their own self-interest.

In contrast, KHT2 (see Table 17.2) shows the distributional profile common for resource reallocations incentivized through public policy. The example shown might be taken to represent an infrastructure investment to provision a quasi-public good such as a toll road. The beneficiaries are willing to pay B = 100 to use the toll road, which is higher than the toll

Table 17.2   Infrastructure investment, KHT2

	Beneficiary	Contractor/ Operator	Stakeholders Financing the Project	Net
Benefit	B (100)			B(100)
User Charge ("toll")	$-T1(25)$	T1(25)		0
Subsidy		T2(25)	$-T2(-25)$	0
Project Opportunity Cost		$-C1(-50)$		$-C1(-50)$
Financing Opportunity Cost			$-C2(-10)$	$-C2(-10)$
Net	$B - T1$ $(100 - 25$ $= 75)$	$T1 + T2 - C1$ $(25 + 25 - 50$ $= 0)$	$-(T2 + C2) =$ $(-25 - 10 =$ $-35)$	$B - C1 - C2$ $(100 - 50$ $- 10 = 40)$

charge of T = 25. The contractor who builds and operates the road receives the toll, and also a public financing share. Together, these financial streams just cover the resource opportunity costs of providing the infrastructure and operating it. Taxpayers provide the public financing share, and also incur a loss from the market distortion that is caused by this financing, for example, the "deadweight cost" of taxation. The final net column shows that the value of the road services is larger than the construction and financing opportunity costs, so that the project passes the benefit-cost test. Summing the net effects at the bottom of the KHT also produces this benefit-cost comparison.

The key distributional distinction between this public project and the private market exchange is that some stakeholders lose. A lot of ink has been spilled in the BCA literature about the philosophic justification for an economic efficiency standard that allows for these kinds of losses (known as the Potential Pareto standard, or the Kaldor-Hicks standard).[6] My own justification is pragmatic. Given the heterogeneity of public preferences and the technical attribute of public goods that force everyone to consume at the same level, losses from public provision are inherent unless all losers are compensated. It is well recognized, however, that complete compensation is not feasible in the general case; some losses are inevitable. Under these circumstances, the Pareto test, like a unanimous vote, is impossible to pass. Majority voting is a practical alternative to unanimous consent, enabling public decision-making when voting is the method for preference aggregation. Although the Kaldor-Hicks standard combines information differently than voting processes, it also provides a practical way to aggregate preferences when losses are an inevitable aspect of public decision-making.

The standard approach in benefit-cost analysis is to conduct the evaluation exclusively from the perspective of the right-hand column of the KHT, that is, to compare aggregated benefits against the aggregated costs. This effectively isolates the efficiency analysis from the distributional effects. However, even in this standard approach, the distributional effects cannot be entirely excluded. For one thing, a "financial sustainability analysis" has to be conducted to assess whether private revenues from user charges will cover the opportunity costs incurred by the infrastructure provider. KHT2 shows that the user charge does not fully cover opportunity costs, so the project is not privately sustainable. In short, the indicated public subsidy is essential for making the project viable. Additionally, the magnitude of the project's benefit will reflect the size of the user charge. The benefits from road use will be higher if the user charge is lower – more people will use the toll road in this case – and lower if the user fee is higher. This point is well recognized in the BCA literature: a benefit-cost analysis of a transportation project will estimate transportation demand. Of course, the level of the toll charge will also influence the financial effect on the project supplier, impacting the project's sustainability. In sum, this example shows that efficiency and equity are not likely to be fully separable in practice.

A FRAMEWORK FOR DISTRIBUTIONAL ACCOUNTING

Standard BCA values the input-output relationship linking resources used to project outcomes, ignoring distributional effects. That is, the standard evaluation focuses on the right-hand column of the KHT. This approach may reflect a historical legacy. BCA was used in the nineteenth century by French engineers to assess public works projects, and started to be used in the United States in the 1930s and 1940s to evaluate large infrastructure such as dams, irrigation canals, roadways and pipelines (Wiener and Ribeiro, 2016). The construction of this kind of infrastructure was an engineering feat. The benefit-cost analysis of these projects focused on technical input-output relationships defining the production function.

In the past three decades, BCA has diversified to the evaluation of health, environmental and social policies. The social nature of production processes is especially salient in these contexts. Expected outcomes cannot be divorced from the behavior of individuals. Whether a vocational training program has benefits larger than its costs depends on whether the incentive structure of the program is such that prospective trainees will want to participate. Whether a rural clinic offers significant benefits from disease reduction depends on the private incentives residents scattered throughout a region have to travel to the clinic. A distributional analysis in these cases is essential to accurately specifying the input-output relationship itself.

An accounting of distributional effects also offers policy-relevant information. I will illustrate using a fictitious example of an employment-training program, shown in KHT3. This program is based on a public-private partnership between a state employment-training department and participating firms. The state employment-training department and the firm jointly pay a training wage to unemployed individuals who enroll in the program. The employment-training department incurs an administrative cost to operate the program, while the firm is responsible for the training itself. Trainee time has an opportunity cost, while offering no productivity benefit in the training period. Input taxes are paid on training inputs, and the trainees pay wage taxes. Taxes are collected by a combination of state and federal governments. All these effects are shown in KHT3 under the transfer and cost headings for the training year. Additionally, there is a social benefit – avoided social service costs – when trainees are occupied in training.

After the training program is over, the firms hire the workers that they have trained. The principal benefit is the enhanced productivity the new employees create, and a continuing societal benefit in social cost savings. Workers continue to incur time opportunity costs. Wages are paid by firms and received by workers; wage taxes are paid, and workers lose the welfare payments they had during their non-working period. All of these effects are displayed in KHT3 (see Table 17.3).

Conceptually, the entries in KHT3 can be regarded as either annualized values, or as present values. Also note the implicit assumption that firms and trainees are residents of the state where the training program is conducted.

Here are some relevant points:

1) The KHT shows the benefit-cost comparison in the right-hand column, revealing the essential efficiency picture. The bottom cell in this column gives the net-efficiency effect.
2) The comprehensive distributional picture is shown in the rest of the table *at the level of stakeholder disaggregation chosen.* More or less detail could have been shown. For example, just the net effect on stakeholders in the bottom row of the tableau could have been presented – effectively, aggregating all rows in the KHT into one. The impact on the federal government could have been disaggregated as was done for the state government. In general, the level of representation is an editorial decision about the information useful to display.

Table 17.3 *Worker training program, KHT3*

	Trainees	Firms	State Government			In-State Public	Federal Government	Net
			Welfare Department	Revenue Department	Employment Training-Dept.			
Training Year								
Benefit								
Social benefit						4,000		4,000
Costs								
Trainee time	-8,000							-8,000
Administration cost					-4,000			-4,000
Training cost		-11,667						-11,667
Transfers								
Input tax		-2,333		1,167			1,167	0
After-tax training wage	13,600	-6,800			-6,800			0
Tax on training wage		-1,200		800	-1,200		1,600	0
Operational Period								
Benefits								
Productivity		281,498						281,498
Social benefit						35,392		35,392
Cost								
Time	-63,706							-63,706
Transfers								
After-tax regular wage	198,885	-198,885						0
Tax on regular wage		-35,097		11,699			23,398	0
Welfare	-138,029		69,015				69,015	0
Net	2,749	25,516	69,015	13,666	-12,000	39,392	95,180	233,518

70,681

Fiscal Impact on State Aggregated

3) Summing across the cells in the bottom row of the KHT gives the net-efficiency effect as the sum of the net effects on stakeholders. This aggregation underlies the standard Kaldor-Hicks criterion.

4) Distributional effects are policy relevant for two reasons. First is the standard normative question about the desirability of the observed distribution and whether changes in transfer payments in the tableau should be made to increase equity. Second is a positive issue: for a program to be viable, no stakeholder whose voluntary participation is essential can end up as a loser. In the present case, the positive net effects on trainees and firms satisfy this constraint. However, a Monte Carlo simulation representing net effects probability distributions would improve confidence in the assessment of stakeholder incentives (See Chapter 19 for more on Monte Carlo simulation).

5) By treating state and federal governments as stakeholders, a fiscal impact assessment is embedded within the analysis. Fiscal impacts are policy relevant given financing constraints. The financing efficiency gain from the net positive fiscal impact of this program could also have been represented (the flip side of the financing cost shown in KHT2).

6) KHT3 represents a national accounting perspective. The state accounting perspective could have been shown by deleting the federal column, and recomputing the net column on the right-hand side of the tableau. The net value of this training program will be lower from the state than the national perspective. Welfare payment losses and additional tax payments fall fully on stakeholders within the state accounting domain, but the state only recovers a fraction of these losses (the part of the welfare originally paid by the state, and the part of the taxes that are paid to the state).

7) Practitioner-produced benefit-cost analyses are sometimes unclear about the accounting stance, or use inconsistent accounting stances within the same benefit-cost analysis. The latter is a particular problem with "benefit-cost analyses" of regional infrastructure projects. Inconsistently specified accounting domains produce uninterpretable information. A well-specified KHT, like that shown in KHT3, can help avoid this problem.

8) KHT3 adds insight about the structure of the program and increases transparency about the program's effects. This representation reduces the probability that the public or politicians will double count, for example, by adding the plus side of transfer payments to bona fide benefits properly measured. This kind of confusion is common in practitioner-produced BCAs.[7]

9) It should not be difficult to construct a KHT at this level of disaggregation. The fiscal impact assessment requires keeping track

of paid taxes – a necessity for shadow-pricing the inputs – as well as changes in welfare payments. The benefits and costs have to be computed in any event, and their distribution among stakeholders is logical.

CONCLUSION

Standard benefit-cost analysis provides essential information, comparing the aggregated willingness to pay for a public good to the opportunity costs of producing it. However, the lack of distributional detail in standard benefit-cost analysis has the potential to bias the specification of the input-output relationship, if the incentive structure for stakeholder participation is not clearly identified. Moreover, ignoring distributional effects leaves out policy-relevant information. The Kaldor-Hicks Tableau provides an accounting framework that brings relevant distributional information into the picture in a coherent and transparent way.

NOTES

1. This idea was offered as advice for making a decision about a job offer in a letter Ben Franklin wrote to Joseph Priestley. See B. Franklin (1956).
2. See T. Gayer and W.K. Viscusi (2016).
3. See M. Greenstone (2017).
4. See US Environmental Protection Agency (2014).
5. See A. Sinden (2014).
6. For a thoughtful review see J.D. Graham (2008).
7. See A. Boardman et al. (1993) and S. Farrow (2013).

REFERENCES AND RECOMMENDATIONS FOR ADDITIONAL READING

Boardman, A., A. Vining and W.G. Waters (1993), "Costs and benefits through bureaucratic lenses: Example of a highway project," *Journal of Policy Analysis and Management*, **12**(3), 532–55.

Farrow, S. (2013), "How (not) to lie with benefit-cost analysis," *The Economists' Voice*, **10**(1), 45–50.

Franklin, B. (1956), *Mr. Franklin: A Selection from His Personal Letters*. New Haven, CT: Yale University Press.

Gayer, T. and W.K. Viscusi (2016), "Determining the proper scope of climate change policy benefits in US regulatory analyses: Domestic versus global approaches," *Review of Environmental Economics and Policy*, **10**(2), 245–63.

Graham, J.D. (2008), "Saving lives through administrative law and economics," *University of Pennsylvania Law Review*, **157**, 395–540.

Greenstone, M. (2017), "Statement of Michael Greenstone, before the United States House Committee on Science, Space, and Technology, Subcommittee on Oversight Hearing on 'At What Cost? Examining the Social cost of Carbon,'" February 28.

Howe, C.W. (1987), "Project benefits and costs from national and regional viewpoints: Methodological issues and case study of the Colorado-Big Thompson Project," *Natural Resources Journal*, **27**, 5–20.

Krutilla, K. (2005), "Using the Kaldor-Hicks Tableau format for the teaching and practice of project appraisal and policy analysis," *Journal of Policy Analysis and Management*, **24**(4), 864–75.

Krutilla, K. and J.D. Graham (2012), "Are green vehicles worth the extra cost? The case of diesel-electric hybrid technology for urban delivery vehicles," *Journal of Policy Analysis and Management*, **31**(3), 501–32.

Sinden, A. (2014), "Cost-benefit analysis, Ben Franklin, and the Supreme Court," *UC Irvine Law Review*, **4**(4), Article 4.

US Environmental Protection Agency (EPA) (2014), Guidelines for Preparing Economic Analyses. December 17, 2010 (updated May 2014). National Center for Environmental Economics, Office of Policy. US Environmental Protection Agency.

Wiener, J.B. and D.L. Ribeiro (2016), "Environmental regulation going retro: Leaning foresight from hindsight," *Journal of Land Use and Environmental Law*, **32**(1), 1–72.

18. Case studies in the classroom: Lessons learned

Stuart Shapiro

ABSTRACT

Using case studies to teach benefit-cost analysis (BCA) brings out aspects of the practice of BCA that cannot be effectively taught in lectures. Case studies also allow students to demonstrate what they have learned from earlier lectures. I detail my experience using Regulatory Impact Analyses (RIAs) from the federal government, analyzed and presented by students, to reinforce lessons from lectures on the quantitative aspects of BCA and to teach lessons about how understanding an analysis is more than a mechanical exercise. Among the lessons highlighted by the case studies are how one can combine two policies to obscure the net costs of one, how precision can mask inaccuracy, the use of co-benefits and confusion about baselines. Case studies can be invaluable in presenting a holistic view of benefit-cost analysis.

SETTING

Case studies play a critical role in my benefit-cost analysis (BCA) class. They give the students an opportunity, after nine weeks of classroom instruction and discussion, to engage with actual analyses used by the government to assist in decision-making. Students regularly cite the experience of diving into an analysis as extremely helpful to their learning. The evaluations of the course and of the graduate program highlight the value of these case studies.

Students in the class are primarily from the Masters of Public Policy program. The students are not economists and rarely have any taken any economics, besides an introductory microeconomics course; the course is not intended to teach them to conduct BCAs. Rather, the intention is to make them wise consumers of benefit-cost analyses and to be intelligent skeptics of the analyses conducted by others.

The class begins with nine weeks of traditional instruction in the important ideas behind benefit-cost analysis. We cover the philosophical roots of BCA in utilitarianism, the ethical debates over BCA, consumer and producer surplus (and alternative methods of measuring welfare in markets), secondary markets, techniques such as averting behavior, hedonic methods and contingent valuation, discounting, risk and uncertainty, and finally values of a statistical life (VSLs) and other measures for valuing reductions in morbidity and mortality. In this way, the class is fairly standard.

CASE STUDY COMPONENT OF THE COURSE

At about the sixth week of the semester, the students in the class are broken up into four to six groups of four students each. Each group is assigned a regulatory impact analysis (RIA) done by an agency of the federal government in the past year.[1] The students are grouped based on their interests to the extent possible. Students interested in the environment are given RIAs from the Environmental Protection Agency (EPA) or the Department of Energy (DOE). Students interested in security issues are given one from the Department of Homeland Security (DHS).

During the ninth week of the class, I do a case study for them. I go through an RIA (usually one from several years ago that was done reasonably well by the agency). Then, over the next three to four weeks, the students take over the class. Each session has one or two groups present on their RIA, explaining the issue being analyzed, highlighting the strengths and weaknesses of the analysis, and whether they would recommend the agency be allowed to move ahead with the regulation based on the RIA. In addition to presenting to the class, each individual student writes a memo on the RIA with their individual views on the regulation in question.

I have noticed numerous patterns emerge from years of these case studies. Below I summarize these lessons by describing how the cases highlight the students' absorption of the technical materials. Then I move on to discussing what the cases reveal about what students do not pick up from the first two-thirds of the course. What I have learned is that there are certain lessons that cannot be easily taught by just telling students what to watch out for. Much like some people can only learn through experience, the same is true of our students. The case studies give them that experience.

A MAJOR POSITIVE FINDING: STUDENTS ABSORB THE TECHNICAL LESSONS

I am impressed every year by how students, who at the beginning of the course had only vague notions about discounting, uncertainty and the value of a statistical life, can read an RIA in which these concepts are integral. Not only that but also they can grapple with arguments about how the agency chose the discount rate and offer relevant criticisms about that choice. They can discuss intelligently the choice by the agency for the value of the VSL and how the agency dealt with uncertainty.

This success says something both about the nature of teaching BCA and about how agencies do their RIAs. Subjects like basic economics, discount rates, uncertainty and VSL are all eminently teachable. While each of these subjects has many aspects which can be complex, the basic idea behind them is not terribly difficult for students with a Masters level education and some microeconomics in their background. If all there were to doing a BCA was checking the technical boxes, then individuals with this level of background would be able to comment intelligently on agency analyses.

This is why skilled agencies in turn are usually very careful to make sure they follow Office of Management and Budget (OMB) guidance (OMB, 2003) relatively closely on these subjects. No agency wants to offend OMB (or potentially reviewing courts) by making the simple and avoidable mistakes of not discounting future benefits (or doing so in an indefensible manner), by not monetizing mortality risks, and by ignoring uncertainty. While these topics were all the subject of considerable controversy over the years (see, for example, Ackerman and Heinzerling 2005 or Revesz and Livermore 2008), they are now controversial only in the details.

If an agency or anyone conducting a BCA wants to obscure their intent, it must turn to other techniques within its RIAs. Identifying the errors associated with these techniques, some of which have been noted by critics of federal RIAs, is not so easy to teach. Only by seeing these issues first-hand can students begin to understand them. It is in teaching the understanding of these techniques that using case studies of actual analyses is most useful.

USING CASE STUDIES TO UNDERSTAND THE NUANCES OF BENEFIT-COST ANALYSIS

Combining Two Policies to Make the Less Economically Attractive One Look Better

In several cases over the years, I have seen my students "fooled" by RIAs that combine analysis of a policy that has low or even negative net benefits with analysis of a policy that has high net benefits. The resulting analysis shows net benefits and obscures the fact that an alternative of just implementing the high net benefit policy would have far greater gains to social welfare. The alternatives analyzed by the regulating agency do not include eliminating the policy with net costs or very low net benefits.

One example of this is a regulation by the Mine Safety and Health Administration (MSHA) that addressed the issue of exposure to coal mine dust for miners.[2] The regulation affected both surface mines and underground mines. Because exposures are much more severe in underground mines, the benefits of reducing dust exposure for underground miners are much greater for these reductions than for reducing surface miner exposure (the costs for underground mines are eight times as high as those for surface mines but the benefits to miners who work underground are at least 20 times as high compared with those who work above ground). This is also true of the net benefits. While the costs for underground and surface mines are calculated separately as are the number of lives saved, the monetized value of lives saved is not. The analysis shows very high net benefits, but these net benefits are largely driven by the benefits that accrue to workers in underground mines.

Another example comes from the EPA and the nature of the benefits are quite different from the MSHA example.[3] In this case, EPA readily notes that it is promulgating two rules together, one requiring Maximum Achievable Control Technology (MACT) for all boilers classified as "major sources," and then a separate standard for two specific categories of boilers. The MACT standard has very high net benefits while the range of estimates for the specific standards is largely negative. EPA does not try to hide this distinction but reports the combined total as the total value of net benefits and does not include an alternative of simply promulgating the MACT standard.

In both of these cases, my students did not pick up on the combining of policies on their own. Once it was pointed out they quickly understood that MSHA and EPA may have reached a different policy decision if an alternative of promulgating only the policy with the high net benefits was highlighted. One can stand in front of a classroom and tell students to be aware of this method of making a questionable policy look like it has net benefits, but until they see it done, they will be unlikely to absorb the lesson.

Using Dense Precise Analysis to Give the Appearance of Good Analysis

Training students to use data and economics to analyze a policy question leaves them particularly open to being fooled by reams of data and complicated analysis. Over the years, I have noticed my students sing the praises of numerous analyses that were nearly 1,000 pages in length but do not grapple with some of the more critical questions that are fundamental to whether the policy has net benefits. The students see that not only are all the boxes checked (discounting, treatment of uncertainty, VSL and so on), but also that the agency has looked in excruciating detail at the impact of their regulation on particular sectors or particular markets.

The primary example of this are the analyses of energy efficiency standards by the DOE (one example is the standard for residential boilers).[4] The "Technical Support Document" for the residential boiler standard, which includes the RIA also includes background documents totaling 890 pages. On the surface, it is very difficult (for me, not to mention my students) to determine what in these 890 pages is necessary to understand the conclusions of the RIA, and what is less critical. Hence the students generally need to wade through the entire document.

However, the central issue in the benefit-cost analysis of nearly all the energy efficiency standards is how to treat "internalities." The primary benefit (often outstripping the benefit from reduced risk from climate change) is the fact that people will save money on their electric bills that, in the long run, will outweigh their increased expenditure on more energy efficient appliances. For this to be counted as an economic benefit, one must assume that the individuals making the decision to purchase an appliance are not the best judges of their own welfare (Mannix and Dudley 2015).

But this issue is usually given a sentence or two within an analysis of nearly 1,000 pages. My students almost always miss it entirely (even though over the past few years, we have talked about internalities in class). The students get so wrapped up in understanding the complexities of the analysis and deciding which numbers in one chapter correspond to the numbers used in a subsequent chapter of the analysis that it is difficult for them to see a large issue that the agency barely mentions. Like the issue of combining policies, the use of complexity in analysis is easy to warn students about but much more difficult for students to understand until they have been fooled by it.

The Use of Co-benefits

The Environmental Protection Agency has issued many regulations designed to curb exposure to various pollutants that also reduce exposure to particulate matter. Particulate matter is a particularly hazardous pollutant. In some of the analyses of these regulations, the quantified benefits of reducing the targeted pollutant do not outweigh the costs of doing so. Once the benefits of reducing emissions of particulate matter are added in to the analysis however, the benefits usually far exceed the costs. Scholars of the regulatory process have termed these "co-benefits."

Putting aside the controversial issue (Smith 2011) of whether counting the benefits arising from reducing particulate matter across different regulations is legitimate, the use of co-benefits raises another issue. This is particularly true if these co-benefits are changing the sign of the net-benefit calculation. If, the benefits of regulating particulate matter are so great, why not design the regulation to target particulate matter rather than the pollutant in question? In the RIA, why not include alternatives that are designed to reduce particulate matter?

One prominent example of this use of co-benefits was the RIA for the EPA regulation of mercury emissions.[5] EPA estimated the costs of this rule as $9.6 billion. The benefits were estimated to have a range between $37 and $90 billion, nearly all arising from particulate matter reductions. When my students were assigned this as a case study, they were impressed by the large net benefits (as a side note, the EPA RIA devotes equal space to the calculation of the $90 billion in benefits to reduction from particulate matter and the less than $1 billion in quantified benefits from reductions in mercury emissions – highlighting the issue discussed earlier of using volume to mask key issues). They did not, until it was pointed out, think about the implications of relying on co-benefits to generate a high net benefits number for the mercury rule.

This is another example of the type of technique used in RIAs to ensure that individual regulations have positive net benefits that is hard to teach in the absence of case studies. Co-benefits do exist and by all means should be counted as part of the overall benefits of a regulation. But their use raises questions about the regulatory approach to a particular problem. I've found that these questions are best discovered by students by responding to and dissecting actual analyses that rely upon co-benefits.

Baselines

I always discuss baselines with my students during the lecture portion of the class. I emphasize both the need to measure costs and benefits against a common baseline and the ability to manipulate the final results of an analysis by changing the baseline. While I try to give examples in class, it is clear from the class' reactions that the issue of choosing a baseline does not resonate in the same way as other subjects where there are formulas or acronyms. This issue is discussed in more detail in Chapter 3 of this volume.

A few well-placed questions during the student presentations of the case studies however, drive the point home much more effectively. Asking students how the analysis would change if the Department of Transportation assumed that fewer plane crashes would occur in the absence of a new air-plane safety regulation[6] drives the point of the baseline home very quickly.

Homeland security regulations are also excellent examples of the importance of the baseline as the agency must always (unless they are doing a break-even analysis rather than a benefit-cost analysis) make a choice about how many terrorist attacks will occur in order to measure the benefits of a new security measure. Simply increasing that assumption by one significant attack increases the benefits without affecting the costs of prevention.

WHAT INDIVIDUAL CASE STUDIES CANNOT SHOW STUDENTS ABOUT BCA

I have read hundreds of regulatory benefit-cost analyses over my career as a desk officer at the Office of Information and Regulatory Affairs (OIRA) and as a professor. Some of the things that I have learned have come from seeing many analyses, and are both hard to communicate in a lecture, and impossible to understand from a detailed study of just one RIA. Two lessons in particular that arise from reading multiple analyses are questions of consistency and the use of the same benefits in multiple analyses.

Agencies that do many benefit-cost analyses such as the EPA, the DOE and the Food and Drug Administration often confront the same questions repeatedly. When I was an OIRA desk officer, an agency changing its approach to analyzing benefits or costs immediately raised warning signs. In addition, different agencies often choose different answers to fundamental questions such as the choice of a value for a VSL or a discount rate. Different circumstances may indeed merit different choices for these parameters. But they may not. It is only in reading multiple analyses that these inconsistencies can be spotted and more thoroughly questioned.

Agencies also often issue multiple regulations designed to target the same regulatory problem. The EPA issues regulations to reduce particulate matter exposure, and, as described earlier, issues other regulations that claim particulate matter emission reduction as a co-benefit. The MSHA issues multiple regulations intended to protect the lives of miners. The Department of Homeland Security issues regulations to reduce the risk of a terrorist attack. Whether these multiple analyses claim the same benefits (or costs for that matter) is impossible to know when a student is exposed to only one case study of a benefit-cost analysis.

CONCLUSION

My experience in using case studies to teach benefit-cost analyses has been very positive. In addition to the substantive ideas that students are exposed to from reading and reporting on individual RIAs, there is a clear pedagogical benefit from having them engage with analyses directly. As fascinating as I may be in front of a classroom, there is an inevitable dryness that comes with lecturing about economics. The case studies force students to grapple with the questions associated with benefit-cost analysis themselves.

The case studies serve two purposes from my perspective. First, I can see how well the students have absorbed the material that makes up the bulk of the lectures. On that count, I have been gratified to see how well students have understood concepts that do not come naturally to most of them. Second, it allows me to show students that even if all of the technical aspects of an analysis are well defended, there can be other issues. Doing an analysis is more than getting the formulas right. As students move from looking for the "right" answer to a policy question to evaluating trade-offs between different answers, I believe this is a critical lesson.

As the examples cited above hopefully make clear, I have learned which issues in particular can confuse students (and presumably others engaged in the policy process). In this sense, supervising the case studies has taught me some important lessons as well.

Finally, as noted earlier, the students regularly report that they enjoy the case studies. This along with their observations during a wrap-up session after the cases have all been presented tell me that the two purposes of using the case studies have been fulfilled. In one semester, an instructor is not going to make economists out of students who generally have taken only one microeconomics course. But the case studies help me fulfill the central goal of the class, making them intelligent consumers of BCA who can ask intelligent questions when reading an analysis.

NOTES

1. RIAs are regulatory impact analyses which include an analysis of benefits and costs required for major federal regulations. See Chapter 6 for a brief overview.
2. The economic analysis can be found at http://www.msha.gov/endblacklung/docs/REAFinalRule.pdf (last viewed June 1, 2017).
3. The economic analysis can be found at https://www.regulations.gov/document?D=EPA-HQ-OAR-2006-0790-2317 (last viewed June 1, 2017).
4. The economic analysis can be found at https://www.regulations.gov/document?D=EERE-2012-BT-STD-0047-0036 (last viewed June 5, 2017).
5. See https://www3.epa.gov/ttnecas1/regdata/RIAs/matsriafinal.pdf (last viewed June 7, 2017).
6. See http://www.regulations.gov/#!documentDetail;D=FAA-2010-0100-1352 for example (last viewed June 8, 2017).

REFERENCES AND RECOMMENDATIONS FOR ADDITIONAL READING

Ackerman, F. and L. Heinzerling (2005), *Priceless: On knowing the price of everything and the value of nothing*. New York: The New Press.

Farrow, S. (2013), "How (not) to lie with benefit-cost analysis," *The Economists' Voice*, **10**(1), 45–50.

Mannix, B.F. and S.E. Dudley (2015), "Please don't regulate my internalities," *Journal of Policy Analysis and Management*, **34**(3), 715–18.

Office of Management and Budget (OMB) (2003), "Regulatory impact analysis: A primer," 2003.

Revesz, R.L. and M.A. Livermore (2008), *Retaking rationality: How benefit-cost analysis can better protect the environment and our health*. Oxford: Oxford University Press.

Smith, A. (2011), "An evaluation of the Pm2. 5 health benefits estimates in regulatory impact analyses for recent air regulations," NERA Economic Consulting, December.

19. Simulation: Incorporating uncertainty

Scott Farrow

ABSTRACT

Simulation is an increasingly accessible method to investigate uncertainty in an analysis. This chapter supports that conclusion, explains the concept behind simulation and presents class exercises using both standard Excel as well as more advanced spreadsheet simulation tools.

WHY SIMULATION?

Most benefit-cost analyses (BCAs) are forecasts where either or both the base case and the project or policy contain a large element of uncertainty (here used synonymously with risk). Analysts and decision-makers often find useful an empirical uncertainty analysis based on the variability for parameters such as willingness to pay, elasticity, cost and so on. Simulation is the modern extension of sensitivity analysis where the model is first resolved and then key outcomes, such as net present value, are recomputed for different values of uncertain input variables.

The process of simulation provides a template for the systematic, statistical exploration of uncertainty. The outcome of the simulation provides information to the analyst and decision-maker about the statistical properties of both intermediate and final outcomes. For instance, information about the statistical distribution for social costs could be reported as well as that for the net benefits. Many decision-makers are interested in expected values, which simulation may reveal are not at the central estimate of the base case if some input variables are skewed, while many decision-makers are also interested in the dispersion or the probability that the outcome exceeds some target level.

DESCRIPTION AND OBJECTIVES

Simulation uses statistical distributions defined by the analyst for key input data. Typically, computerized software then samples from the identified distributions for the input data to recalculate the value of selected output variables. Several software packages can store the result of each resolved "trial" and synthesize information about the resulting distribution of the outcomes. It is possible to do simulations where the analyst does more him- or herself, but Excel add-ins or other software are likely to meet the requirements of most users in practice.

The objectives of this module are: (1) to understand the usefulness of quantitative information about uncertainty in a BCA, (2) to internalize that statistical distributions for inputs are typically just another equation integrated into the BCA model, (3) to understand how Monte Carlo simulation samples from the statistical distributions are given to it and (4) to be able to communicate the results of a simulation.

This module first defines a simple base case of net benefits where there is uncertainty about the number of lives that might be saved annually by a project, the value of a statistical life and cost. The data-gathering problem to define statistical distributions is discussed. An equation for a probability density function (statistical distribution) is presented and demonstrations indicate how values from that distribution are selected and used as alternative inputs into the benefit-cost model. More automated approaches using Excel add-in software are demonstrated. Typical methods for communicating the results to decision-makers including graphs and tables are presented.

BACKGROUND

In the area of statistics, students should review from their statistical courses the meaning of a univariate probability density and cumulative distribution function. Specific functions that will be used include the continuous uniform distribution, the triangular distribution (not often taught in statistics but useful in simulation) and the normal distribution. In this introduction, variables will be assumed to be independent of each other, but software typically allows correlations among inputs.

Management Science texts such as Powell and Baker (2017) often have a chapter on simulation which may be useful for the students, although simulation is seldom covered in econometrics texts (an exception is Barreto and Howland 2006).

CLASS EXERCISE

Simulation can be applied to almost any portion or complete benefit-cost analysis. A basic three equation, three variable net benefit model is used here to focus on the technique and interpretation of simulation. Consider a possible regulation or investment of one alternative size that is forecast to save Q lives (avoid premature deaths) per year. Using the shadow pricing approach, your organization uses a value of a statistical life, V (see Chapter 9) and the regulation or project is estimated to cost C for that year. The deterministic base case for the change in net benefits for this one year (more later on present value) will then be:

$$\text{Social Benefit} = Q*V$$
$$\text{Social Cost} = C$$
$$\text{Net Social Benefit} = \text{Social Benefit} - \text{Social Cost} \qquad (19.1)$$

Your base case point forecast typically includes the expected (mean) value of Q, V and C (US OMB 1992; Arrow et al. 1996). But uncertainty almost certainly exists for each of Q, V and C. It is also possible in this case that the variables are independent of each other in the sense that some costs are incurred and then nature randomly determines the number of deaths avoided while the shadow price V is believed not to change with the magnitude of premature deaths averted.[1] Simulation goes further than plugging in a few alternative values for these variables. Simulation requires the analyst to: (1) review evidence to determine what statistical distribution is associated with each variable, potentially including a custom distribution like a histogram based on local data, (2) design a simulation using the software available to re-run the model "numerous" times and evaluate the resulting distribution of the outcomes of interest. The outcomes in this case would at least be the Net Social Benefit, although the intermediate outcome of Social Benefit may also be of interest to the analyst and decision-maker.

Student Exercise 1: "Brute Force" Simulation

A. Tools and task: Uses basic Excel to generate N (here 25) observations and then evaluate the N simulated outcomes.
B. Base case data
   Quantity (the change in premature deaths) = 100
   Value of a statistical life = 5 million dollars in a given year's dollars
   Cost = 525 million dollars.
C. Distributions of inputs. Assume that extensive work and literature reviews indicate that each variable has the following distributions:

Quantity: Uniform integer distribution between 75 and 125

Value of a statistical life: Continuous uniform distribution with bounds [2 million, 10 million]

Cost: Normal distribution with mean = \$525 million and standard deviation of \$75 million.

D. Creating N trials. Create 25 observations of Net Social Benefit given the information above. This is typically done by giving each trial a row, computing the variables and the outcome for that observation or trial in various columns so that the net benefits are eventually computed in some column to the right. Many spreadsheet designs are possible (Powell and Baker 2017).

E. Evaluate the simulation. When the 25 observations (rows) exist for each variable, what is the mean, min and max? Is the mean the same as the mean of the base case? Why or why not? Will every student have the same value? Why or why not? Students could go on to report other statistics for the simulations distribution (perhaps using Descriptive Statistics in Excel); they could also generate a histogram and address questions such as what is the probability that the Net Social Benefit will be larger than zero or some other anchoring point.

F. Tools and hints: Standard Excel functions of rand, randbetween (min, max) and Norm.Inv can be used in this example. The continuous uniform distribution above will require defining a linear equation with intercept equal to the lower bound plus rand multiplied by the difference between the high and low value. Norm.Inv returns the value X (here Cost) given a probability from the cumulative standard normal with a given mean and standard deviation.

Student Exercise 2: Software-enabled Simulation Using Excel Add-ins

A. This exercise uses add-ins for Excel such as Analytic Solver, @Risk, Oracle Crystal Ball or other software with which the instructor may be familiar.

B. Entering input distributions. Using the same information as above, select the appropriate distribution from the menu of distributions and enter the parameters as required by the particular software (example below). Instructors can also vary the distribution chosen and select appropriate parameters. One common distribution used in benefit-cost practice is the triangular distribution (which as a more advanced exercise can also be programmed in standard Excel based on values of the minimum, maximum and most likely value).[2]

C. Defining output: Each software requires the output cell to be defined.

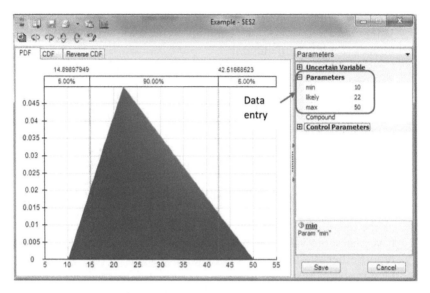

Source: Author using Frontline Systems/Analytic Solver (2017).

Figure 19.1   Example of input data entry for a triangular distribution

D. Running the simulation: There will be a default number of trials (which could be altered by the instructor), along with various report options.
E. Interpreting the simulation: The software facilitates answering questions such as "What is the probability that net benefits will be negative?". With the simulation software this can often be answered by selecting a threshold value in a requested report or graphic. With the "brute force" method, one could sort the outcomes and find the percentage of the sample that exceeds a threshold value.
F. Examples of data entry and output windows using Analytic Solver (2017) are shown below in Figures 19.1 and 19.2. Several other Excel add-in programs have similar data entry and output windows.

Discounting

Instructors or students may wish to incorporate discounting. Some thought should be devoted to whether or not each year is a new random draw from various parameters instead of a replica of the first year. The discount rate could also be modeled with a known discount rate, or input as a random variable in its own right. Each year may become its own outcome and the result is the present value of each year.

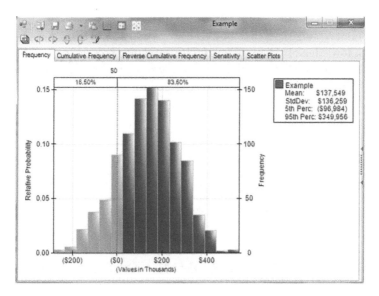

Source: Author using Frontline Systems/Analytic Solver (2017).

Figure 19.2   *Example of simulated output after 1000 trials*

KEY LEARNING OUTCOMES

- Simulations require credible construction of a base case model.
- Simulations can be implemented relatively easily.
- Additional data are required: The analyst must not only obtain a point estimate for uncertain variables, but also obtain enough information to justify use of some form of a statistical distribution for key inputs. The information may come from a literature review, original data gathering or other sources.
- Statistical distributions are most often just another equation from which values of a variable are sampled.
- A statistical distribution for the outcome variable(s) is computed based on variations in the input data structured to correspond to the input distributions.
- Interpreting simulation output involves interpretation of a statistical distribution including, but not limited to, the mean, range, variance, probability of exceeding or not exceeding some value such as zero.
- The ability to communicate the results of a simulation is an important and separate skill.

- Simulation provides a structured approach to incorporating uncertainty (and risk) that is likely more consistent with the analyst's knowledge of the problem and the available data.
- Decision-makers are often vitally interested in the risk or uncertainty associated with outcome variables.

NOTES

1. More complex models might embody different regulatory size "treatments" and so there may be a relation between the planned investment size and the resulting lives saved, perhaps in discrete regulatory alternatives.
2. See for instance, "Triangular distribution, generating triangular-distributed random variates," Wikipedia available at wikipedia.org/wiki/Triangular_distribution, accessed January 11, 2018.

REFERENCES AND RECOMMENDATIONS FOR FURTHER READING

Analytic Solver (2017), *Analytic Solver*. Frontline Systems, Inc. Available at solver.com/analytic-solver-platform, accessed January 11, 2018.

Arrow, K., M. Cropper, G. Eads, R. Hahn, L. Lave, R. Knoll, P. Portney, M. Russell, R. Schmalensee, V.K. Smith and R. Stavins (1996), "Is there a role for benefit–cost analysis in environmental, health, and safety regulation?," *Science*, **272**(April): 221–2.

Barreto, H. and F. Howland (2006), *Introductory Econometrics: Using Monte Carlo Simulation with Microsoft Excel*, Cambridge: Cambridge University Press.

Farrow, S. (2012), "A missing error term in benefit-cost analysis," *Environmental Science and Technology*, **46**(5): 2523–8.

Farrow, S., E. Wong, R. Ponce, E.M. Faustman and R.O. Zerbe (2001), "Facilitating regulatory design and stakeholder participation: The FERET template with an application to the Clean Air Act," in S. Farrow and P. Fischbeck (eds), *Improving Regulation: Cases in Environment, Health and Safety*, Washington, DC: Resources for the Future Press.

Frontline Systems, Inc. (2017), *Frontline Solvers Optimization and Simulation User Guide*. Accessible at https://www.solver.com/products-overview, accessed January 11, 2018.

Powell, S. and K. Baker (2017), *Business Analytics: The Art of Modeling with Spreadsheets*, 5th edition, Hoboken, NJ: Wiley.

US Office of Management and Budget (OMB) (1992), "Guidelines and discount rates for benefit–cost analysis of federal programs," OMB Circular A-94, Washington, DC.

Index